Inequalities in Study Abroad and Student Mobility

Bringing together a range of contributions from diverse international scholars, this edited volume explores issues of inequality in student mobility to consider how schools, universities, and colleges can ensure equitable access to international study and exchange.

Featuring evidence-based accounts of students' experiences and exploring opportunities for study abroad in school and university contexts, *Inequalities in Study Abroad and Student Mobility* analyses how pedagogy and student support services can be designed to accommodate linguistic, cultural, ethnic, and socio-economic differences. Chapters foreground issues of access and opportunity and offer unique insights to inform institutional policy in developing more effective, inclusive, and equitable ways to internationalize exchange and study abroad programs and initiatives for all.

This timely volume will benefit researchers, academics, and postgraduate students in the fields of international and comparative education, as well as educators and school leaders working within secondary and higher education settings concerned with multicultural education.

Suzan Kommers is a Research Associate at Nuffic, the Dutch Organization for Internationalization in Education, the Netherlands. Suzan Kommers received her PhD from the University of Massachusetts Amherst in which she primarily investigated internationalization of the higher education system.

Krishna Bista is an Associate Professor in the Department of Advanced Studies, Leadership and Policy at Morgan State University, USA. Krishna is Founder/Executive Editor of the *Journal of International Students* and the founding Chair of the Comparative and International Education Society (CIES) Study Abroad and International Students SIG.

Routledge Studies in Global Student Mobility

Series Editors: Krishna Bista and Christopher Glass

Routledge Studies in Global Student Mobility offers a scholarly forum for original and innovative research which explores, explains, and increases understanding of issues and opportunities relating to international student mobility in K-12, higher education, and beyond. Consisting in peer-reviewed authored and edited volumes, the series advances theoretical understanding and identifies best practices for educators and professionals involved in study abroad.

As an interdisciplinary scholarly venue, the series showcases new ideas and fresh perspectives relating to international student mobility, study abroad, exchange programs, student affairs from the US and around the world, and from a wide range of academic fields, including student affairs, international education, and cultural studies.

This series is produced in collaboration with the CIES SIG Study Abroad & International Students, STAR Scholars Network, and Open Journals in Education (OJED).

Books in this series include:

Inequalities in Study Abroad and Student Mobility
Navigating Challenges and Future Directions
Edited by Suzan Kommers and Krishna Bista

For more information about this series, please visit: https://www.routledge.com/go/routledge-studies-in-global-student-mobility

Inequalities in Study Abroad and Student Mobility

Navigating Challenges and Future Directions

Edited by
Suzan Kommers and Krishna Bista

Routledge
Taylor & Francis Group
NEW YORK AND LONDON

First published 2021
by Routledge
52 Vanderbilt Avenue, New York, NY 10017

and by Routledge
2 Park Square, Milton Park, Abingdon, Oxon, OX14 4RN

Routledge is an imprint of the Taylor & Francis Group, an informa business

Library of Congress Cataloging-in-Publication Data
A catalog record for this title has been requested

ISBN: 978-0-367-42788-7 (hbk)
ISBN: 978-0-367-85513-0 (ebk)

Typeset in Baskerville
by codeMantra

Contents

About the Editors

Krishna Bista is a scholar of international higher education. He is an Associate Professor in the Department of Advanced Studies, Leadership and Policy at Morgan State University, Maryland. His research focuses on college student experiences, faculty–student relationships, and cross-cultural teaching and learning strategies in higher education. Previously, Dr. Bista served as the director of Global Education at the University of Louisiana at Monroe, where he was Chase Endowed Professor of Education in the School of Education. Dr. Bista is founding editor of the *Journal of International Students*, a quarterly publication in international education. He is also founding chair of the Study Abroad and International Students SIG at the Comparative and International Education Society (CIES). He has reviewed several book projects related to educational research, international, and comparative education series for Routledge, Sage, Palgrave MacMillan, and Bloomsbury publications. His latest books are *Higher Education in Nepal* (Routledge, 2020) and *Global Perspectives on International Experiences in Higher Education: Tensions and Issues* (Routledge, 2019).

Suzan Kommers received her PhD from the University of Massachusetts Amherst. She primarily investigates internationalization of higher education and questions on how to provide equitable educational opportunities to all students. Dr. Kommers' research interests include disparities in study abroad opportunities and the effect on students' academic and career outcomes. Her research has been published in journals such as *The International Journal of Higher Education Research, The Journal of International Students*, and *Research in Higher Education.*

Figures

Tables

Acknowledgements

We are most grateful to Elsbeth Wright, our acquisitions editor at Routledge Publishing for her encouragement, coordination, and support through the project. Special thanks to Dr. Chris Glass and colleagues in the *Routledge Student Mobility Series* as well as at the STAR Scholars Network. We also appreciate the support of colleagues whom we worked with over the years at the Open Journals in Education, a consortium of the professional journals, the Comparative and International Education Society's Study Abroad and International Students SIG, and the *Journal of International Students.*

We would also like to acknowledge the help of all the scholars who were involved in this project and, more specifically, the authors and reviewers who took part in the review process. Without their support, this book would not have become a reality. At Morgan State University, Dr. Bista would like to thank his colleagues for their encouragement and support including graduate students and graduate assistants in the Department of Advanced Studies, Leadership and Policy.

We would also like to thank Bawool Hong, Christof Van Mol, Gerardo L. Blanco, Giorgio Marinoni, Grace K. Stephenson, James E. Callaghan, Joshua S. McKeown, Paul J. Cardwell, Ravi Ammigan, William I. Brustein, Wondwosen Tamrat, and Yenbo Wu for their feedback on the early draft of this book as well for their endorsements.

Special thanks to the following reviewers who assisted us in reviewing manuscripts received for this book, *Inequalities in Study Abroad and Student Mobility: Navigating Challenges and Future Directions.* It could not be possible to finalize the selected chapters without their evaluations and constructive feedback.

Chapter Reviewers:

Aamir Taiyeb, University of Toronto, Canada
Abigail Parrish, Bishop Grosseteste University, U.K.
Adam Thomas Grimm, Michigan State University, U.S.A.
Adinda van Gaalen, Ghent University, Belgium
Adriana Medina, University of Maryland, U.S.A.
Alia Ammar, Drexel University, U.S.A.
Anita Gopal, The George Washington University, U.S.A.

Anne Maree Payne, University of Technology Sydney, Australia
Armineh Soorenian, Leeds, U.K.
Baoyan Cheng, University of Hawai'i at Manoa, U.S.A.
Charity Clay, Xavier University of Louisiana, U.S.A.
Christopher Johnstone, University of Minnesota, U.S.A.
Crystal Green, University of California, U.S.A.
Dawn Joseph, Deakin University, Australia
Duy Pham, Educational Testing Service, U.S.A.
Emily Schell, Stanford, U.S.A.
Erik Byker, UNC Charlotte, U.S.A.
Erika Saito, Pepperdine University, U.S.A.
Eva Burbo, Tomsk State University, Russia
Eva Janebová, University of Minnesota, U.S.A.
Evan Mickey, University of Illinois, U.S.A.
Gerry Fry, University of Minnesota, U.S.A.
Hatice Altun, Pamukkale University, Turkey
Janet Gao, The George Washington University, U.S.A.
Jayme Scally, University of Hawai'i at Manoa, U.S.A.
Jennifer Marcy, Michigan State University, U.S.A.
Jiaqi Li, Wichita State University, U.S.A.
Julie Ficarra, SUNY Cortland, U.S.A.
Kayoko Enomoto, The University of Adelaide, Australia
Ling Chen, University of Massachusetts Amherst, U.S.A.
Louise Michelle Vital, Lesley University, U.S.A.
Maki Kato, Mori Arinori Institute for Higher Education and Global Mobility, Japan
Manca Sustarsic, University of Hawai'i at Manoa, U.S.A.
Melissa Mace, Maryville University, U.S.A.
Melissa Whatley, North Carolina State University, U.S.A.
Metrice Harris-Weedman, Lancaster University, U.K.
Michael Kung, University of Florida, U.S.A.
Mitchell Williams, Old Dominion University, U.S.A.
Peggy Gesing, Eastern Virginia Medical School, U.S.A.
Peter Ghazarian, Ashland University, U.S.A.
Piet Kommers, UNESCO Learning Technologies, The Netherlands
Piyachat Dhephasadin Na Ayudhaya, Nakhon Ratchasima Rajabhat University, Thailand
Raquel Guimaraes, Federal University of Parana, Brazil
Richard Johnson, RMIT University, Australia
Richard Warner, The University of Adelaide, Australia
Rita Berger, University of Barcelona, Spain
Rita Kasa, Stockholm School of Economics in Riga, Latvia
Rosa Acevedo Villarreal, University of Minnesota, U.S.A.
Rosalind Raby, California Colleges for International Education

Santiago Castiello, University of Arizona, U.S.A.
Sharon Glazer, University of Baltimore, U.S.A.
Sherrie Lee, Tertiary Education Commission, New Zealand
Shuai Gao, The George Washington University, U.S.A.
Shuning Liu, Teachers College Muncie, U.S.A.
Stephen Wanger, Oklahoma State University, U.S.A.
Susan Boafo-Arthur, Goodwin University, U.S.A.
Taylor Woodman, University of Maryland, U.S.A.
William Geibel, UCLA, U.S.A.
Xiaoli Jing, McGill University, Canada
Xin Zhao, University of Sheffield, U.K.
Yukari Takimoto Amos, Central Washington University, U.S.A.
Yuko Ida, University of Hawai'i at Manoa, U.S.A.
Zachary Taylor, The University of Texas at Austin, U.S.A.

Dr. Bista and Dr. Kommers' collective work provides critical reflections and implications for underlying issues within internationalization of higher education. In a post COVID-19 world, these reflections and implications should help enlighten many scholars and educators, and encourage forthcoming research."

— *Bawool Hong, Research Assistant, Korea University, South Korea*

"This book is a valuable addition to our understanding of the relationship between inequalities and international education – both at home and abroad. Besides offering insights from cases around the Western world, all chapters also offer useful implications for daily practice."

— *Christof Van Mol, Assistant Professor, Tilburg University, Netherlands*

"*Inequalities in Study Abroad and Student Mobility* presents a remarkable set of voices that, taken together, provide a deep, critical, and valuable analysis of some of the most pressing issues for international higher education. The contributions that Bista and Kommers have brought together are well positioned to lead the way toward a new internationalization that is guided by values and principles."

— *Gerardo L. Blanco, Associate Professor, Boston College, USA*

"The COVID-19 crisis made the risk of growing inequalities in higher education even more visible. *Inequalities in Study Abroad and Student Mobility* is a must-read book addressing the topic of inequalities in internationalization and study abroad in a holistic manner. Covering not only higher education but also secondary education, the book does not limit itself to highlighting the problems, but also proposes solutions. The International Association of Universities promotes an inclusive, fair, and ethical process of internationalization of higher education, and we can only welcome this book and praise its editors and authors."

— *Giorgio Marinoni, Manager of Higher Education, International Association of Universities, France*

"A helpful read that examines study abroad from several angles. The focus on equity brings a new theoretical depth to discussion of mobility that is often missing."

— *Grace Karram Stephenson, Postdoctoral Fellow, University of Toronto, Canada*

"An impressive and important collection. The editors have assembled twelve strong contributions that not only lay out the challenges inherent in study abroad access in an unbalanced and vulnerable world, but offer well-reasoned prescriptions for greater equity, effectiveness, and sustainable positive impact. Packed with solid data, and copious bibliographies highlighting the best work in the field to date, the collection is essential reading for students, faculty, professionals, and policy-makers seeking to make a difference in – and through – study abroad."

—*James E. Callaghan, Assistant Vice-President, Georgia College & State University, USA*

"This book makes an important contribution, particularly now as student mobility faces new restrictions worldwide. The issues raised in *Inequalities in Study Abroad and Student Mobility* should be of concern to educators and policy makers everywhere so that the many benefits of international education are achieved in the broadest way, and in as many places as possible."

—*Joshua S. McKeown, Associate Provost, State University of New York at Oswego, USA*

"This book brings together an impressive collection of international scholars, providing evidence-based accounts of inequalities in student mobility. The book is an important contribution to an under-explored dimension of study abroad."

— *Paul James Cardwell, Professor of Law, University of Strathclyde, UK*

"This book serves as an important resource for international educators and practitioners at a critical time when institutions are grappling with inequality issues in study abroad and student mobility. It offers both practical and research-driven insights that can guide institutional policy and practice in promoting diversity, empathy, and inclusive internationalization on campus."

— *Ravi Ammigan, Associate Deputy Provost, University of Delaware, USA*

"*Inequalities in Study Abroad and Student Mobility* sheds light on a critically important issue that has been far too often ignored, namely, social inequality in study abroad. Utilizing a comparative cross-national approach, this edited volume offers a highly welcomed examination of a gnawing concern for all of us engaged in international education."

— *William I. Brustein, Vice President, West Virginia University, USA*

"Despite the abundant literature on international mobility, the issue of inequalities in student mobility has been rarely treated in an organised fashion. Apart from bridging this enigmatic gap, the book provides valuable insights about how the various dimensions of inequality within the wider sphere of internationalization should be understood and addressed. I congratulate the editors and authors for an exemplary accomplishment."

— *Wondwosen Tamrat, President, St. Mary's University, Ethiopia*

"Global student mobility has led to a democratization of knowledge, information, and promotion of culture sharing and exchange. At the same time, however, it keeps reproducing social stratification and reinforcing the existing unequal socioeconomic structure, in both developing and developed countries. The great efforts demonstrated by this book to address the worldwide issue of social mobility, equity, and inclusion in student mobility are to be highly commended."

— *Yenbo Wu, Associate Vice President, San Francisco State University, USA*

Foreword

Dr. George Mwangi is an Associate Professor in higher education. Her scholarship broadly centers on (1) structures of opportunity and educational attainment for underrepresented populations along the P-20 education pipeline; (2) impacts of globalization and migration on U.S. higher education at the student, institution, and policy levels; and (3) African and African Diaspora populations in higher education. Some of her recent research projects emphasize the educational experiences of Black immigrant collegians; the role of family and community in college access and success; broadening underrepresented student participation in STEM; and higher education cross-border partnerships. Dr. George Mwangi worked for a number of years as a college administrator including positions in undergraduate admissions, multicultural affairs, student conduct, and academic advising. She has also engaged in education research and policy work for organizations including the Council for Opportunity in Education, the Pell Institute for the Study of Opportunity in Higher Education, and Higher Education for Development.

I am honored to write this foreword for *Inequalities in Study Abroad and Student Mobility: Navigating Challenges and Future Directions*. Prior to becoming a faculty member, I spent a number of years as an administrator in college admissions and student support services. Much of my practitioner work focused on equity and inclusion regarding domestic diversity issues in the United States. However, as a graduate student studying higher education, I also became interested in how higher education institutions pursue and foster global engagement, given that universities are consistently working outside of their national borders. I realized that while scholarship on domestic or local education issues often explicitly discussed diversity, equity, and inclusion as goals, I did not often see the equity and inclusion lens fully grounded within international education scholarship or internationalization practice in education. Instead, I often saw internationalization being connected to goals for improving rankings and institutional prestige and as a mechanism for revenue generation. While these goals are not inherently bad, they should not be at the center of why internationalization is pursued. The internationalization of education has been critiqued for promoting an elitist, hegemonic, and neoliberal agenda (Altbach, 2004; de Wit & Jones, 2018; Knight, 2012; Stier, 2004), and while this can be true, I do not believe that we should give up on internationalization as a means for creating powerful and positive outcomes for students and society. Over my career, I have been intentional in seeking out scholars and practitioners who feel the same. Now, as a faculty member who continues to study the global nature of higher education, I believe that it is more important than ever that internationalization practices and processes, such as study abroad and student mobility, should lead to positive societal change and improved equity for students and communities. *Inequalities in Study Abroad and Student Mobility* is exactly the kind of book that I would love to have had when I was an education practitioner or as a graduate student, in being able to develop an equity-driven framing of how education institutions can and should pursue global engagement.

Dr. Krishna Bista and Dr. Suzan Kommers have brought together an edited volume that provides a platform for engaging in key questions such as: What should study abroad look like in institutional practice? What purpose does sending and receiving students around the world serve? Who do these efforts serve? How can scholars engage in inquiry that uncovers and informs the ways in which greater equity can be achieved through study abroad and student mobility? The 12 chapters within their book use empirical inquiry that begins to provide responses to these and other critical questions focusing on equity in student mobility and study abroad. The book begins with four chapters that address the question: How do equity issues in international student mobility play out on a global scale? The authors – Adinda van Gaalen, Hatice Altun, Lien Pham, and Kayoko Enomoto, Richard Warner and Julia Miller – demonstrate that equity issues arise in the unintended outcomes of internationalization, the consideration of international higher education as a public or private good, the social positioning of "students of the new global elite," and in investigating geo-cultural equity in global student mobility. Next, authors Manca Sustarsic, Baoyan Cheng, Yuko Ida, and Melissa Whatley grapple with inequality in students' opportunities to gain international experiences. Their chapters highlight the student mobility in secondary schools and higher education, as well as across diverse student populations and country contexts. Equality in Study Abroad and Student Mobility concludes with four chapters focused on inclusion in study abroad, promoting diversity, and alternatives to traditional study abroad formats. In these final chapters, the authors – Eva Janebová, Christopher Johnstone, Melissa Mace, Dawn Joseph, Richard Johnson, Sharon Glazer, and Rita Berger – focus on resources, such as technology tools and collaborative partnerships, as well as processes, such as internationalization at home and inclusive internationalization, to center diversity and inclusion as key outcomes of study abroad. Across all of the chapters, the authors challenge readers to interrogate common internationalization practices and (re)imagine more equitable approaches to study abroad and student mobility. Scholars and practitioners alike will benefit from reading the analyses within the chapters and in seeing the innovative frameworks and methodological approaches used by the researchers in the book.

The issues and concerns addressed in *Inequalities in Study Abroad and Student Mobility* are situated within a number of paradoxes that are impacting and being impacted by higher education. First, society is becoming both more global, given the forces of globalization, and yet more insular due to growing nationalism around the world. In parallel, within higher education, colleges and universities are expected to have some sort of global connection via internationalization; and yet, there are also media discourses debating whether the internationalization of education is in demise due to sociopolitical climates reflecting greater xenophobia, nationalistic policies, and border control (for example, Fischer, 2019; Helms, 2019). Second, colleges and universities around the world are broadening participation to students of diverse backgrounds and, at the same time, are still experiencing high levels of inequity in terms of student retention and degree completion. In the last two decades, there has been a rapid expansion of higher education globally, with universities increasingly serving more diverse students (Altbach, Reisberg, & Rumbley, 2009). Yet, as universities expand access to higher education within their respective countries, there is a growing need for effective strategies that create equitable and inclusive educational environments as well as promote the success of students from underrepresented and minoritized backgrounds (Altbach et al., 2009). Given this second paradox, it is important that researchers and practitioners amplify the impact of educational inequity and the importance of broadening participation as global issues rather than solely as national or local ones. Third, higher education continues to straddle the line between being a force for public social good and being a corporatized entity. For example, internationalization has become a big business for study abroad agencies and international student recruiters, some who market internationalization as a commodity that can be bought through students' (as consumers) purchasing power (Stein, Andreotti, Bruce & Susa, 2016). At the same time, research within the chapters of this book demonstrates the positive student and social outcomes that can result from global engagement and connectedness. Higher education institutions can do better to embody the role of a public social good by targeting increased equity as a goal of internationalization.

Given the many paradoxes impacting education internationally, I view the research within this book to be more important than ever. As a global society, we are continuing to face vast inequities that exist within higher education systems around the world stemming from xenophobia, racism, nativism, and other social and economic forces. These inequities can be reified by many of the ways in which internationalization efforts are pursued in educational spaces. Study abroad and student mobility are major examples of how the privileged few can obtain global access to greater learning opportunities and social mobility through education. However, *Inequalities in Study Abroad and Student Mobility* provides a check on the ways in which study abroad and student mobility reproduce social stratification, with the authors offering alternative approaches that can engender more equitable outcomes. Similarly, the choices that scholars and practitioners make in how we engage in work related to international education and the internationalization of education can help to reduce inequality. Our scholarship and practice should remain not only relevant in today's globalized world but also useful for transforming and mitigating inequity. This equity-based approach to internationalization, which grounds the studies in this book, will continue to push forward the reimagining of what educational spaces can positively achieve within the globalized world in which we live.

Chrystal A. George Mwangi
Associate Professor, University of Massachusetts Amherst

References

Altbach, P. G. (2004) Globalization and the university: Myths and realities in an unequal world. In National Education Association (Ed.), *The NEA 2005 almanac of higher education* (pp. 63–74). Washington, DC: National Education Association.

Altbach, P. G., Reisberg, L., & Rumbley, L. E. (2009). *Trends in global higher education: Tracking an academic revolution. A report prepared for the UNESCO 2009 World Conference on Higher Education*. Paris: UNESCO.

de Wit, H. & Jones, E. (2018). Inclusive internationalization: Improving access and equity. *International Higher Education, 94*, 16–18.

Fischer, K. (2019, March 28). How international education's golden age lost its sheen. *The Chronicle of Higher Education*. https://www.chronicle.com/interactives/2019-03-28-golden-age

Helms, R. M. (2019, April 15). Going, going, gone? Internationalization's past, present, and future. *Higher Education Today*. https://www.higheredtoday.org/2019/04/15/going-golden-gone-internationalizations-past-present-future/

Knight, J. (2012). Five truths about internationalization. *International Higher Education, 69*, 4–5.

Stein, S., Andreotti, V., Bruce, J., & Susa, R. (2016). Towards different conversations about the internationalization of higher education. *Comparative and International Education, 45*(1), 1–18.

Stier, J. (2004). Taking a critical stance toward internationalization ideologies in higher education: Idealism, instrumentalism, and educationalism. *Globalisation, Societies and Education, 2*(1), 1–28.

Contributors

Hatice Altun, PhD, is a Lecturer in the School of Foreign Languages, Pamukkale University, Turkey. Her major research interests lie in areas of bi/multilingualism, discourse analysis, study-abroad, and higher education research.

Rita G. Berger, PhD, is an Associate Professor of Organizational Psychology and Vice-Coordinator of the Master Erasmus Plus on Work, Organizational and Personnel Psychology at the Universitat de Barcelona. She has nearly 20 years of experience in teaching, research, and consulting. Her expertise is in teams, leadership, and stress from a cross-cultural perspective, and her research has received funding from the European Commission. She has been a visiting professor in Germany and the USA. Finally, Dr. Berger is a reviewer for several international journals.

Krishna Bista is a scholar of international higher education. He is an Associate Professor in the Department of Advanced Studies, Leadership and Policy at Morgan State University, Maryland. His research focuses on college student experiences, faculty-student relationships, and cross-cultural teaching and learning strategies in higher education. Previously, Dr. Bista served as the director of Global Education at the University of Louisiana at Monroe, where he was Chase Endowed Professor of Education in the School of Education. Dr. Bista is founding editor of the *Journal of International Students*, a quarterly publication in international education. He is also founding chair of the Study Abroad and International Students SIG at the Comparative and International Education Society (CIES). He has reviewed several book projects related to educational research, international and comparative education series for Routledge, Sage, Palgrave MacMillan, and Bloomsbury publications. His latest books are *Higher Education in Nepal* (Routledge, 2020), and *Global Perspectives on International Experiences in Higher Education: Tensions and Issues* (Routledge, 2019).

Baoyan Cheng, EdD, is an Associate Professor in Comparative/International Education at University of Hawaiʻi at Manoa. Her major research interests lie in the area of comparative and international education with a special focus on China, cross-cultural issues, and international student mobility.

Kayoko Enomoto is a Senior Lecturer, Head of Department, Asian Studies and Director, Student Experience in the Faculty of Arts at the University of Adelaide, Australia. Her major research interests lie in the areas of higher education research, language education, intercultural education, and innovative teaching practices.

Sharon Glazer, PhD, is a Professor of Cross-Cultural Industrial-Organizational Psychology at the University of Baltimore, and has over 25 years of teaching, consulting, and research experience, with expertise in cross-cultural practice and research, particularly related to occupational stress. She has been a visiting professor in France, Italy, Spain, Portugal, Hungary, and New Zealand. She was elected Fellow of the Society for Industrial & Organizational Psychology (SIOP), International Association for Applied Psychology, and the International Academy for Intercultural Research. Currently, Dr. Glazer is a co-editor of a book and monograph series on *Culture, Organizations, and Work* and co-Chair of the SIOP International Affairs Committee.

Yuko Ida is pursuing a MEd in Educational Foundations at the College of Education, University of Hawai'i at Mānoa. With seven years of teaching experience as a public elementary school teacher in Okinawa and Nagoya, Japan, her research focuses on equity and social justice issues in education as well as impacts of globalization on educational policies and practices. Ms. Ida holds a BA in Education from the University of the Ryukyus in Okinawa, Japan.

Eva Janebová is an international educator with scholarly experience from Columbia University and University of Minnesota, Charles University and the University of New York Prague. For the last 4 years, she served as the Manager of Strategic Partnerships Project at the Faculty of Education at Masaryk University in Brno in the Czech Republic. Eva has over 18 years of experience as an educator in academia and has served as academic advisor to the Council for International Education Exchange, the Czech Ministry of Education and JAMK in Finland. She has overseen the design of a hundred plus international courses, delivered presentations at NAFSA, EAIE and trainings related to intercultural and international education and various universities, including the University of Minnesota where she was the very first Mestenhauser Fellow in 2018. Her PhD thesis on Internationalization of Higher Education won the Charles University 2008 Bolzano award for the most distinguished social sciences thesis. Her professional commitment is to build capacities of Czech universities to make internationalization an institution-wide process inclusive to all.

Dr. Richard Johnson currently teaches in undergraduate and postgraduate programs in the School of Education, RMIT University. Richard's research and teaching interests include intercultural teaching and preparing teacher education undergraduates to make the transition to the profession.

Christopher J. Johnstone is an Assistant Professor of Comparative and International Development Education at the University of Minnesota. His research spans three areas – inclusive education, inclusive internationalization, and inclusive development. Johnstone is the faculty director of his university's Leadership and Intercultural and International PhD program, a program designed for developing scholar-practitioners as international education leaders. His work has appeared in international development and higher education journals, and he is the recent editor of the *Sage Handbook on Diversity and Inclusion in Education* (2019). He has participated in multiple international fellowships including Fulbright (Czech Republic and India) and Endeavour (Australia). Most recently, Johnstone led a global evaluation of UNICEF's inclusive education initiatives from 2019 to 2020.

Dr. Dawn Joseph is an Associate Professor in the Faculty of Arts and Education at Deakin University. She teaches in undergraduate and postgraduate programs in the School of Education. She is a member of the editorial boards of international and national refereed journals. Her research and publications focus on teacher education, music education, community music, African music, cultural diversity, and ageing and well-being in the Arts.

Suzan Kommers received her PhD from the University of Massachusetts Amherst. She primarily investigates internationalization of higher education and questions on how to provide equitable educational opportunities to all students. Dr. Kommers's research interests include disparities in study abroad opportunities and the effect on students' academic and career outcomes. Her research has been published in journals such as *The International Journal of Higher Education Research, The Journal of International Students* and *Research in Higher Education.*

Melissa K. Mace, EdD, is a scholar-practitioner at Maryville University in St. Louis, United States where she serves as an Assistant Vice President for Enrollment and a Dissertation Chair for the School of Education, Higher Education Leadership Program. Her major research interests include comprehensive internationalization, global education, and internationalization of the curriculum. She co-developed the Institutional Assessment Rubric on Comprehensive Internationalization in Higher Education (IARCIHE).

Julia Miller, PhD, is a Senior Lecturer in the School of Education in the Faculty of Arts at the University of Adelaide, Australia. Her major research interests lie in the areas of phraseology, lexicography, and innovative teaching practices.

Lien Pham is a Senior Lecturer in the Graduate Research School at the University of Technology Sydney. Her research and publications are in the fields of international education and development in East and Southeast Asia, participation and social change combining critical theory and political philosophy. She has consulted for various Australian government agencies on policy-focused research and evaluations, and for multilateral organizations including UNESCO Bangkok on educational policy reforms.

Manca Sustarsic is a PhD Candidate in the Educational Foundations department at University of Hawai'i at Manoa. Her research interests lie in the area of international student mobility and secondary school exchange programs.

Adinda van Gaalen (PhD Candidate, Ghent University) is senior policy officer at Nuffic. Her interests are in the areas of internationalization strategies, policy development, ethics, and intercultural competence development. Adinda is both an advisor to the board of Nuffic and an advisor to higher education institutions in developing internationalization strategies. She also works as a researcher, trainer, and auditor. Previously Adinda worked at the Amsterdam University of Applied Sciences.

Richard Warner is an Adjunct Lecturer in the School of Education in the Faculty of Arts at the University of Adelaide, Australia. His major research interests lie in the areas of cultural dimensions of academic writing, learning through transcultural reflective practices, and role of pathway programs for English as an Additional Language students.

Melissa Whatley, PhD, is a Postdoctoral Research Scholar in the Belk Center for Community College Leadership and Research at North Carolina State University. She applies advanced quantitative analytic approaches to improve our understanding of issues surrounding access and equity in U.S. international higher education. Her research focuses especially on international education at community colleges.

1 Study Abroad and Student Mobility

From Educational Experience to Emerging Enterprise

Suzan Kommers and Krishna Bista

> We live in a globalizing world. That means that all of us, consciously or not, depend on each other. Whatever we do or refrain from doing affects the lives of people who live in places we'll never visit.
>
> – Zygmunt Bauman

Introduction

Global challenges such as climate change, the refugee crisis, and the global spread of the Coronavirus (COVID-19) create anxiety and disruption in human thoughts and institutions. At the same time, it offers windows to rethink our values, behaviors, and systems. As Bauman (2001) illustrated, the world is interconnected, meaning that the decisions by one person on one side of the world can greatly impact people on the other side of the planet. We need political support for global solutions that can effectively address today's global challenges. People thereby need to feel a sense of cohesion and shared responsibility that goes beyond national boundaries (Deardorff, 2006; Paige, Fry, Stallman, Josić, & Jon, 2009).

One of the common ways higher education institutions try to provide students with the opportunity to encounter different worldviews is by encouraging them to do a part of their undergraduate degree in a foreign country (Paige et al., 2009; Take & Shoraku, 2018). Study abroad was historically described as an educational experience that addresses global issues by making students more aware of their global responsibilities and encouraging them to contribute to a more humane world (Reilly & Senders, 2009). Over the past decades, however, the focus of study abroad and student mobility has shifted from mostly an educational experience to an emerging enterprise. In this introductory chapter of the book, we discuss what the commercialization of study abroad meant for the equity in study abroad and student mobility. Is the business model of international higher education gradually pulling away from the goal it was meant to serve? How can scholars, policymakers, and educational practitioners ensure that study abroad is not reinforcing the social inequality present in societies and the world?

Commercialization of Study Abroad

Colleges and universities have increasingly started outsourcing study abroad and exchange programs to third-party vendors and private businesses, often promoting the tourism element over the educational purpose (Pipitone, 2018). Glossy posters of exotic locations try to convince students to study abroad, encounter new people, places, and languages at a destination of their choice. Offering study abroad as a packaged experience often means that this experience is stripped of the educational context and has little preparation and few reintegration programs upon return (Bolen, 2001; Weinberg, 2007). While such an abroad experience may be attractive to students, just sending students to a location abroad is not sufficient for reaching the learning goals often envisioned (Pedersen, 2010). It is mostly the educational guidance and mentoring that helps students recognize the variety and complexity in intercultural encounters (Holmes, Bavieri, & Ganassin, 2015), making abroad meaningful to students' future lives and careers (Doyle et al., 2010). Without proper educational guidance, students often remain unaware of what they have learned and fail to apply their experiences in their work (Messelink, Van Maele, & Spencer-Oatey, 2015).

Apart from study abroad being stripped of its educational context, the commercialization has impacted the goal the abroad experience is argued to serve. Study abroad has been marketed as a way for students to gain a competitive edge in the job market (Bolen, 2001). The extra costs involved with studying abroad in terms of program fees, visa applications, travel, and living are often on top of students' already expensive education and would therefore need to be 'worth it'. Indeed, students reported earning a higher salary as a key motivating factor for them to study abroad (Punteney, 2016). Also, in national policies, the main rationale for sending students abroad is for them to develop new skills and knowledge that would help the workforce (Helms, Brajkovic, & Rumbley, 2016). With the growing emphasis on the effect of study abroad on students' labor market success, there is a growing body of literature addressing the effect of study abroad on students' career outcomes (Salisbury, An, & Pascarella, 2013; Waibel, Rüger, Ette, & Sauer, 2017).

The effect of study abroad on career outcomes is often described in terms of indirect effects.

Research has indicated study abroad allows students to develop intercultural competency and provides them with the experience to communicate effectively and appropriately in intercultural situations (Lokkesmoe, Kuchinke, & Ardichvili, 2016; Pedersen, 2010; Peng, Dyne, & Oh, 2015; Salisbury et al., 2013; Williams, 2005). This, in turn, would make students more successful in their later careers. Moreover, study abroad is suggested to relate to students' career outcomes indirectly through the social and cultural capital such experience results in. Employers recognized the importance of cross-cultural understanding in an increasingly global workforce (Crossman & Clarke, 2010; Molony, Sowter, & Potts, 2011) and believed that students who gained international experiences through study abroad were superior in professionally relevant competencies (Teichler & Janson, 2007). While study abroad is often assumed to benefit students' later careers, research shows this effect may be more nuanced. Labor market returns vary according to factors such as the level of study, the type of mobility, and prestige hierarchies of the host country (Van Mol, Caarls & Souto-Otero, 2020).

The often-assumed effect of study abroad on career success is problematic for two reasons. First, the studies finding an effect of study abroad on career success such as job income often do not account sufficiently for the selection effect of only certain students going abroad, potentially making the effect a result of pre-existing social inequalities (Waibel et al., 2017). Second, in case study abroad actually positively impact students' careers, this means that students who do not have equal opportunities to participate in study abroad, miss out on the enhanced educational opportunities, meaning that study abroad creates inequitable chances for upward social mobility. In sum, the shift of study abroad from a learning experience to an enterprise and way to gain upward social mobility signifies the importance of examining study abroad practices in terms of equity, accessibility, and socioeconomic inequality.

Inequality in Study Abroad Opportunities

Studying abroad requires financial, social, and cultural resources, making it much harder for students of low socioeconomic status to participate (Dessoff, 2006; Lörz, Netz, & Quast, 2016; Salisbury, Paulsen, & Pascarella, 2011). The inequality in study abroad opportunities means that some students are shut out of key learning experiences. Moreover, with the increasing consensus that study abroad gives students an advantage on the job market, inequitable opportunities to study abroad can create inequity in later career outcomes. With mostly students from higher socioeconomic status going abroad, study abroad might reinforce existing social inequality rather than making the world more compassionate and socially just. The inequalities in study abroad opportunities become apparent upon reviewing the federal policies on study abroad, which show that some students – primarily already disadvantaged students – miss out on the learning and career advantages.

The United States has been described as an example of a country that has very little regulation in terms of outgoing student mobility. This provides a prime example showing that by not providing any regulations and financial support, study abroad will only be accessible to the elite. The U.S. Department of Education has had almost no involvement with the campus internationalization initiatives (e.g. study abroad, transnational research collaboration) at American colleges and universities. There are limited opportunities for students and faculty to receive student aid/travel support, to support their research and collaboration, and to prioritize strategic goals and policies in relation to the national interest (Ruther, 2014; Trilokekar, 2015).

Even though higher education institutions have promoted study abroad and internationalization in their mission and vision statements, they often did not translate this into practical steps and equivalent federal funding (Ruther, 2014). The lack of federal funding for study abroad resulted in a lack of a strategic approach in the regulation and organization of outgoing student mobility (de Wit, 2002). The extra expenses required from students at most institutions in the U.S. create a heavy financial burden on the student, which in many cases, makes study abroad unaffordable. The lack of federal funding strategies on study abroad can subsequently create large disparities in study abroad opportunities.

Conversations about study abroad have mainly focused on study abroad in response to the demands of changing economic and occupational structures. However, to fully address study abroad and student mobility, there needs to be a better understanding of the inequity in educational and occupational outcomes of study abroad and how such inequities might make study abroad a reproducer of social inequality. Only by examining how study abroad and student mobility reinforces social stratification, research can work towards finding ways to make internationalization practices like study abroad more effective and more socially just (George Mwangi et al., 2018). What are alternatives to study abroad programs that exceed the primacy of local face-to-face lecturing and tutoring? Will blended distance education and collaborative online international learning overrule traditional student mobility? These questions are touched in this book to help us proceed further in the 21st century.

Organization of the Book

Each chapter of the book provides a broad range of inequality issues and thereby responds to the growing need for insights into how to increase equity in study abroad and student mobility. The chapters presented in this book will bring a fresh perspective on how our current internationalization efforts are serving some students while disadvantaging others. The entire book is divided into three parts.

The first section of the book includes four chapters that discuss how equity issues in international student mobility play out on a global scale. In Chapter 2, Adinda van Gaalen provides an overview of the undesired consequences of internationalization of higher education following the People, Planet, Prosperity (3P) values framework of the United Nations. Hatice Altun addresses a specific aspect of the global power dynamic by exploring the social and educational trajectories of 'students of the new global elite' in an intercultural setting in Chapter 3. Lien Pham describes the challenges of social equity in international education within Vietnam specifically in Chapter 4. In Chapter 5, Kayoko Enomoto, Richard Warner, and Julia Miller describe Australian students' learning experience while on Japanese exchange to discuss the balance between institutional and individual students' responsibilities to prepare students embarking on study abroad.

The second section of the book addresses the inequality in students' opportunities to gain international experiences. The first two chapters in this part focus on inequality in internationalization in secondary education. In Chapter 6, Manca Sustarsic and Baoyan Cheng explore equity issues in secondary school student mobility by discussing how social and cultural capital gets transmitted through merit-based exchange programs. In Chapter 7, Yuko Ida examines how the promotion of International Baccalaureate education in Japan resulted in an increase in inequality in the educational system. Moving the focus to inequality in students' opportunities to gain international experiences in postsecondary education, in Chapter 8, Melissa Whatley describes how postsecondary institutions relate to students' abroad going, particularly in terms of their location and the duration of their time abroad.

The final section of the book addresses the question of how to make study abroad more inclusive by promoting diversity and exploring alternatives to study abroad. In Chapter 9, Chris Johnstone provides an overview of the recent literature on inclusive internationalization, comparing the U.S. and European policy and practice. In Chapter 10, Melissa Mace reviews the literature around aspects of internationalization at home and offers recommendations for a global education context that permeates all areas of the student experience. In Chapter 11, Dawn Joseph and Richard Johnson examine an example of an alternative to study abroad, discussing benefits and challenges in relation to the value of promoting diversity through international partnerships. Finally, Sharon Glazer presents a quick guide on how to develop virtually abroad programs in Chapter 12.

Study Abroad and Student Mobility: It's Time to Reinvent

While internationalization practices like study abroad are often implemented to make the world a better place, study abroad and student mobility are increasingly commercialized, creating a growing concern about equity issues. At the same time, recent developments such as the climate crisis and the COVID-19 outbreak also show that education practices that require students to travel may not be sustainable in the long run. This book is a response to the growing need for reinventing study abroad and student mobility. This book is meant to be insightful to both researchers and administrators working in the area of internationalization of higher education, and for educators and practitioners that deal with the results of increasing student mobility on a day-to-day basis. Collectively, all contributors offer insights and practical tips to inform institutional policy in developing more effective, inclusive, and equitable ways to internationalize their campus programs and initiatives both for students and faculty members. By addressing both the scientific and practical implications of the research, we hope that the book can serve as a tool for discussion and further reflection within international education offices, graduate classrooms, and as a foundational reference for forthcoming research and scholarship.

Looking Towards the Future

The time we live in both emphasizes the importance and challenges in relation to the future of study abroad and student mobility. Collectively, contributors in this book acknowledge the dynamics of study abroad and alternative opportunities to reimagine study abroad and student mobility. Apart from making study abroad more accessible, education should work on creating alternatives for study abroad that do not require students to leave their home communities. Education carries a large responsibility to prepare the next generation for a globalized world. The world cannot rely anymore on students' capacity to travel and study overseas. To enable the learning that is so necessary, alternatives to study abroad and student mobility should be developed. As scholars in the field, we hope to support our fellow scholars, administrators, and educators in their aspiration to approach issues of inequality and gain guidance on how to work towards policy and pedagogy to make study abroad more socially just. This book provides an overview of the equity issue in study abroad and student mobility and some concrete examples of how to address these issues in different situations.

Internationalization at home practices provides students with opportunities to gain international experiences while staying at their home campus (Beelen & Jones, 2015). Educators and policymakers have noticed the need to provide internationalization experiences at home and started to implement alternatives. For example, at the State University of New York, the Collaborative Online International Learning Center offers programs related to cross-cultural communication skills and global understanding virtually. Many emerging platforms such as the United Planet offer distance and faraway classrooms to bring in diverse and intercultural perspectives to educate future global leaders. Soliya, a technology-based learning platform headquartered in New York, offers interactive cross-cultural exchange and learning opportunities. Colleges and universities around the world seem to be interested in exploring ways to give their students a more international outlook to prepare for the 21st-century workforce. Emerging commercial programs such as Youth for Understanding, GoAbroad, Virtual Exchange Coalition, and many others are some examples of exchange programs or virtual initiatives where students get an opportunity to engage with fellow students from different cultures and languages. This is an alternative educational practice that can help students develop intercultural competencies by having them collaborate online with international students. Not much is yet known on the effectiveness of such online learning practices and virtual exchanges. Future research should investigate how these educational experiences result in intercultural learning and how such experience compares to students studying abroad in the traditional way.

References

Bauman, Z. (2001). Whatever happened to compassion? In T. Bentley & D.S. Jones (Eds.), *The model universe (pp. 51–56)*. London, UK: Demos.

Beelen, J., & Jones, E. (2015). Europe calling: A new definition for Internationalization at Home. *International Higher Education, 83*, 12–13. doi: 10.6017/ihe.2015.83.9080

Bolen, M. (2001). Consumerism and US study abroad. *Journal of Studies in International Education, 5*(3), 182–200. doi: 10.1177/102831530153002

Crossman, J. E., & Clarke, M. (2010). International experience and graduate employability: Stakeholder perceptions on the connection. *Higher Education, 59*(5), 599–613. doi:10.1007/s10734-009-9268-z

Deardorff, D. K. (2006). Identification and assessment of intercultural competence as a student outcome of internationalization. *Journal of Studies in International Education, 10*(3), 241–266. doi:10.1177/1028315306287002

DeGraaf, D., Slagter, C., Larsen, K., & Ditta, E. (2013). The long-term personal and professional impacts of participating in a study abroad program. *Frontiers: The Interdisciplinary Journal of Study Abroad, 23*, 42–59.

Dessoff, A. (2006). Who's NOT going abroad? *International Educator, 15*(2), 20–27.

de Wit, H. (2002). *Internationalization of higher education in the United States of America and Europe*. Santa Barbara, CA: Greenwood Publishing Group.

Doyle, S., Gendall, P., Meyer, L. H., Hoek, J., Tait, C., McKenzie, L., & Loorparg, A. (2010). An investigation of factors associated with student participation in study abroad. *Journal of Studies in International Education, 14*(5), 471–490. doi:10.1177/1028315309336032

George Mwangi, C. A., Latafat, S., Hammond, S., Kommers, S., Thoma, H., Berger, J., & Blanco-Ramirez, G. (2018). Criticality in international higher education research: A critical discourse analysis of higher education journals. *Higher Education,* 76(6), 1091–1107. doi:10.1007/s10734-018-0259-9

Helms, M. R., Brajkovic, L. & Rumbley, L. E. (2016). National policies for higher education internationalisation: What campus leaders and practitioners need to know. *Internationalisation of Higher Education: Policy and Practice, 3*, 1–18.

Holmes, P., Bavieri, L., & Ganassin, S. (2015). Developing intercultural understanding for study abroad: Students' and teachers' perspectives on pre-departure intercultural learning. *Intercultural Education, 26*(1), 16–30. doi:10.1080/14675986.2015.993250

Lokkesmoe, K. J., Kuchinke, K. P., & Ardichvili, A. (2016). Developing cross-cultural awareness through foreign immersion programs. *European Journal of Training and Development, 40*(3), 155–170. doi:10.1108/ejtd-07-2014-0048

Lörz, M., Netz, N., & Quast, H. (2016). Why do students from underprivileged families less often intend to study abroad? *Higher Education, 2*, 153–174. doi:10.1007/s10734-015-9943-1

Messelink, H. E., Van Maele, J., & Spencer-Oatey, H. (2015). Intercultural competencies: What students in study and placement mobility should be learning. *Intercultural Education, 26*(1), 62–72. doi:10.1080/14675986.2015.993555

Molony, J., Sowter, B., & Potts, D. (2011). 2011 QS global employer survey report. http://www.iu.qs.com/product/qs-global-employer-survey-report-2011/

Paige, R. M., Fry, G. W., Stallman, E. M., Josić, J., & Jon, J. (2009). Study abroad for global engagement: The long-term impact of mobility experiences. *Intercultural Education, 20*, 29–44. doi:10.1080/14675980903370847

Pedersen, P. J. (2010). Assessing intercultural effectiveness outcomes in a year-long study abroad program. *International Journal of Intercultural Relations, 34*(1), 70–80. doi:10.1016/j.ijintrel.2009.09.003

Peng, A. C., Van Dyne, L., & Oh, K. (2015). The influence of motivational cultural intelligence on cultural effectiveness based on study abroad. *Journal of Management Education, 39*(5), 572–596. doi:10.1177/1052562914555717

Pipitone, J. M. (2018). Place as pedagogy: Toward study abroad for social change. *Journal of Experiential Education, 41*(1), 54–74. doi:10.1177/1053825917751509

Punteney, K. (2016). International careers: U.S. undergraduates' motivations and concerns. *Journal of International Students, 6*(2), 478–500. https://eric-ed-gov.silk.library.umass.edu/?id=EJ1094890

Reilly, D., & Senders, S. (2009). Becoming the change we want to see: Critical study abroad for a tumultuous world. *Frontiers: The Interdisciplinary Journal of Study Abroad, 18*, 241–267.

Ruther, N. L. (2014). *Barely there, powerfully present: Thirty years of U.S. policy on international higher education.* New York, NY: Routledge.

Salisbury, M. H., An, B. P., & Pascarella, E. T. (2013). The effect of study abroad on intercultural competence among undergraduate college students. *Journal of Student Affairs Research and Practice, 50*(1), 1–20. doi:10.1515/jsarp-2013-0001

Salisbury, M. H., Paulsen, M. B., & Pascarella, E. T. (2011). Why do all the study abroad students look alike? Applying an integrated student choice model to explore differences in the factors that influence White and minority students' intent to study abroad. *Research in Higher Education, 52*(2), 123–150. doi:10.1007/s11162-010-9191-2

Take, H., & Shoraku, A. (2018). Universities' expectations for study abroad programs fostering internationalization: Educational policies. *Journal of Studies in International Education, 22*(1), 37–52. doi:10.1177/1028315317724557 130

Teichler, U., & Janson, K. (2007). The professional value of temporary study in another European country: Employment and work of former ERASMUS students. *Journal of Studies in International Education, 11*, 486–495. doi:10.1177/1028315307303230

Trilokekar, R. D. (2015). From soft power to economic diplomacy? A comparison of the changing rationales and roles of the U. S. and Canadian federal governments in international education. https://cshe.berkeley.edu/publications/soft-power-economic-diplomacy-comparison-changing-rationales-and-roles-u-s-and-canadian

Van Mol, C., Caarls, K., & Souto-Otero, M. (2020). International student mobility and labour market outcomes: An investigation of the role of level of study, type of mobility, and international prestige hierarchies. *Higher Education*, 1–27.

Waibel, S., Petzold, K., & Rüger, H. (2018). Occupational status benefits of studying abroad and the role of occupational specificity – A propensity score matching approach. *Social Science Research, 74*, 45–61. doi:10.1016/j.ssresearch.2018.05.006

Waibel, S., Rüger, H., Ette, A., & Sauer, L. (2017). Career consequences of transnational educational mobility: A systematic literature review. *Educational Research Review, 20*, 81–98. doi:10.1016/j.edurev.2016.12.001

Weinberg. (2007). Quantity or quality in study abroad? Inside in Higher Ed. https://www.insidehighered.com/views/2007/05/08/quantity-or-quality-study-abroad

Williams, T. R. (2005). Exploring the impact of study abroad on student's intercultural communication skills: Adaptability and sensitivity. *Journal of Studies in International Education, 9*(4), 356–371. doi:10.1177/1028315305277681

Part I

How Do Equity Issues in International Student Mobility Play Out on a Global Scale?

2 Mapping Undesired Consequences of Internationalization of Higher Education

Adinda van Gaalen

Introduction

The traditional domestic role of higher education (HE) has influenced by a globalized context, which means that decisions made in one part of the world affects the other parts (Held, McGrew, Goldblatt, & Perraton, 2003). This is also true for internationalization of higher education (IoHE): its effects are not always noticed, for instance, because they are experienced by stakeholders in another geographical area. However, an awareness of both desired and undesired consequences of internationalization is developing within the HE-field.

Literature on this topic includes a wide variety of themes, among which are education abroad (Dvorak, Christiansen, Fischer, & Underhill, 2011; Hughes-Warrington, 2012), international student mobility and recruitment (Anderson, Monjeau, & Rau, 2015; Hulme, Thomson, Hulme, & Doughty, 2014), language of instruction (Hughes, 2008), sustainable development (Campbell & Mawer, 2019), curriculum (Robinson & Lee, 2007), international branch campuses (IBCs) (Waters & Leung, 2017; Wilkins, 2017), intercultural practice (Killick, 2018) and partnerships (Helms Matross, 2015). If higher education institutions (HEIs) wish to uphold the values they stand for, they should recognize and act upon potential undesired consequences. Particularly, public HEIs need to safeguard the support for internationalization from the general public and politicians. While some undesired consequences – such as exclusion – are extensively discussed in the literature, others – such as the carbon footprint of academic traveling – gain much less attention. Furthermore, a model enabling HEIs to identify the potential undesired consequences of their activities is lacking thus far. The premise of this chapter is that ethical IoHE can be achieved by an HEI by finding harmony in attending to all its values.

The growing number of stakeholders involved in the context of HE as well as the history of IoHE has led to a range of understandings, rationales, ideologies and foci on IoHE at various levels within the HE sector (Bamberger, Morris, & Yemini, 2019; Stier, 2004). According to Robinson and Lee (2007), both globalization and the variety of stakeholders may result in uneasy ethical situations. These are situations in which a decision must be made between various choices within IoHE that are in mutual conflict and yet equally (un)desirable.

In this chapter, a decision or act is considered ethical if it is acceptable to the larger community because it complies with moral norms or standards of behavior (Jones, 1991). If a choice must be made between alternatives that support different values, this is called a dilemma. Dilemmas also appear when a choice must be made between two or more alternatives that each breach a different value or if there is a situation in which one value is breached and yet another value is supported. Recognizing the interdependence and relatedness between values, it is important to avoid oversimplifying a dilemma, privileging one value over all others or overlooking key stakeholders (see also: Scholars at Risk, 2017). It is therefore important to recognize that ethical frameworks are historically and socially rooted and therefore show great variations. What may be considered ethical in one social setting may be unethical in another.

Conceptual Approach

Without claiming that one particular set of values and ethics could serve all HEIs worldwide, this chapter examines how a value framework can provide a moral compass for internationalization strategies. Such a framework should be based on an individual HEI's values to support a more conscious and comprehensive approach to IoHE. The People, Planet, Prosperity (3P) framework is used as a lens to map undesired consequences across four main clusters of internationalization activities, including outgoing credit mobility (OCM), incoming diploma mobility (IDM), internationalization of teaching and learning (ITL) and transnational education (TNE). The choice of clusters is based on priorities set by HEIs in Europe, as reported in surveys by the European University Association (EUA) (2013), the International Association of Universities (IAU) (Egron-Polak & Hudson, 2014) and the European Association of International Education (EAIE) (Sandström & Hudson, 2018). TNE was added to this list because it is 'a complex and high-risk operation' (Stafford & Taylor, 2016, p. 626) and has increased, albeit moderately, in size since 2000 (Wilkins, 2017).

OCM refers to students staying abroad for a short time of study, research or internship, with the aim of obtaining credits that are recognized by the home institution. Various alternative terms are used in literature, such as 'outgoing student mobility', 'study abroad' and 'education abroad'. Incoming diploma mobility (IDM) is used to refer to students from another country who aim to earn a full degree from the host country HE system. Alternative terms include 'incoming degree mobility' and 'international degree students'. Internationalization of teaching and learning (ITL), as used in this chapter, is best described by Leask's definition of internationalization of the curriculum: 'the incorporation of an international and intercultural dimension into the content of the curriculum as well as the teaching and learning processes

[. . .]' (Leask, 2009, p. 209). ITL is part of the broader concept of internationalization at home (IaH). TNE, used interchangeably with 'offshore education' (Knight, 2016), refers to offering degree programs to students located in another country (Shams & Huisman, 2012). It includes academic courses or programs abroad, IBCs, overseas joint ventures, franchises (Egron-Polak & Hudson, 2014), joint or multiple degree programs (Engel et al., 2015) and distance education (Wilkins, 2017).

Research Method

The research was conducted through an iterative process of literature review. It focused on generating a comprehensive overview of undesired consequences of internationalization. The initial search – via Web of Science – used the search terms 'ethic/ethics', 'sustainability' and 'social responsibility' (terms closely related to the SDGs) in combination with the terms 'internationalisation/internationalization' and 'higher education'. This search resulted in 19 papers. The first step was to search these titles, then to read the abstracts and finally to fully read the publications found. In this step, articles were excluded on topics that are not exclusively linked to IoHE and are indeed part of another extensive body of literature such as corruption and research ethics. Literature on the teaching practice – for instance, global ethics education, education for sustainable development and decolonization of the curriculum – are not the focus of this chapter on governance and policies and were therefore excluded. Finally, articles at the micro-level were excluded as this book chapter focuses on the institutional and national policy levels. After filtering out these publications, a total of 12 relevant articles remained.

This approach has its limitations. A literature search in English only may lead to publications from primarily Anglo-Saxon countries. As these countries are the main receiving countries in terms of IDM and the most active suppliers of TNE, they do not necessarily experience the same type and scale of desired and undesired consequences as non-Anglo-Saxon countries do. Moreover, values in Anglo-Saxon countries likely do not represent the full range of values in HE worldwide. Therefore, in the second step in which additional literature was found through the references in the first selection of literature, special attention was paid to non-Anglo-Saxon and particularly non-Western countries. Also helpful were the literature suggestions of the Critical Internationalization Studies Network. The second search focused on titles including terms such as 'brain drain', 'inequality' and 'carbon footprint' as well as related terms. Also, new search terms were identified including 'dilemmas', 'contradictions', 'ambiguities', problems', 'gaps', 'paradoxes' and 'SDGs'. In the third step, these were combined with the term 'internationalisation/internationalization' in a new search in Web of Science. In addition, 'Internationalisation/internationalization' was combined with terminology related to ethics including 'moral values', 'morality', 'integrity' and 'principles'. Steps two and three resulted in an additional 105 publications of which 85 articles were selected as relevant for this research.

Table 2.1 3P Framework

People	*Planet*	*Prosperity*
Universally accessible education	Promoting sustainable travelling	Equal (job market) opportunities
Respecting race, ethnicity and cultural diversity, and fostering intercultural understanding	Sustainable consumption and production patterns	Reduction of inequalities of outcome
Protecting and educating on human rights	Sustainable use of natural resources	Income growth for the most vulnerable
Respecting human dignity		Planned and well-managed migration policies
Shared responsibility		

Note: Table based on UN (2015).

The complete list included 124 publications of which 97 are relevant titles (a list can be requested from the author). The chosen approach yielded a rich set of publications, but obviously – due to the broad remit of the SDGs – a relevant study may have been missed. In light of the purpose of this study, however, it can be assumed that a sufficient amount of studies has been covered to map undesired effects of internationalization.

This chapter uses the UN (2015) value framework, 3P, for the purpose of offering an example. This framework was selected on the basis of its relevance for the public sector, its broad scope and its international character. The 3Ps can be directly linked to the three main dimensions of the world we live in: society, environment and economy. The UN created this framework through intensive consultation with stakeholders around the world and explains each value by giving some examples, some of which are particularly relevant to HEIs in a global setting (see Table 2.1).

Using any particular framework has some weaknesses. First, values are not fixed. Instead, there is a continuous need to (re)negotiate shared values and conceptualizations in diverse settings. Second, a common value – even when acknowledged by almost 150 countries worldwide – is not necessarily applied identically across cultures or HEIs. Third, there is no single set of values within any national or institutional setting. Fourth, how values are conceptualized is partly dependent on a person's position and context. Therefore, it must be noted that even a value framework developed in an international consultation process is not by definition a universally applicable framework in HEIs.

Still, this framework provides a starting point for exploring little researched territory. Given the exploratory nature of this topic, this mapping is not meant to be complete but instead a first attempt to discuss values and resulting dilemmas in internationalization in a more comprehensive way.

Results

The articles reviewed address a number of internationalization activities that have been categorized for the purpose of the analysis into Outgoing credit mobility, Incoming diploma mobility, Internationalization of teaching and learning and Transnational education. The framework of analysis is formed by the 3P criteria (see Table 2.1). This section gives an overview of the undesired effects reported in the literature for each of these criteria.

Outgoing Credit Mobility (OCM)

In terms of *people* criteria, OCM often includes careful selection of partners based on comparability, excluding those HEIs which are not considered to offer the same value (Clifford & Montgomery, 2014; Lumby & Foskett, 2016). This leads to a narrow focus and increasing homogeneity rather than diversity of HEIs being promoted. At the student level, Jefferess (2008) points out another dilemma. Internships in developing countries can lead to feelings among students of responsibility to aid or educate others (developing benevolent identities). These feelings may result in unequal relationships and even exploitative forms of intervention that fail to respect cultural diversity.

OCM may also negatively affect the *planet* due to a high level of fossil fuel consumption and carbon emissions caused by academic traveling (Dvorak et al., 2011; Ilieva, Beck, & Waterstone, 2014). This seems contradictory to the aim of many OCM programs to develop global citizenship in students (Long, Vogelaar, & Hale, 2014).

Finally, in terms of *prosperity*, literature reports a number of undesired effects of OCM. It generally caters to a relatively small and homogenous group of students with at least one parent who has an HE degree. This is further stimulated by HEIs actively promoting OCM as a strategy of distinction (Sidhu & Dall'Alba, 2017). This selectivity of studying abroad may result in a limited and select group of students benefiting from internationalization activities (Salisbury, Paulsen, & Pascarella, 2011), which can intensify social and economic inequality (Tannock, 2013).

Incoming Diploma Mobility (IDM)

IDM leads to a number of undesired effects in terms of *people*, according to a review of the literature. Degree programs abroad are particularly accessible for students with certain backgrounds and nationalities (Enslin & Hedge, 2008), in other words, those who can afford it rather than those who qualify (Hulme et al., 2014). As a consequence, home students meet a partial, skewed and elite representation of students who have grown up in other countries (Tannock, 2013). In addition, it can lead to social segregation and resentment towards students who can afford to study abroad but perform lower than students in the national system (Andersson, 2017).

In addition, there is a hierarchy of international students. Some are seen as valued talented guests, whereas others – like refugees – are not as welcome (Kenway & Fahey, 2009).

International students are often presented by HEIs to add value to the learning environment of domestic students. At the same time, international students may be considered to be a special needs group in terms of pedagogy (Doherty, 2006). Tange (2016) suggests that presenting international students as special needs groups reduces complex issues to differences between native and international, whereas other variables may play significant roles as well (Tange, 2016). Making this distinction between international and domestic students can potentially lead to increased (real or perceived) inequality between these groups of students. Domestic students may, for instance, perceive international students as taking their place in their program of choice (Tannock, 2013). International students have, in some locations, become subject to surveillance, racism, increasing restriction and divisive rhetoric (O'Connor, 2017). Lumby and Foskett (2016) explain that too much heterogeneity may result in calls to protect the host culture as there is a limit to the level of otherness accepted by staff and students.

Finally, the dominance of Anglo-Saxon countries in IDM leads both to a risk of re-colonialization (Ilieva et al., 2014) and to decreased linguistic, cultural and curricular diversity of education. IDM may thus intensify inequality between HE systems. Systems with higher prestige usually attract the most students on a global scale adding to their prestige.

IDM requires traveling which often results in a carbon footprint (Shields, 2019), an effect related to the *planet* criteria. This is particularly the case if travels are not limited to one trip to the host country and one trip back home. International students may pay various visits to their home country and also travel within the host region. In addition, any visits from family and friends also add to the carbon footprint of the individual degree mobility.

A number of ethical issues in IDM relate to aspects of *prosperity*. The growing focus on student recruitment – in some countries – has turned HE into an economic sector in its own right (Stier, 2004). The HE market, however, is skewed by a language advantage/barrier, thus excluding non-English speaking communities from the global HE offer and its benefits (Hughes, 2008).

Another ethical concern is the question of who pays and who profits in IoHE (Sidhu & Dall'Alba, 2012). In financial terms, (students from) poor countries invest their resources in rich countries' consolidated academic programs rather than in sustaining their own educational system. Foreign scholarships enhance this effect, as students are often required to spend the grant in the donor country rather than in their home country. This also leads to a generation of scholars who are trained in practices and academic cultures that may not be fully applicable in their own country (Anderson et al., 2015). Foreign degrees may also be unjustly valued higher or lower than those from local institutions, leading to unequal competition on the labor market. Finally, students deciding not to return home may, depending on the context, cause a brain drain (Beerkens, 2014).

Internationalization of Teaching and Learning (ITL)

In terms of the *people* criteria, Clifford and Montgomery (2014) found that lecturers are concerned that ITL could be a new form of colonialism, lacking historical context and privileging the Western perspective. As the role of English in HE is increasing, the users of this language tend to become more oriented towards English-speaking academic systems (Altbach, 2004). This undermines respect for pluralism, which is an important value underpinning many internationalization efforts (Stier, 2004). Leask acknowledges this pitfall of internationalization and explicitly states that internationalization of the curriculum is not an effort to develop a curriculum that 'looks the same everywhere and can be taught anywhere to anyone' (2015, p. 12) but instead to prepare students to work and live in a global society.

Turner (2009, p. 243) states that 'the use of one group of students as an internationalizing source for another is doubtful unless the benefits to all concerned are reciprocal and unequivocal'. English as a Teaching Language (ETL) may open up education for a wider group of students but may also harm educational accessibility for domestic students and raises concerns about second-language effects on the learning process and the quality of education (Beerkens, 2014). ETL may also create inequality in the relationship between native and non-native speakers, particularly when considered a proxy for lower academic ability (Harrison, 2015).

Undesired consequences in terms of *planet* criteria are limited for this internationalization category as ITL generally involves little to no traveling. However, it does often include virtual cooperation which also has a carbon footprint though much smaller.

In theory, ITL allows all students to benefit from internationalization efforts and is therefore aligned with the principle of equality as an element of *prosperity*. According to Harrison (2015, p. 424), however, 'there is accumulating evidence that even IaH is unequally distributed with strong differences in willingness (or ability) to benefit'. International and intercultural skills should thus be acquired as a part of the core curriculum rather than through elective courses (Beelen & Jones, 2015). Finally, some HEIs simply replace local cases for international cases that are actually just as local but from elsewhere (Ljosland 2008, cited by Fabricius, Mortensen, & Haberland, 2017, p. 587).

Transnational Education (TNE)

The *people* criteria can be enhanced and damaged by IBCs and distant learning as it can increase accessibility of HE but it can also erode and prevent the development of indigenous capacity for research and innovation

(Khoo, 2011) with associated implications in terms of prosperity. According to McNiff (2013), this is a new form of colonialism and a threat to diversity. Distance learning courses often require a fee, digital skills and good internet connections. As a result, 70% of participants in MOOC's have a bachelor's degree or higher (Patru & Balaji, 2016). In addition, Wilkins (2017) raises the issue of academic freedom in IBCs.

Some forms of TNE such as IBCs and joint degrees may require staff or student mobility with undesired consequences for the *planet* criteria.

Hiring local staff can also have ethical implications in terms of *prosperity criteria*. It may cause local HEIs to lose quality staff or it can negatively influence the quality offered in the IBC (Shams & Huisman, 2012). IBC programs can also lead to classification and demarcation of students if presented as an alternative for a competitive local HE system (Waters & Leung, 2017). If the IBC program is presented as identical to the original program in the home country when in reality it is not, this can potentially lower the value attributed to the diploma (EAIE, 2013). On the bright side, one could argue that this is an adaptation of the quality of the education to the host system rather than imposing a model developed in another system often perceived as 'higher' quality. Doubts have also been raised regarding the value of degrees in multiple and joint degree programs as a result of double-counting of workload towards more than one qualification (Bamford, 2012) (Table 2.2).

Discussion and Conclusions

This mapping exercise reveals that various types of dilemmas can be distinguished in IoHE. First, they may be caused by a contradiction within a single policy measure: e.g. the carbon footprint contradicting the aim to instill global citizenship. Second, a dilemma can arise when activities result in both positive and negative outcomes depending on the value from which the results are viewed. Long-term mobility, for instance, is generally more sustainable in terms of the environment but less accessible than short-term mobility. Third, a dilemma occurs in case of a contradiction between short-term and long-term gains of IoHE. For instance, when TNE with a short-term focus leads to (longer-term) disinvestments in the HE system of the hosting country. Fourth, ethical dilemmas emerge from the fact that IoHE has features of both a public good and a commodity. Recruitment of international students can eventually lead to brain drain if education is considered a public good or to brain gain when considered a commodity. Fifth, a dilemma occurs when ethical behavior at a meso or macro-level is unethical behavior at micro-level or vice versa. Scholarship programs may try to prevent brain drain for the sake of a nation state by requiring grant holders to return home after graduation. However, this prompts the question of whether it is ethical to force individuals to leave behind the (social) life and network they may have built, in their host country.

A complicating factor in solving dilemmas is that there are often more than two perspectives on them. Recruiting students, for instance, may lead

Table 2.2 Mapping of Undesired Consequences by IoHE Activity

	People	*Planet*	*Prosperity*
Outgoing credit mobility	Unequal student opportunities Over-simplified views of cultures reinforced Exclusion of students and/or HEIs Less diversity of HEIs Unequal relationships	Carbon emissions through academic traveling High level of fossil fuel consumption	Global inequality reinforced Intensifying social and economic inequality
Incoming degree mobility	Exclusion because of equal or unequal treatment (discrimination and racism) Treatment of being in deficit Unequal access (domestic students pushed out) Decreased linguistic, cultural and curricular diversity	Carbon emissions Fossil fuel consumption	Brain drain Unequal labor market competition Poor countries subsidize education in rich countries Mismatch between international education content and local application
Internationalization of teaching and learning	Decreased diversity of curricula Cultural homogenization, undermining respect for pluralism Exploiting students' cultural background as an educational resource for other students ETL decreasing access for local students ETL creating inequality between native and non-native speakers		Benefits unequally distributed among students Mismatch between delocalized educational programs and local needs
Transnational education	Degrees incompatible with local or home country norms and standards Classification and demarcation of students Cultural imperialism threatening diversity	Carbon emissions Fossil fuel consumption	Power imbalances Counterproductive to developing capacities of host country

not only to brain drain but also to enhanced access if it increases the HE offer in a country. Countries may learn from benchmarking with foreign providers of HE (Enslin & Hedge, 2008). Furthermore, in countries with insufficient highly skilled jobs, non-returnees decrease the competition on the labor market while at the same time sending remittances and helping to promote cross-national cooperation. It is therefore important that internationalization policies in HE consider all possible effects and do so from a wide variety of perspectives.

Implications

This chapter shows how a values framework can be used to identify undesired effects of IoHE. Such an exercise can, for instance, be applied to developing and implementing internationalization strategies. It supports a more conscious, systematic and comprehensive approach to IoHE and to dealing with ethical dilemmas. However, contradictory views on the consequences of IoHE often exist within one country and even within one institution on a daily basis as no single values framework but rather a variety of ambitions and indeed perspectives on ethical behavior exist.

The 3P values framework may provide inspiration for HEIs when (re)viewing their internationalization activities based on their own values framework. A mapping of desired and undesired consequences of internationalization activities is a starting point for consideration and debate. The challenge for any HEI trying to achieve ethical internationalization seems to be to find harmony in attending to all its values. As it is much easier to distinguish irresponsible choices in IoHE than to determine what responsible choices are, further research is needed on transforming undesired outcomes into responsible strategic choices.

References

Altbach, P. G. (2004). Globalisation and the university: Myths and realities in an unequal world. *Tertiary Education and Management, 10*(1), 3–25. doi:10.1007/978-94-6209-338-6

Anderson, C. B., Monjeau, A., & Rau, J. R. (2015). Knowledge dialogue to attain global scientific excellence and broader social relevance. *BioScience, 65*(7), 709–717. doi:10.1093/biosci/biv046

Andersson, R. (2017). The Sandwich model. A successful case of capacity building. In E. Egron-Polak, H. Teekens, L. Purser, & M. F. Green (Eds.), *Internationalisation of higher education* (pp. 1–14). Berlin, Germany: DUZ Academic Publishers.

Bamberger, A., Morris, P., & Yemini, M. (2019). Neoliberalism, internationalization and higher education: connections, contradictions and alternatives. *Discourse: Studies in the Cultural Politics of Education, 40*(2), 203–216. doi:10.1080/01596306.2019.1569879

Bamford, J. K. (2012). *Dealing with difference: Developing an understanding of international postgraduate joint degree programmes in business in London and France*. London: University of London.

Beelen, J., & Jones, E. (2015). Redefining internationalization at home. In A. Curaj, L. Matei, R. Pricopie, J. Salmi, & P. Scott (Eds.), *The European higher education area* (pp. 59–72). Cham, Switzerland: Springer.

Beerkens, E. (2014). 40 years of internationalisation in European higher education: Achievements and challenges. *RIHE International Seminar Reports* 21, 1–24, Hiroshima University.

Campbell, A. C., & Mawer, M. (2019). Clarifying mixed messages: International scholarship programmes in the sustainable development agenda. *Higher Education Policy, 32*, 167–184. doi:10.1057/s41307-017-0077-1

Clifford, V., & Montgomery, C. (2014). Challenging conceptions of western higher education and promoting graduates as global citizens. *Higher Education Quarterly, 68*(1), 28–45. doi:10.1111/hequ.12029

Doherty, C. A. (2006). *The production of cultural difference and cultural sameness in online internationalized education* [Queensland University of Technology]. http://eprints.qut.edu.au/16302/

Dvorak, A. M. W., Christiansen, L. D., Fischer, N. L., & Underhill, J. B. (2011). A necessary partnership: Study abroad and sustainability in higher eEducation. *Frontiers: The Interdisciplinary Journal of Study Abroad, 21*(Fall), 143–166.

EAIE. (2013). Diplomacy and education: Internationalisation or neo-colonialism? *Executive Summary Dialogue 01,* (September), 7. Istanbul: EAIE.

Egron-Polak, E., & Hudson, R. (2014). *Internationalization of higher education: Growing expectations, fundamental values. IAU 4th Global Survey*. Paris, France: IAU.

Engel, L., Sandström, A. M., van der Aa, R., & Glass, A. (2015). Internationalisation in Europe. *The EAIE barometer internationalisation in Europe—extended executive summary*. Amsterdam, The Netherlands: EAIE.

Enslin, P., & Hedge, N. (2008). International students, export earnings and the demands of global justice. *Ethics and Education, 3*(2), 107–119.

European University Association. (2013). *Internationalization in European higher education: European policies, institutional strategies and EUA support.* Brussels, Belgium: EUA.

Fabricius, A. H., Mortensen, J., & Haberland, H. (2017). The lure of internationalization: paradoxical discourses of transnational student mobility, linguistic diversity and cross-cultural exchange. *Higher Education, 73*(4), 577–595. doi:10.1007/s10734-015-9978-3

Harrison, N. (2015). Practice, problems and power in "internationalisation at home": Critical reflections on recent research evidence. *Teaching in Higher Education, 20*(4), 412–430.

Held, D., McGrew, A., Goldblatt, D., & Perraton, J. (2003). Rethinking globalization. In D. Held & A. McGrew (Eds.), *The global transformations reader: An introduction to the globalization debate* (pp. 67–74). Malden, MA: Polity Press.

Helms Matross, R. (2015). *International higher education partnerships: A global review of standards and practices*. Washington, DC: ACE.

Hughes, R. (2008). Internationalisation of higher education and language policy: Questions of quality and equity. *Higher Education Management and Policy, 20*(1), 1–18.

Hughes-Warrington, M. (2012). The ethics of internationalisation in higher education: Hospitality, self-presence and "being late." *Educational Philosophy and Theory, 44*(3), 312–322. doi:10.1111/j.1469-5812.2010.00674.x
Hulme, M., Thomson, A., Hulme, R., & Doughty, G. (2014). Trading places: The role of agents in international student recruitment from Africa. *Journal of Further and Higher Education, 38*(5), 674–689. doi:10.1080/0309877X.2013.778965
Ilieva, R., Beck, K., & Waterstone, B. (2014). Towards sustainable internationalisation of higher education. *Higher Education, 68*, 875–889. doi:10.1007/s10734-014-9749-6
Jefferess, D. (2008). Global citizenship and the cultural politics of benevolence. *Critical Literacy: Theories & Practices, 2*(1), 27–36.
Jones, T. M. (1991). Ethical decision making by individuals in organizations: An issue-contingent model. *The Academy of Management Review, 16*(2), 366–395.
Kenway, J., & Fahey, J. (2009). Academic mobility and hospitality: The good host and the good guest. *European Educational Research Journal, 8*(4), 555–559. doi:10.2304/eerj.2009.8.4.555
Khoo, S. (2011). Ethical globalisation or privileged internationalisation? Exploring global citizenship and internationalisation in Irish and Canadian universities. *Globalisation, Societies and Education, 9*(3–4), 337–353. doi:10.1080/14767724.2011.605320
Killick, D. (2018). Critical intercultural practice: Learning in and for a multicultural globalizing world. *Journal of International Students, 8*(3), 1422–1439. doi:10.32674/jis.v8i3.64
Knight, J. (2016). Transnational education remodeled. *Journal of Studies in International Education, 20*(1), 34–47. doi:10.1177/1028315315602927
Leask, B. (2009). Using formal and informal curricula to improve interactions between home and international students. *Journal of Studies in International Education, 13*(2), 205–221. doi:10.1177/1028315308329786
Leask, B. (2015). *Internationalizing the curriculum*. New York, NY: Routledge.
Long, J., Vogelaar, A., & Hale, B. W. (2014). Toward sustainable educational travel. *Journal of Sustainable Tourism, 22*(3), 421–439. doi:10.1080/09669582.2013.819877
Lumby, J., & Foskett, N. (2016). Internationalization and culture in higher education. *Educational Management Administration & Leadership, 44*(1), 95–111. doi:10.1177/1741143214549978
McNiff, J. (2013). Becoming cosmopolitan and other dilemmas of internationalisation: Reflections from the Gulf States. *Cambridge Journal of Education, 43*(4), 501–515. doi:10.1080/0305764X.2013.831033
O'Connor, S. (2017). Problematising strategic internationalisation: Tensions and conflicts between international student recruitment and integration policy in Ireland. *Globalisation, Societies and Education, 7724*, 1–14. doi:10.1080/14767724.2017.1413979
Patru, M., & Balaji, V. (2016). *Making sense of MOOCs: A guide for policy-makers*. Paris: UNESCO.
Robinson, S., & Lee, S. (2007). Global ethics on the ascent. In E. Jones & S. Brown (Eds.), *Internationalising higher education* (pp. 25–41). London: Routledge.
Salisbury, M. H., Paulsen, M. B., & Pascarella, E. T. (2011). Why do all the study abroad students look alike? Applying an integrated student choice model to explore differences in the factors that influence white and minority students'

intent to study abroad. *Research in Higher Education, 52*(2), 123–150. doi:10.1007/s11162-010-9191-2

Sandström, A. M., & Hudson, R. (2018). *The EAIE barometer internationalization in Europe Second edition.* Amsterdam: EAIE.

Scholars at Risk. (2017). *Promoting higher education values. A guide for discussion.* New York, NY: Scholars at Risk.

Shams, F., & Huisman, J. (2012). Managing offshore branch campuses. *Journal of Studies in International Education, 16*(2), 106–127. doi:10.1177/1028315311413470

Shields, R. (2019). The sustainability of international higher education: Student mobility and global climate change. *Journal of Cleaner Production, 217,* 594–602. doi:10.1016/j.jclepro.2019.01.291

Sidhu, R., & Dall'Alba, G. (2017). 'A strategy of distinction' unfolds: Unsettling the undergraduate outbound mobility experience. *British Journal of Sociology of Education, 38*(4), 468–484. doi:10.1080/01425692.2015.1131143

Sidhu, R. K., & Dall'Alba, G. (2012). International education and (Dis)embodied cosmopolitanisms. *Educational Philosophy and Theory, 44*(4), 413–431. doi:10.1111/j.1469-5812.2010.00722.x

Stafford, S., & Taylor, J. (2016). Transnational education as an internationalisation strategy: Meeting the institutional management challenges. *Journal of Higher Education Policy and Management, 38*(6), 625–636. doi:10.1080/1360080X.2016.1202811

Stier, J. (2004). Taking a critical stance toward internationalization ideologies in higher education: Idealism, instrumentalism and educationalism. *Globalisation, Societies and Education, 2*(1), 1–28. doi:10.1080/1476772042000177069

Tange, H. (2016). Inclusive and exclusive knowledge practices in interdisciplinary, international education. *International Journal of Inclusive Education, 20*(10), 1097–1108. doi:10.1080/13603116.2016.1155660

Tannock, S. (2013). When the demand for educational equality stops at the border: Wealthy students, international students and the restructuring of higher education in the UK. *Journal of Education Policy, 28*(4), 449–464. doi:10.1080/02680939.2013.764577

Turner, Y. (2009). "Knowing Me, Knowing You," Is there nothing we can do? *Journal of Studies in International Education, 13*(2), 240–255. doi:10.1177/1028315308329789

United Nations. (2015). *Transforming our world: The 2030 agenda for sustainable development.* New York, NY: United Nations.

Waters, J. L., & Leung, M. W. H. (2017). Domesticating transnational education: Discourses of social value, self-worth and the institutionalisation of failure in 'meritocratic' Hong Kong. *Transactions of the Institute of British Geographers, 42*(2), 233–245. doi:10.1111/tran.12163

Wilkins, S. (2017). Ethical issues in transnational higher education: The case of international branch campuses. *Studies in Higher Education, 42*(8), 1385–1400. doi:10.1080/03075079.2015.1099624

3 Proxy Power Attained through Wealth

Social and Educational Trajectories of Students of the New Global Elite

Hatice Altun

Introduction

Studying abroad has become immensely powerful in restructuring inequalities and privileges as a wing of the global culture industry, committed to the symbolic production of elite status. As international students operate themselves in segmented spaces, their countries of origin often imply global class hierarchy (Kelly, 2012), positioning them in various ways that twist the world economic order. Their social class plays an important role in reconstructing their second-language identities and the ways they exercise agency. However, social class, particularly elite status, remains largely underexplored in applied linguistics. Block (2012) argues that social class, one important identity inscription, has been understudied unlike other identity constructs such as race, gender, etc. To address this gap, the study draws on Bourdieusian conceptualization of social class to explore how 'relational and emergent' elite-class positionings of Turkish undergraduate international students studying in global university contact zones impact their social-class identity.

Literature Review

Bourdieu's four capitals and his notions of habitus and hexis offer a framework to understand class as an emergent practice and symbolic behavior in various settings. Considering *habitus* as "a durable way of standing, speaking, walking and thereby of feeling and thinking" (Bourdieu, 1991, pp. 69–70) (e.g., how one carries one's body around, the way one speaks, wears, watches, listens to), and *hexis*, a sense of acceptability and legitimacy in different social contexts, I draw on Bourdieu's sequence of capital metaphors to explore class in this study. In the constitution of class, *habitus* and *field* are *symbolic capitals* for they are socioculturally shaped, value-laden products of habitus-mediated activities in social fields, and therefore, class is relational and emergent (Bourdieu, 1986). *Economic capital* directly relates to a traditional disposition of class, e.g., personal wealth; *cultural capital* refers to possession of cultural resources to create particular class effects as an association to certain institutions, settings and artifacts, e.g., right or wrong accent, taste or attitude in a particular setting like music, books and art, or connection with certain professional associations; and *social capital* refers to these institutional contacts and relationship with more powerful others, and there is a parallel relationship with cultural capital of these others and social capital; the stronger the cultural capital of others, the stronger the social capital accrued by being in connection with those others (Bourdieu, 1986). Social class in this study is understood in the light of these capitals, and thus a synthesis of wealth, occupation, education and symbolic attitude is useful to develop a comprehensive understanding of class and identity. Hence the participants are identified as members of upper class both based on family income and sociocultural and historical class positioning emanating from their symbolic, cultural and social capitals.

Bourdieu (1986) and Bernstein (2000) observe that middle-class or upper-class children benefit more from education systems in capitalist economies than their working-class counterparts. Heller (2006) also found in her study of a French immersion school in Toronto that social-class differences emerge at several levels, and results were supportive of Bourdieu and Berstein. Similarly, Vandrick (2011) observes that although working-class children and economically disadvantaged English as a Second Language (ESL) students who are minorities and immigrants are sometimes oppressed and marginalized because of their language status and social class and need extra empowerment, students of the new global elite are quite comfortable with their privileges and already know that they will step into positions of wealth, power and influence when they return to their countries. They compose a large proportion of ESL students at many American universities. However, they may also suffer from some marginalization as foreigners who cannot use English fluently and rarely as people of minorities. Thus, even these students sometimes experience discrimination or the burdens of being an outsider at American colleges. Vandrick (1995) adds that usually these problems are balanced by the students' privileges. Even so, there is an essential need to develop an understanding about how their identity is affected by this clash: oppressed outsider versus privileged insider or both at once. Therefore, to occupy the stated niche about the interplay between social class and identity constructs pertaining to privileged international students, the current study explores the effects of social class on Turkish international students' social-class identities.

Research Method

In this chapter, I discuss a segment of data from a larger corpus compiled from 2014 to 2016, as part of a longitudinal mixed-method study of 10 Turkish undergraduate students in the U.S. The study presented here focuses on four of the participants due to their more noticeable elitist identity carvings.

I used data gathered through interviews, personal narratives, diaries and field observations as evidence for contestation and negotiation of many facets of the participants' social-class identities. For the analysis of the interviews and journal entries and observations, I employed narrative analysis, a method for interpreting texts with a common storied form. Aware that I would be interrogating cases (rather than population-based samples), I tried to make conceptual inferences about a social process, i.e., an identity construction via close observation. Given that, I picked up Wolcott's (1994) further analysis technique and tried to form descriptions from the data as well as relating the description to the literature; i.e., I analyzed each participant's narrative by finding themes connecting their second-language identity and other social categories (social class, gender and ethnicity). This allowed me to recognize the distinct discourses taken up by my participants. In several excerpts presented in the following parts, I studied these linguistic instantiations of how the participants perceived, positioned and composed themselves in relation to their social-class identity in a global contact zone.

Participants

They are four male Turkish undergraduate students pursuing an engineering degree in the U.S. They were exchange students who originally studied at the same public university in Turkey and were already friends when I encountered them. I met with participants on a monthly basis and interviewed them mostly in Turkish about their specific experiences. Then I translated the data. Thanks to these ethnographic interviews, I achieved an extensive understanding of their emotional reactions, world-views, sense-making, history, etc. I gave them English pseudonyms: Brian, Michael, Kiel and David.

The common construct that adequately shaped the groups' identity construction was their wealth. All of them were raised in affluent environments, and their privileged background has always provided them with opportunities. They had high accessibility to many kinds of resources. First, they were able to enroll in a prestigious university in Turkey, thanks to their economic power. Thus, they paid much more to gain access to a prestigious program. They also had the privilege to study at a university in the U.S., again thanks to their wealth. They can not only pay high tuition and other daily expenses but also have traveled to other countries and are familiar with the culture and lifestyle in those places. Apart from many other Turkish international students studying in the U.S.-based universities, who usually come from either Turkish-American families or study here as graduate students on scholarship due to their successful educational background, participants (based on their own acknowledgment) have never been academically outstanding but always had the best opportunities, thanks to their families' wealth. In that sense, the university they studied in the U.S. is another privileged environment where successful students from all over the world study.

Results

Theme One: Carving Elite Identities

All participants demonstrated a genuine and credible identity formation process with regard to discursive enactments of their social-class privileges. They manifested an exclusivity, superiority and distinction as acts of identity. Their elitist stance-taking was particularly revealed in the structures of feeling, which are useful tools because they are analytically accessible through discourse when members of a community of practice try to articulate their experiences as they are changing over two years during their stay in a global contact zone. Therefore, I analyzed structures of feelings that provide the discourse whereby an elite status/identity is enacted.

Kiel characterized elite consumption patterns: he traveled for leisure (e.g., backpacking through Tibet, touring Italy with 'buddies', getting a culinary class in Umbria, partying on Costa del Sol, weekend runaways in Vegas), shopped for promoting symbolic and material markers of privilege and status (e.g., he gifted Hermes scarves and purses to his friends. While watching the movie "Blue Jasmine," he commented on Kate Blanchet's Channel jacket as "These are produced in one pattern only so that they could be very distinctive") (field notes 2, September 2014) and constantly positioned himself as an arbiter of good taste through evaluative remarks: "I appreciate good food, good music, and luxury things" (Interview 2, October 12, 2015). The extract below exemplifies his way of thinking clearly:

KIEL: I had a list of the restaurants I wanted to go in New York when I first came to America. And I think I went to most of them. I feel accomplished. There were Jean George, Le Bernardine, and Pastis. And I am really happy that I went to Pastis because they closed it now.

HATICE: What is so special about that restaurant?

KIEL: It is a French restaurant and they say it has a special meat with a special sauce. But I love the Crème Brule I had there, it was the best Crème Brule in my life, and I really like that place, the aura and interior design. It was old and a bit dark and mystic (Interview 2, October 12, 2015).

The feeling adjectives and direct opinion markers he used (accomplished, really happy, special, the best, really like) augmented his positive self as a superior, privileged person. His stance-taking is based on the assumption that there is a shared attitude or values between the listener (positioning the hearer also as 'elite') and himself, thus creating a sense of in-group membership.

It was also quite salient to observe the simple binary distinction of "good" (elite) and "bad" (nonelite) in his narrative throughout the year.

> When I go to New York, to the Meatpacking district, I see people wearing good clothes. They're taking care of themselves and I like people who

> make their hair, wear makeup because I want to take care of myself, but you know, if I do that here, it would be hilarious, so I got used to the fact that I can just wear my bad pajamas and go to school, at some point. But when I go to the Meatpacking district, I felt like myself again because it feels like Istanbul.
>
> (Interview 2, October 12, 2015)

In this extract, we note his implied insinuation of the U.S. city he lives in as down-market, and the metaphoric privileging of the district is very self-identifying. Again, the feeling adjectives associated with both ends ('elite' and 'nonelite') are self-explanatory.

Michael has also adopted a "good" (elite) and "bad" (nonelite) narrative. "I like New York; I like the western side more because the eastern side is a bit boring. I like Las Vegas although it might be a bit overrated for some but I like it" (Interview 2, October 14, 2015). His direct opinion markers made it clear that he positions himself as powerful positive elite and others as not-qualified nonelites. When he traveled to Cancun during the spring break, he claimed for himself the cultural capital of 'cosmopolitan' identity. He wrote in his journal:

> Cancun was a nice break [. . .] I enjoyed the place except for the horrible crowd of cheap vacationers. Wherever we went, I tried to mix with locals and wore traditional clothes (the locals are quite short), so I tried to assimilate myself. But it backfired at some point, we were stopped by the local police and we weren't able to find the documents of the rental car. The vulgar and ignorant police asked for bribe and we gave some 20 dollars (500 something in Mexican Pesos), it wasn't much but annoying. The joy of the greedy policemen was worth seeing, though, when they received the money.
>
> (Diary entry 6, April 14, 216)

Michael in fact reveals an orientation to engage with local people and their culture. However, his journal entry also displays his lack of willingness and competence in achieving this when circumstances got worse with the police. We can see that in his description of the local police officer (vulgar, ignorant and greedy) as 'a local person.' We can assume that he uses those adjectives due to their unlawful actions but in the previous parenthetical insinuation of the locals being short and Mexican money equivalence of dollars is convincing that he has racist remarks and no sympathy for the local people in understanding how global inequalities may affect those people's lifestyles. Bourdieu (1991) explains that this kind of linguistic maneuver can be seen as a form of condescension: a higher-class person tries to show herself in the social practices of a lower-class group. Yet, such condescension only rivets hierarchical relations of inequality. He also built his elitist stance on the contrast with underlying social judgement of mass tourists and exotic locals, despite the negative evaluation of the locals disguised in parentheses.

During my field observations, I noticed that the participants enjoyed sharing their in-group characteristic of being inherently affluent and positive affinity about the valued objects that display elite stance, which are exploited for their existing cultural capital. In this regard, I want to explore a voice recording made by Michael to be used as part of the quantitative data analysis of the original study because it speaks volumes about the contemporary class-status of my participants.

MICHAEL: This time when I was coming from Turkey, although I had lots of miles in my Miles&Smiles card I had to fly at the premium seats because there were no seats available in the business class. It was so discomforting. The seat seemed to shrink around me the entire journey and it was so unbearable and suffocating.

KIEL: Once I had to travel in the economy and I almost cried because the seats were so narrow and annoying. I couldn't sleep all night. [. . .] Can you imagine? Me! Sitting at the economy class!

MICHAEL: The light was disturbing and I missed the soothing purple light trying to read during the flight. But at least before the flight, they let me use the business lounge.

BRYAN: Yes, that business lounge is always lifesaving. When we were going to Turkey for winter break, I took Ashley with me to the lounge since she was flying in the premium, they normally don't allow her but as my guest, they allowed me to take her with me (Authentic data recording 2, February 11, 2016).

This extract is a neat reminder that class privilege is always historical because it is deeply set in our minds and ways of being (Thurlow & Jarowski, 2009). When I first listened to this extract, it occurred to me that these subjects and I – being neither rich nor poor, I consider myself of middle class, but I might be falling in the lower end of the middle class when my ways of being are considered – don't have much in common when it comes to privileges. They have always felt to be the righteous owner of the 'privilege.' So, they were quite surprised when treated as 'non elites' and thought their well-deserved right was usurped. Disapproval of my participants was clearly seen through the lens of negative feeling structures ("discomforting, unbearable, suffocating, made me cry, narrow, annoying") about the economy class. Their claim of superiority is encoded in an indirect lexicon as well, as Bourdieu (1991) notes that dominant cultural capital is not overt but generally invisible and insidious. The names of the credit cards in the audio recording can be indexed as another kind of shared cultural capital since they are not explained in the conversation but used with their functions as free-mile providers for flights. Their shared sentiment can be read as a form of condescension, too. Their appeal for exclusivity expressed through negatively evaluated airplane economy class section and the annoying comparison of the business class to the premium strike us as highly unrealistic, but their privileged class mindset is justified by an underlying "I deserve it" presumption of privilege, as is seen in Kiel's exaggerated tone of resentment ("Can you imagine? Me! Sitting at the economy class!"). Not surprisingly, the elitist mindset entails the positive evaluation of excess and self-indulgence. Thus, the inconspicuous boundary drawn between haves and have-nots by my participants seems like a key to maintaining their elite status in their daily lives.

Theme Two: Seeking Refuge in Wealth

These students' firm sense of privileged identity helps them deflect or emphasize negative experiences they have gone through in the U.S., particularly in relation to their language barrier and insufficient school performance. Bryan, for example, recounted that when he was sitting with his friends at Starbucks in Boston, an old man asked where he was from and while he was introducing himself, he said where he lived in the U.S. but he was not able to pronounce "live" correctly and the word sounded like "leave." Upon hearing this, the old man got angry with him and discriminated him by saying

> All immigrants, who cannot even pronounce "leave" and "live" correctly, came to our most beautiful cities and they have the privilege to enjoy themselves here with us, at the same Starbucks where I have spent my last 10 years.
>
> (Interview 4, February 16, 2015)

Although Bryan mentioned the racist remarks of the old man, he didn't feel disturbed because other nice memories overweight the few negatives in Boston. Or when Michael was harshly criticized by his professor about his inefficiency in class, which he believed might be caused by his computer's keyboard (a Turkish one, about which his professor remarked 'How can you manage to work on this alien keyboard?'), he paid no attention because both or all my participants were quite secure in their own sense of being privileged and didn't feel pressure on themselves by the others' comments.

As stated earlier, they paid a lot more money to gain access to a prestigious program. However, they still felt the need to rationalize their paying more tuition by underlining that "Our instructors are more qualified than the regular classes', and all are professors, because they receive more money for their teaching from the department." (Bryan) (Interview 4, December 10, 2015). In that sense, the American university they studied in is another privileged university environment. However, what they encountered at the university in the U.S. was somewhat disheartening for them because although they were in a privileged environment, as they were used to, they couldn't enjoy this privilege due to their incompatibility with the schooling system and their lack of command over English. They were used to getting a passing grade in Istanbul without much effort, yet in the U.S., they suffered from being ordinary students although they had enough money "to manipulate and deceive the professors." In one of the interviews, Bryan once told me that when he was not able to do an assignment, he asked a smart and hardworking student he found on Craig's list to do it. But when the student asked for a little amount for the assignment, Bryan, ready to pay much more, was surprised and gave more notwithstanding. He said:

> He didn't struggle with the questions in the assignment like us. And when he finished, he asked for 20 dollars blushingly, probably he thought he asked for too much, but I was even ready to give 200 dollars. So, as a favor, I gave 50 bucks to him. When he saw that amount, he got freaked out and kept asking "Are you sure, Are you sure?" [Echoes the boy, laughing.] The students here are usually poor kids and they are usually losers [laughs].

In his original wording in Turkish, Bryan really withered the efforts of the engineering student, mocking him and mimicking his surprise when he gave more money than expected. He used a Turkish slang "ezik" (loser) to describe the student's 'misery.' Once more, he took his entitlement for granted for the solutions to the problems he encountered. His bitter remarks revealed that he was in fact seeking refuge in his economic capital. Though he was the one in need, he pretended as if that student needed his help due to lack of economic capital. However, I must acknowledge that I never saw him speaking so recklessly elsewhere with other people. Probably due to the rapport I developed with him during these two years, he was this much careless and senseless yet speaking his true mind without wearing a mask of pretension.

Similarly, David admitted that

> American graduates are real engineers but we just save the day and survive. We have no option but to finish our school and go back. But Americans, on the other hand, have to graduate well-qualified because they have to fight against the violent competition in America.
>
> (Interview 6, February 20, 2016)

Although disturbed by the fact that they don't have advanced engineering skills like American students, he still seeks refuge in his wealth by arguing that American students have no options but to be successful in order to get a job in the job market in the U.S. However, they have no problem with recruitment because many of them are going to take over the family businesses so they have the convenience of not being very hardworking.

Michael also had the same privileged mindset and narrated a story about a local's surprise when he noticed that he was all alone in Chicago as a young adult from Turkey. He recounted it as follows:

> I met a girl in Chicago when we went on a Thanksgiving vacation. I was waiting for my friends and she started chatting with me. After learning

> that I was alone in America studying for my engineering degree, she got amazed and admitted she never traveled out of her city in the US, let alone abroad. She was particularly impressed upon hearing I am from Turkey because she probably thought Turkey as a third-world country
> (Interview 5, February 6, 2016)

His remarks had two edges: First, he empowered himself by acknowledging that he traveled more than a local though he was coming from a less-developed country. The other is about the woman's attitude about his country of origin. He might be exaggerating the situation but he somehow confronted the implied comment by the local that he was coming from a less-developed country yet still he travels a lot. No matter what others thought, Michael felt, similarly, entitled to be privileged.

Discussion and Conclusions

Based on the participants' discursive enactment of elite social-class standing, it can be argued that their social class has impacted their identity construction in two ways. First, they had to negotiate between the two opposite positionings: oppressed outsider and privileged insider. As outsiders, they were marginalized because of their lack of language competency and sometimes due to their national identity and different culture. Yet, as insiders in their own Turkish community of practice, they had a strong sense of privilege and entitlement which enabled them to develop a self-assured, comfortable and sometimes disdainful demeanor. Their ever-privileged status in Turkey created an expectation on their part that they should be granted with the same privilege in the U.S. too. Theirs was a clash of two historical class positionings, i.e., two habitus. Turkey, a less-developed country, operates as an economic-class society, where disagreement occurs between economically determined groups such as property owners and laborers, whereas the U.S., an advanced multinational-state, is a status-conventional society, where identity politics has constituted the main focus. So, they had to balance this clash during their socialization in the U.S., yet oftentimes, they avoided such confrontations and took their wealth as a refuge for their second-language identity.

Block (2015) argues that engagement with social class in the ever-increasingly complex 21st-century societies should be articulated in relation to intersectional thinking. "Intersectionality" (Crenshaw, 1991) is how to interpret the ways that different types of discrimination and inequality overlap and/or are inextricably linked due to various class recognitions in various societies. Thus, it is impossible to understand some of my participants' feelings without considering the multiple overlapping and interlinked social dimensions. These dimensions include (1) the way my participants are positioned in Turkish society as upper-class people, (2) their social and institutional positionings in the local community as ESL learners on alien visas, (3) their status as people culturally different, coming from a relatively Eastern culture, (4) their immersion in gender politics both in Turkey and the U.S. and (5) their ethnic positionings as Turkish people. These various marginalization dimensions didn't work with the same force on my participants and neither are they all equally oppressive. My participants' powerful class positioning and their subjective awareness of their class helped them disregard the other dimensions of their marginalization.

Thurlow (2018) reminds us that class privilege is a historical phenomenon and "deeply ingrained – marked on our bodies and rooted in our minds" (p. 8). So, I may argue that they became quite habituated into a more extensive narrative of self and lifestyle, which in turn have shaped the participants' habitus. However, in our deterritorialized global contact zone, the habitus becomes transnationalized (Darvin & Norton, 2014): "Bearing the imprint of both countries of origin and countries of settlement, this transnationalized habitus allows migrants to discern and act based on the interplay of dispositions by these distinct spaces" (p. 113).

In that sense, the participants' mobility (touristic and educational) was one of the most important characteristics of their elite identities. Urry (2007) argued that mobility is the most central concept of culture and identity in relation to class in late-modern societies. Parallel with Bourdieu's capitals, he offers 'network capital,' which highlights the extent to which an individual or group's access to economic resources is related to the degree of mobility. These people thus obtain status not only in their local contexts but in the global contexts. Despite being citizens of nation-states, they literally and psychologically detach themselves from their local contexts and contribute to the gap between the haves and have-nots in the global world (Urry, 2007).

Thus, my participants' identity alignment can also be viewed from Urry's perspective, and their transnational elite identity enactments can be seen as a perpetuation of world economic disorder. In essence, the participants have revealed the visual and behavioral manifestations of elite stance. I observed that these identificational meanings and visual manifestations of elitist stance have lasted through repetition and routinization in their daily practices. They had a clear sense of entitlement, and it can be easily observed that they felt it quite natural, given that they should be among the wealthy people. They didn't question why they were wealthy or why others didn't deserve to be wealthy, as if it was the natural order of the universe. They became quite habituated into a more extensive narrative of self and lifestyle, which in turn shaped their transnational habitus.

Implications

English language education has an agenda to improve social justice by focusing on race, gender, identities and ethnicity. Social class goes unacknowledged in educational contexts as a parameter of injustice though it has a significant role in the field. Hence, social class and its relation to English language teaching should be problematized in the fields of curriculum development, language policies and teacher preparation. If such problematization is neglected, educational institutions will keep on serving new world economic disorder, which improves few people's lives while negatively affecting many.

The participants' discursively enacted elite identity makes us contemplate on the status of teachers instructing elites in the classrooms. The participants questioned the authority of the instructors who were oftentimes coming from a lower social class. An English teacher may wonder if she is perpetuating social inequality by teaching English to wealthy students. Teachers act through their own agencies, and they are unavoidably affected by the forces of the social structures. Thus, when my participants, assuming that I came from a lower-class status, recommended me to eat at upscale restaurants in order to gain perspective about the lives of affluent people, or comparing my Esprit watch to their Rolex in terms of promptness, they exemplified the unavoidable perpetuation of global social inequalities. Hence, one might wish that English language teaching should develop an agenda for the exploration and implementation of more egalitarian social systems.

References

Bernstein, B. (2000). *Pedagogy, symbolic control and identity: Theory, research, critique.* London, UK: Rowman & Littlefield.

Block, D. (2012). Economizing globalization and identity in applied linguistics in neoliberal times. In D. Block, J. Gray, & M. Holborow (Eds.), *Neoliberalism and applied linguistics* (pp. 56–86). New York, NY: Routledge.

Block, D. (2015). Social class in applied linguistics. *Annual Review of Applied Linguistics, 35*, 1–19. doi:10.1017/S0267190514000221

Bourdieu, P. (1986). The forms of capital. In J. F. Richardson (Ed.), *Handbook of theory of research for sociology of education* (pp. 241–258). New York, NY: Greenwood Press.

Bourdieu, P. (1991). *Language and symbolic power.* Cambridge, UK: Polity Press.

Crenshaw, K. (1991). Mapping the margins: Intersectionality, identity politics, and violence against women of color. *Stanford Law Review, 43*(6), 1241–1299.

Darvin, R., & Norton, B. (2014). Social class, identity, and migrant students. *Journal of Language, Identity & Education, 13*(2), 111–117. doi:10.1080/15348458.2014.901823

Heller, M. (2006). *Linguistic minorities and modernity: A sociolinguistic ethnography* (2nd ed.). London, UK: Continuum.

Kelly, P. (2012). Migration, transnationalism, and the spaces of class identity. *Philippine Studies: Historical and Ethnographic Viewpoints*, 60(2), 153–186.

Thurlow, C. (2018). Queering critical discourse studies or/and performing 'post-class' ideologies. In J. Flowerdew & J. Richardson (Eds.), *The Routledge handbook of critical discourse analysis* (pp. 111–117). London, UK: Routledge.

Thurlow, C., & Jarowski, A. (2009). Taking an elitist stance: Ideology and the discursive production of social distinction. In A. Jarowski (Ed.), *Perspectives on stance* (pp. 198–209). New York, NY: Oxford University Press.

Urry, J. (2007). *Mobilities.* Cambridge, UK: Polity.

Wolcott, H. F. (1994). *Transforming qualitative data: Description, analysis, and interpretation.* London: Sage Publication.

4 International Education and the Challenges of Social Equity in Vietnam's Transitional Economy

Lien Pham

Introduction

Vietnam has experienced significant growth in the number of students studying abroad in the last three decades. The average year-on-year growth of Vietnamese students outflow worldwide from 1999 to 2012 is about 20%, with the highest increases between 2000 and 2008 (OECD, 2019). The increasing trend has continued, with approximately 130,000 Vietnamese students studying abroad in 2016, an increase of 15% from 2015 (Ha, 2016). This growth reflects the country's consistently strong economic growth since the 1990s when Vietnam, through *Doi Moi* (Renovation), transitioned to a market-based economy with strategic efforts in integrating with the global economy.

In the early years of *Doi Moi* economic reform, most Vietnamese international students studied through bilateral and multilateral scholarships such as the Fulbright program or the World Bank program (Vallely & Wilkinson, 2008). With the rise in private wealth in the last 20 years due to economic growth, there has been a surge in private funding by parents for their children to study abroad. The significant increase in Vietnamese studying abroad, particularly to universities in Europe, North America, and Australia reflect students' and their families' pursuit of employment opportunities and skilled migration in these regions, as well as their perception of the superiority of Western universities, particularly the United States (Pham, 2019; Vietnam Net, 2014).

The rationale for sending students abroad from the government's perspective is to improve education and training development to meet Vietnam's labor market needs of an industrialized market-based economy. Alongside *Doi Moi*'s mission of economic integration with the global economy (The Tenth plenum of the Fifth Central Committee in May 1986, 6th National Congress), international education policies aim for international integration with socialist orientation. The goal is to increase the scale of students sent abroad by the Vietnamese government to train to become teachers and lecturers at all levels and to increase quality educational institutions by improving the quality of teachers and lecturers particularly through Master's and doctoral training. International education is seen as a tool to develop human resources for

Vietnam's transitional economies toward industrialization, modernization, and globalization. At the same time, international education policy specifies the preservation of Vietnamese culture and socialist ideals of citizens' wellbeing, security, health, and protection of rights of the disadvantaged, enhancing equity in material life and moral life of its citizens.

Research on international graduates tend to focus on employability (for example, Campbell, 2010; Crossman & Clark, 2010; Hao, Wen, & Welch, 2016; Harman, 2005), and specifically for Vietnam (for example Nghia, Giang, & Quyen, 2019; Pham, 2019). Studies on non-economic impacts for the individuals or societal benefits as a result of studying abroad received less attention; although there is a shift toward the role of international education for broader social development and related issues of equity and social justice. For example, Paige et al. (2009) found that study abroad positively influences the students' civic engagement, philanthropy, and social entrepreneurship where students have substantial influence on for-profit organizations to be socially responsible. Dassin et al.'s (2018) edited collection of studies highlight the multiple ways that international scholarships in higher education can enable social change by empowering individuals, promoting social mobility and academic diversity, building technical capacity, and contributing to global understanding. The Ford Foundation International Fellowships Program (IFP) Alumni Tracking Study (Martel, 2019) of 1,284 alumni in 22 countries found that alumni are prepared to confront social injustices as well as achieving career success. The 2018 report in the same Alumni Tracking Study Series conducted in Africa and the Middle East region highlighted alumni's personal commitment to social justice and giving back to their communities through professional work or volunteerism (Kallick & Brown Murga, 2018).

Issues of social development and social justice matter for Vietnam, which in parallel with rapid economic growth, have been considered successful in poverty reduction and moving from one of the poorest in the world to a lower middle-income country (World Bank, 2019). Yet, Vietnam still faces challenges in managing equality in poverty reduction, particularly for rural, regional, and ethnic groups, which impact poverty and other welfare indicators (Dang, 2019). Education is important for Vietnam's human capital development and critical in reducing poverty across groups (Dang, 2019). While international education is a policy lever to improve human capital and education in Vietnam, the number of Vietnamese international students abroad (approximately 130,000) represents only 0.14% of the 94 million population (UNESCO, 2019). The majority of these students self-finance their overseas study, with scholarship recipients accounting for 4% of the total number of Vietnamese students abroad (Thanh Nien News, 2014). As Ergin (2019) noted, international education remains accessible for the elites, typically students supported by wealthy parents who are physically mobile.

This chapter explores the challenges of social equity in international education using a case study of Vietnamese international graduates who returned home. The study aimed to investigate: (1) if provision of scholarships in Vietnam targets the elite; (2) whether international education exacerbates economic inequality; (3) if the participants engaged in community development activities when they return to Vietnam; and (4) participants' contribution to Vietnam's development needs. The underpinning assumption of the chapter is that international education is a public good because international graduates make a meaningful contribution to society (de Wit & Hunter, 2015). This means international education has a direct role in the national development of countries that send students abroad. In this regard, the chapter links international education directly to the United Nations' Sustainable Development Goals Target 4.7 "Sustainable Development and Global Citizenship" where international graduates return to their country and make active, purposeful, and responsible contribution to the development of their communities in various dimensions, not just their own economic or social advantages.

After introducing and defining Samuelson's (1954) concept of "public goods", the next section describes the research methods employed in the study. The following section discusses the study's findings, suggesting a broader normative "public good" to Samuelson's "public goods" by including equity issues, and offers some implications for equity policies in providing access to international education and harnessing its benefits in Vietnam.

International Education as a Public Good

Grounded in the way that goods are produced and distributed, Samuelson (1954) defines public goods as non-rivalrous and non-excludable. The term "goods" is used generally to refer to all production including benefits such as educational services. International education fits with this conceptualization because it can be consumed by anyone in any number without being depleted. It is also non-excludable because the benefits cannot be confined to only the international students who received the "goods". Public goods can also be an individual good, for example, when the returnees enter the workforce and their skills and knowledge are transferred to other workers who did not contribute to the cost of education, helping to enhance their productivity and thereby augment the economic returns of the firm overall (Samuelson, 1954).

This concept of public good is relevant to international education in Vietnam and elsewhere, both in terms of improving human resources for market-based economies and for broader civic responsibility. In fact, Vietnam's Ministry of Education and Training policies rationale for international education acknowledge these overlapping benefits of individual and public good. It should be emphasized that public good and individual good are not binary concepts. Rather, the benefits of international education experience are public as well as private because of knowledge and skills application and transfer to others at the individual, institutional, and national level. Furthermore, viewing international education as a composite of individual and public good has implications for broader issues of equity in access to international education experience. I will come back to the conceptualization of equity issues in international education in relation to Samuelson's "public goods" in the Discussion section.

The notion of citizenship used in this chapter also deserves some explanation. Delanty (2001) argued that citizenship is about a person making claim to full participation in the collective group that they belong, which could be the institution, wider community, or the nation. Following Delanty (2011), citizenship is understood here not only as a right or responsibility of a citizen to make that claim because of legislative or national boundaries; rather, citizenship is about the person identifying themselves as part of the collective, and at the same time, they take on the values of the collective and engage in actions to achieve common goals and shared values of the collective. This notion of citizenship is implied if we view international education as a public good. On its own, possession of high skills and knowledge as a result of studying abroad explains very little about the dynamics of international graduates to apply or transfer these skills and knowledge to others in the community in ways that they and the community value.

Method

This chapter draws on a larger tracer study of Vietnamese international graduates who returned home. The study was conducted from 2013 to 2015 employing a mixed-method approach (Creswell & Clark, 2011) of online surveys followed by face-to-face interviews with selected respondents. Survey respondents were recruited using a non-random snowball approach through social media and the researcher's professional and personal networks, as well as contacting various human resources departments at public universities in four major cities of Vietnam as scholarship programs are mostly awarded to university lecturers through Project 911 (see below). The survey aimed to gain an overview of returnees' employment and community activities and their application of overseas-acquired knowledge and skills. There were 247 returnees who fully completed the survey. Semi-structured interviews were conducted with 21 selected survey respondents and 27 members of their networks. The semi-structured interviews aimed to provide a more in-depth understanding of returnees' expectations of the benefits of overseas studies, their motivations to participate in employment and community activities, and their experiences in applying their knowledge and skills in various economic sectors and community groups.

This chapter uses some of the survey responses (n = 247). Descriptive statistics were used to identify the overall distribution of various items and demographic information of respondents. Bivariate analysis was employed to identify differences between returnees who received scholarship and those who self-financed. Chi-square correlation tests were conducted for these two groups to identify significant relationships between respondents' background information for certain items, namely job role, employers, community activities, salaries earned, perception of advantage, and contribution to national development. The comparative analysis between scholarship and self-financing participants aimed to identify differences or similarities between groups and their implications for conceptualizing international education as a public good. The following presentation and discussion of findings draw mainly on the statistical analysis of the survey results and supplemented by interview data from selected survey respondents (n = 21) where relevant to the issue discussed. An overview of international scholarship programs in Vietnam is briefly described for background information.

Brief Overview of Vietnam's International Scholarship Programs

There were 5,422 government scholarships awarded in 2016 (latest available MOET data) for studying in 47 countries.[1] Russia was the most popular destination for Vietnamese government scholarships, followed by France, Australia, and Germany. These scholarships are generally provided from the budget of MOET, the State Budget, and the Country Agreement scholarship, which included Project 911 for doctoral students and Project 599 for undergraduate and postgraduate students. Scholarship schemes also come from various ministries such as the Ministry of Agriculture and Rural Development, Ministry of Industry and Trade, Ministry of Public, and Ministry of Culture, Sports and Tourism. The objectives of the Vietnamese scholarship programs vary depending on the schemes and Ministries. Project 911 aimed at reforming the higher education sector by sending academic staff at universities and colleges abroad. Project 322 also aimed at providing overseas education for public officials at all levels, including Bachelor's, Master's, and PhD degrees. It could be said that most of the talent attraction, development, and retention initiatives from the government through these scholarship programs have mainly targeted improving human resources in the public sector (Liên Hiệp Các Hội Khoa Học và Kỹ Thuật Sơn La, 2012).

Other bilateral scholarships have general aims of supporting developmental needs of Vietnam based on bilateral or regional agreements between governments. For example, Australian Awards Scholarships and Belgium-Vietnam Scholarship aim to reduce poverty and support sustainable development goals; the U.S. Fulbright Vietnamese Student Scholarship Program and the Vietnam Education Foundation, Japanese Government Scholarship, Erasmus Mundus (Europe) aim for cultural and academic exchange. There are other scholarship programs funded by non-government organizations like the Ford Foundation IFP that provide advanced higher education opportunities to emerging social justice leaders from marginalized communities including Vietnam. Although these scholarship programs have specific objectives that tie to donor countries' foreign policies, the broad aims are to develop students' new knowledge and skills for the benefit of Vietnam through work and service to the community. It is thus important to understand scholarship alumni's contribution to Vietnam's development needs through their employment and involvement in community development.

Findings

Access and Selection to International Education

Scholarship alumni were over-represented in the survey with 60% of the 247 respondents receiving scholarships and 40% self-financing their overseas studies. Seventy-four percent of respondents achieved Master's or PhD level, and most of these were scholarship awardees; 24% achieved Bachelor's degrees and 2% achieved diploma qualification, and most of these self-financed. The majority of respondents were from well-educated families with a slightly higher proportion of scholarship recipients with university-qualified parents compared with self-financing returnees. Postgraduates were over-represented in this sample compared with statistics of Vietnamese international students abroad. For example, IIE (2016) reported that 67% of Vietnamese students in the U.S. study primarily at the undergraduate level, 15% at the graduate level, and 18% pursued non-degree programs. The high number of postgraduate qualifications within the scholarship cohort is consistent with bilateral scholarships, for example, the Australia Awards program that mostly provides scholarships for Master's and PhD studies (DFAT, 2013).

The survey respondents' family backgrounds show that irrespective of funding type, those with higher socioeconomic background have access to or are selected to study abroad. This is consistent with Ergin's (2019) observation that most international students worldwide today come from wealthy backgrounds. The majority of students from low and lower middle-income countries (like Vietnam) are still restricted to local education and training institutions which are limited by the quality and relevance for their participation in these countries' industrialization pathways (Chao, 2019; Perkins et al., 2008).

Selections for scholarship also have equity concerns because they are often competitive based on academic tests or English language proficiency. These selection criteria are academic privileges that are often attributable to economic capital (Bourdieu, 1984). In this regard, access and selection to study abroad often carry equity issues from the wider society that privilege social and academic elites. Provision of scholarships by the Vietnamese government, bilateral or multilateral agencies, and host universities amplify and reproduce the socioeconomic inequalities by giving the "privileged" access to international experiences. The reality of international scholarships supporting the privileged class in Vietnam is also distinctive in the Australian Columbo program in the 1950s where Vietnamese academic elites from elite families were sent to Australia to study.

The equity issue in accessing and selecting for international education is a concern given Vietnam's policy of increasing the scale of students abroad to meet the country's development objectives that has led to increased number of Vietnamese government scholarships and scholarships granted by other countries to Vietnamese students to study abroad (VIED, 2016). At the same time, private funding for international education has seen significant increase compared to a decade ago due to an increase in private wealth. In 2008, Vietnamese economists estimated that Vietnamese families are spending at least one billion dollars per year on study abroad (Vallely & Wilkinson, 2008). In 2015, the figure increased to $3 billion a year (Thanh Nien News, 2015).

Participation in the Labor Market

Almost all returnees were working, with 93% employed, 2% working for family business, and 1% not looking for work. The majority (73%) were earning more than 7 million dong per month, 23% earning 3–7 million dong, and 4% earning 3 million dong or less a month. Compared with the Vietnamese Government of Statistics Office (2013) statistics of average salary of 3–7 million dong in urban Vietnam, these returnees were earning relatively high income. There were more scholarship alumni than self-financing in the higher-bracket income group of 9 million dong or more, probably because the majority of scholarship recipients were occupying management levels as a result of postgraduate qualification whereas the self-financing group was employed in entry-level graduate roles, although this differed between economic sectors. There was a statistically significant correlation between the types of funding and income earned. High-income and full-time employment were also consistent with the perception of the majority of survey respondents that international education is advantageous for employment in several aspects, particularly in job appointments, career advancement, and challenging work (see Figure 4.1).

Interview data suggest that while international education was beneficial for job appointment, it was not always advantageous for career advancement; rather, time and personal connections were more important. This may explain why scholarship alumni tended to earn higher income because they returned to the same firm and could leverage their seniority and existing networks. It could also explain why they felt that international education provided them with more opportunities for challenging work. These findings are consistent with the Australia Awards Vietnam tracer studies, which found that reaching managerial positions were often the result of overseas studies with Master's degrees, particularly for those in government positions (DFAT, 2013, 2014). The returnees in this study also reported that international education is often sought for career promotion in government jobs.

Table 4.1 summarizes the distribution of survey respondents by employer type. It shows that the majority of scholarship alumni worked in the public sector in government agencies or state-owned enterprises (SOE), whereas the majority of self-financing alumni worked in the private sector, with more in multinational corporations (MNCs). The interviews also revealed a strong preference among returnees for MNCs. Self-financing undergraduates working in the private sector reported having more challenging work as well as the advantage of overseas studies for appointment of management positions in MNCs or foreign firms although these senior roles often focus

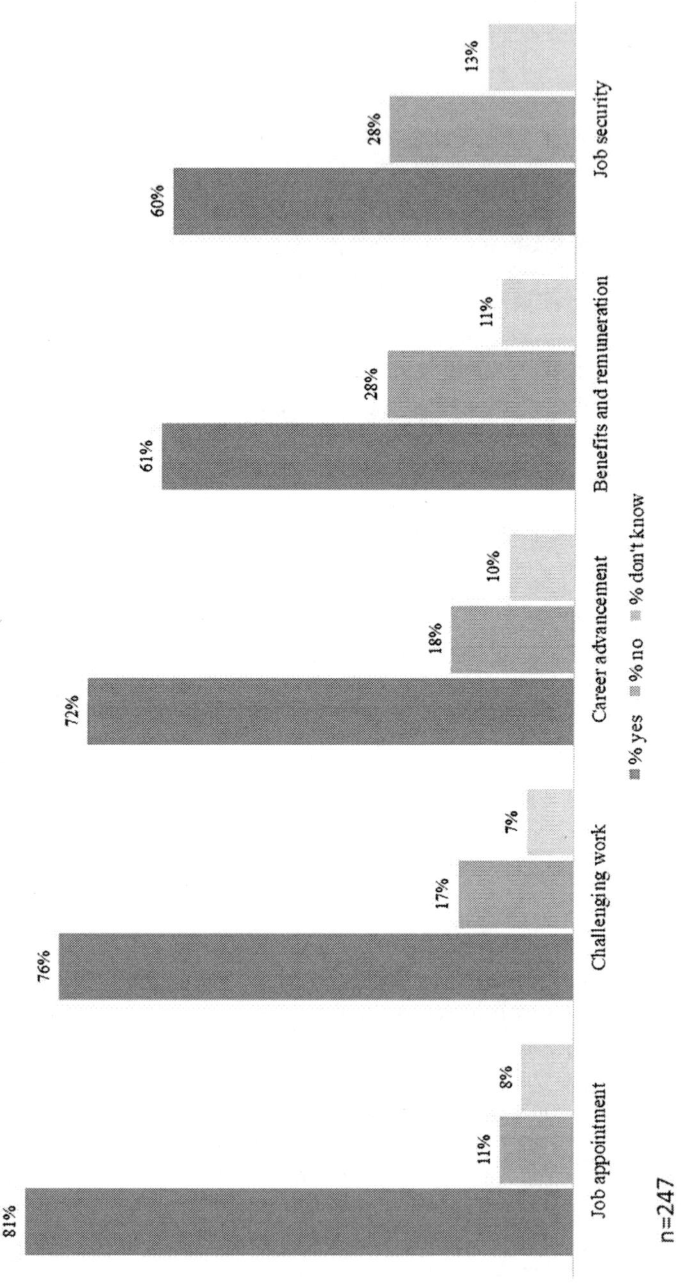

Figure 4.1 Advantages of international education.

Table 4.1 Distribution of Survey Respondents by Funding Type and Employer Type

	Govern-ment Agencies	*SOE*	*Private Sector (Vietnamese firm)*	*Private Sector (MNC/ Foreign firm)*	*NGO/ International Development Agency*	*Family Business*	*Self Employed*	*Other*	*Total*
Scholarship recipients	66	8	8	36	11	0	6	14	149
Self-financing	9	9	22	39	4	2	5	8	98
Total	75	17	30	75	15	2	11	22	247
% of total number of respondents	30%	7%	12%	30%	6%	1%	4%	9%	100%

on transferable skills rather than technical skills (Pham, 2019). These results may explain why there was a high proportion of survey respondents who claimed career advancement as a benefit of international education.

Figure 4.2 shows the distribution of scholarship alumni and self-financing alumni by economic sectors. Graduates who self-financed tended to work in sectors where there are foreign firms or multinationals such as construction, consumer trade, tourism and hospitality, manufacturing, or emerging services like banking and financial services. Public administration, health services, and education and training attracted more scholarship recipients; this may be due to scholarship conditions, particularly in the Project 911 programs, that require lecturers to return and serve at their institutions.

These results suggest that international education confer advantages in the labor market that maintain the economic disparity and elitism conducive to accessing international education discussed earlier. There are other equity implications. As Chao (2019) pointed out, employment opportunities of a graduate in a low or lower middle-income country like Vietnam should be equal to those of a graduate from a middle or high-income country. Although this study did not compare between locally-trained and overseas-trained, the perception of advantages associated with international education in the jobs market suggests that there is equity issue if employment opportunities for local graduates are less than those with international education experiences. Given the strong preference for MNCs or foreign companies because of returnees' perceived advantage in accessing jobs, management roles, higher income, and social status of foreign firms, there is a concern that Vietnamese workers in local firms are not benefiting from the transfer of returnees' knowledge and skills which is one of the rationales for international education policy.

Furthermore, since many returnees in the private sector were willing to forgo opportunities to apply their technical skills to gain jobs in MNCs, they were not fully harnessing their knowledge and skills for their own development as well as collective benefits of improving productivity and technical skills

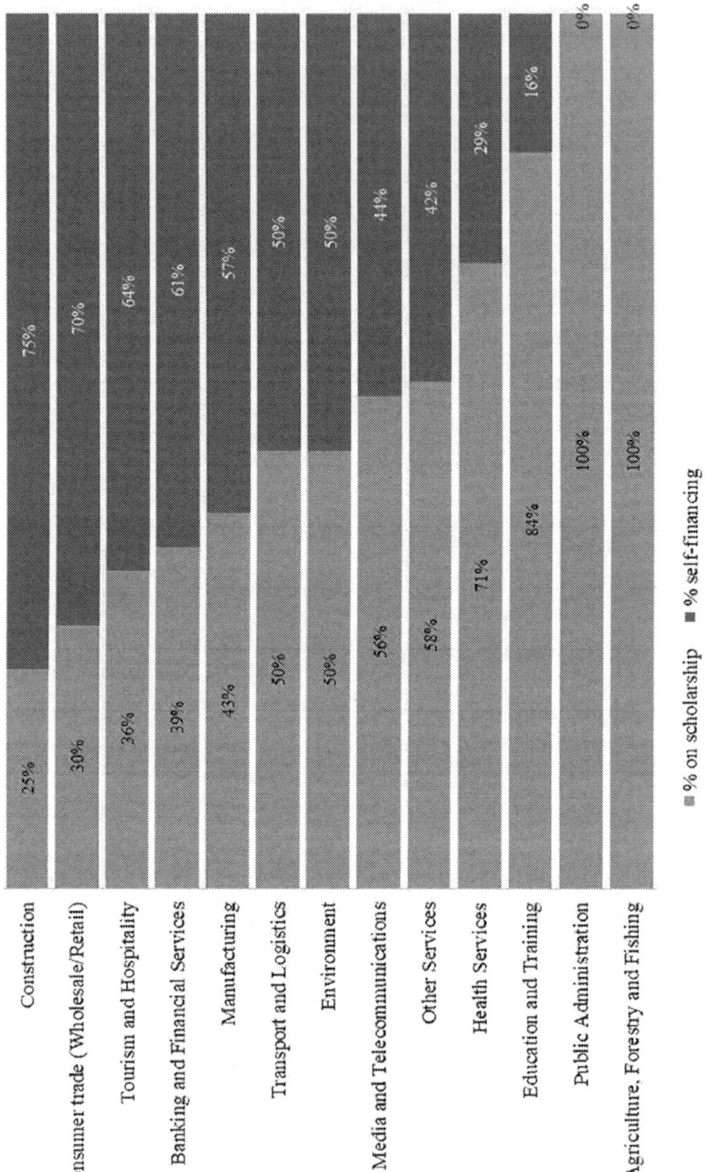

Figure 4.2 Distribution of scholarship alumni and self-financing alumni by economic sector.

development in Vietnamese industries. If the labor market clusters overseas graduates in international firms and locally trained graduates in Vietnamese firms, the latter could apply and further develop technical skills although of lower quality while the former mainly apply transferable skills that may not be relevant or directly enhance their talent, neither group benefit from the transfer and sharing of local and global knowledge and skills. This is a pertinent issue given Vietnam has struggled with a low skill workforce and quality issues in Vietnamese universities (Vallely & Wilkinson, 2008). Much more research is needed to investigate differences between locally-trained and overseas-trained graduates in terms of job opportunities and human resources development for improving the country's productivity.

Engagement in Community Activities

Figure 4.3 shows the proportion of respondents in the scholarship and self-financing cohorts that engaged in community groups and level of participation. In both cohorts, the majority engaged in overseas education alumni groups and professional associations, which suggest their interest in staying connected through employment-related activities. This is consistent with the Australia Awards tracer studies which found that alumni had most contacts with Vietnamese friends they met through their overseas studies, and returnees engaged extensively in professional-linkage activities through private sector firms, NGOs, or development agencies (DFAT, 2013, 2014). Art, music, and recreational and sports were activities that were also popular for both cohorts. Scholarship alumni were more active in community services, political organizations, and humanitarian and charitable organizations. The statistically significant correlation between funding type and level of participation for these three activities may reflect the requirement for community work in Vietnam's public sector jobs.

The majority of returnees did not engage in community development activity, except for humanitarian and charitable activities. If they had membership in a community group, their participation tended to be occasional. The reasons for the lack of active participation in volunteer community work are varied (Pham, 2018, 2019). Some respondents cited lack of time due to work priorities, others were ambivalent about the effectiveness of community activities in Vietnam for community development, and many felt that community activities were not the motivation or expectation for international education. Some felt that the concept of "community" and helping one another already exists in Vietnamese society primarily through families and lineages. There was a consensus among the returnees that international education does not have any direct contribution to the community because it is largely for labor market advantage.

These views suggest that international education is largely understood through concepts of money, position, and personal gain. The notion of service to the community does not align with individualization and academic capitalism (Slaughter & Leslie, 1997) where graduates understand the value

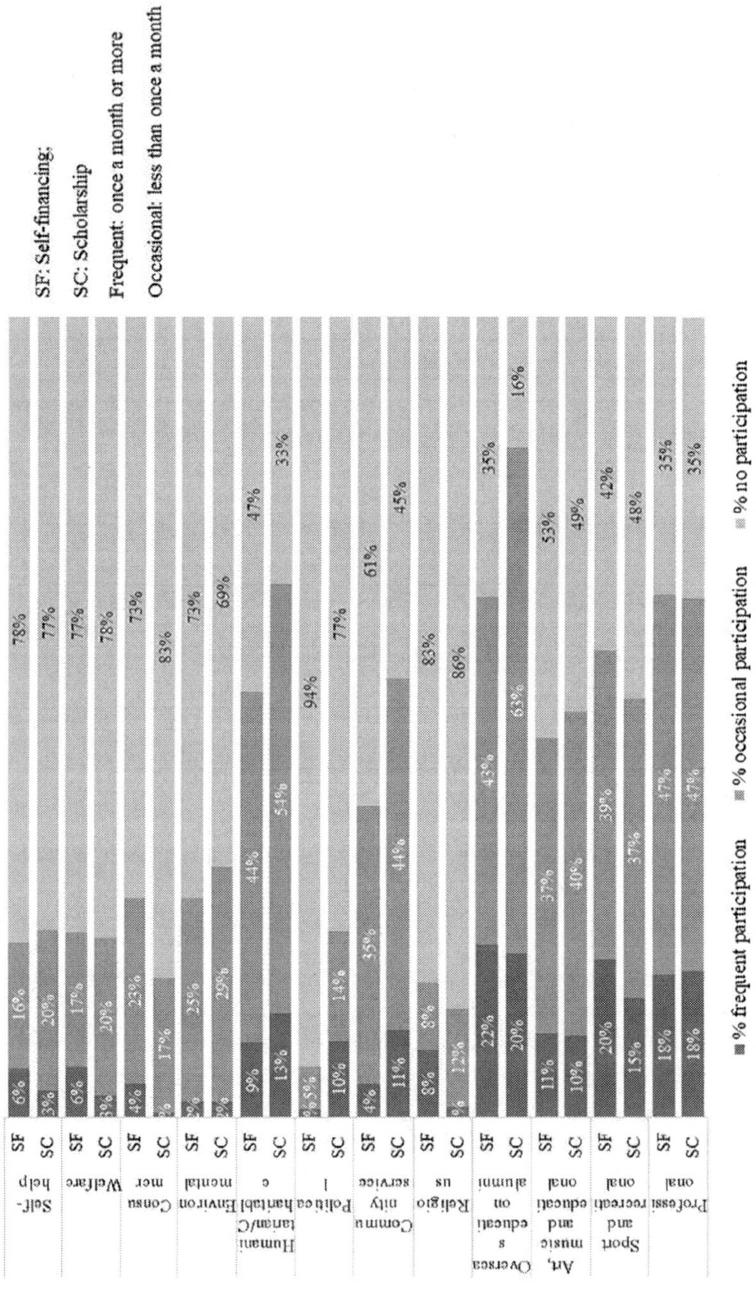

Figure 4.3 Distribution of scholarship and self-financing participants by community group participation.

of their knowledge and skills in relation to the financial return it yields and that they have to prioritize their work often looking to an economic return. As Barnett (2007, p. 25) put it, "the notion of citizenship runs counter to these elements of higher education in the contemporary age". International education relies on exclusivity and scarcity through competition in order to gain positional advantage in society. For these Vietnamese returnees, its value lies in its functions as a vehicle of personal advantage.

Although Vietnam's international education policy aims to preserve socialist orientation alongside citizenship education in the schooling system, reality seems far from such collective thinking. For the returning overseas graduates in this study, there was a contested agenda between fulfilling civic responsibilities and ensuring economic betterment of their families. Although some returnees spoke about the emerging idea of global citizenship because of their time abroad, they rarely felt that they could actualize that in Vietnam. Such tension reflects the broader issues of a transitional economy in needs of human capital while trying to preserve the country's ideals of socialism. It is also derivative of the Vietnamese concept of citizenship, which is less about democratic citizenship, but more about nationalism for legitimacy of the government.

Contribution to Vietnam's National Development

The survey asked returnees about their contribution to Vietnam's development needs through their employment and community activities. The results are summarized in Figure 4.4. There were three areas that the majority felt that their contributions were higher through employment compared with community activities: increasing national production, raising educational levels, and improving national health. These areas are mostly effects of employment, thus affirming the idea that employment is a direct benefit of international education; high contribution to improving education may be attributable to the sample size, with a third of respondents working in the university sector. These results suggest that the policy rationale for international education in terms of labor development and educational improvement for market-based economies are somewhat achieved.

The returnees' perception of contribution to improving national health is interesting in that there was a higher proportion of self-financing compared with scholarship even though there was a lower number of self-financing alumni working in health services (see Table 4.1). Improving democracy and human rights is also an interesting area of contribution because of the higher proportion in self-financing compared with scholarship awardees given that the majority of self-financing worked in the private sector and the majority of scholarship alumni worked in the public sector. These results further support the finding that employment in the private sector is beneficial for these areas of development. However, scholarship recipients contributed more through work than self-financing in improving environmental awareness, improving

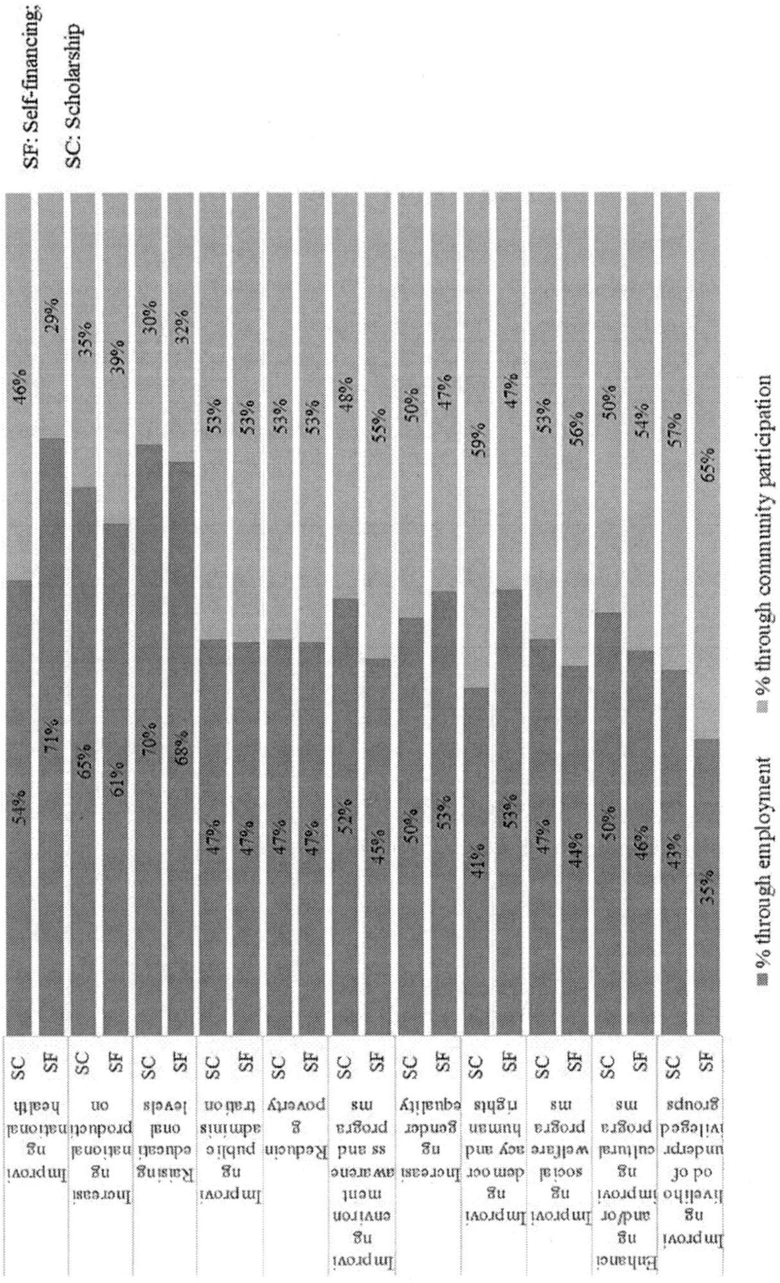

Figure 4.4 Contribution to Vietnam's development needs by type of funding cohort.

social welfare programs, cultural programs, and livelihood of underprivileged groups, which may reflect the nature of their public sector jobs.

Except for improving gender equality, returnees felt that they were contributing to other development areas more through community activities. Given that returnees' engagement in community development activities were mostly occasional, these results suggest that community activities have the potential to contribute to Vietnam's developmental needs if they participate more actively.

Discussion and Implications for Equity Policies

These findings clearly suggest that international education has relevance to Vietnamese society, not only individual benefits, which align with the intention of scholarship programs in contributing to Vietnam's development needs. The analyses have also highlighted equity issues in access and outcomes of international education. This is because contemporary market-based higher education, which international education is firmly located within, promotes self-interest behaviors and acquiring social status based on existing hierarchy for self-promotion and advancement (Marginson, 2011). To address equity concerns in order to harness the benefits of international education for society, Samuelson's (1954) concept of "public goods" needs to incorporate social equity alongside its economic assumptions. Economic gains from international education and transformed economy ought to be sought in consideration of equalizing citizens' opportunities and empowerment (Jonathan, 2001). This would mean direct contribution by returning graduates to enhancing people's lives through community services to create the public or common good. This chapter shows that acquisition of international education can be divisive in terms of labor market advantage and economic gains; it also has energizing potential for social development and collective benefits. Personal advantages and social gains must both be considered explicitly in Vietnam's international education policy and policy for receiving returnees in order to bring about equitable collective benefits. This would align with stipulated objectives of "socialist orientation" in Vietnam's international education policy.

Issues of access to international education reflect past and current social conditions and play a significant part in constructing the future (Bourdieu, 1984). International education confers benefits with more than one kind of value to recipients, and they are scarce resources and have to be competed for. However fair, even on meritocracy grounds, it places a premium on prior relative advantages like economic wealth, education, family status, or personal connections. The findings suggest that scholarship programs, while often presented as providing equal access to international education, in practice, support those from the elite class in Vietnam. Furthermore, in the context of Vietnam's low-quality higher education and lack of skilled human capital, international education can pull a different direction of equity by unfair distribution of access to education and benefits of employment prospects and income. It is not surprising that Vietnamese returnees look to education to gain skills, knowledge to access jobs, and better economic lives. As seen in the results of this study, the status incentive trap of international education plays out in the labor market and in accordance with family expectation, thereby confirms the privileges of those fortunate enough to have access to such experience. It is this confer of advantages that Vietnamese parents seek for their children which tend to be about individual economic security and advancement.

It is, however, unclear whether people will use acquired international education to simply gain their own social advancement or to pay back to society. The experiences of Vietnamese returnees in this study suggest the former over the latter, although there are contested agenda and mixed outcomes and benefits. The contested agenda and ambivalence in the Vietnamese returnees' desire to engage in community development activities are indicative of the problem of countering social equity and economic development in transitional market-based economies. Nevertheless, acknowledging the relation between international higher education and the public good is important given the pertinent role of higher education for development.

There are scope limitations of this study in terms of evaluating outcomes and impacts of specific scholarship programs and the Vietnamese government's rationale for international education policy. It could be said, based on the findings, that if the state's visions for international education encompass both private and public benefits, while parents' motivations are private, and the opportunities to access international education and pathways to benefits are uneven, then, there is a mismatch between private and public expectation and outcomes.

These findings point to the need for policymakers in Vietnam to address equity issues in access and impacts of international education. Regarding access, if scholarship is based on competition, and competition creates status closures that exclude the majority of citizens, then we have to ensure that entry to international education can be organized to function in the collective interests. Policy goals should reconcile equitable opportunities with desires for international education to provide fair access so as to produce the public good and function of international education in the collective benefits. This could be done through admission requirements such as setting quotas or preferential treatment like bonus points for students from rural regions, ethnic minorities, or lower income families. Examples of these initiatives are Brazil's Law No. 10,558 that promotes access to higher education for people from socially disadvantaged groups, specifically targeting Afro-descendants and indigenous peoples; Lao's Education Sector Development Framework 2009–2015 emphasizes equality of access in all of the country's 17 provinces; India's quota-based affirmative action program that targets enrolment of students from scheduled tribes, scheduled castes, and other so-called "backward" classes (UNESCO, 2017).

International graduates gain positional advantage in job access, income, career pathways, challenging work, and job security. The majority of graduates in this study preferred MNCs or foreign firms because of these advantages and social status. Such advantages may create uneven job access and limit the potential of graduates in sharing their overseas acquired skills and knowledge that could be beneficial for human resources development in Vietnamese firms, state enterprises, and government agencies. Given Vietnam's current low-skilled labor force and low-quality universities, skills and knowledge gained from international education that are geared for advanced economies are in demand, which can provide international graduates advantages in the labor market. The implication is a deepening of inequality where elites who gain access to international education gain benefits from better employment opportunities. A key to improving equity in an emerging economy like Vietnam is creating conditions to help workers move out of low-income jobs to those with better income rather than creating a market that distributes people unevenly into jobs based on their socioeconomic backgrounds and existing privileges. Thus, recruitment policies could be used to incentivize returning graduates to work in local Vietnamese firms and SOE to harness their overseas knowledge and skills in specific sectors that are emerging in Vietnam's economy.

Equalizing opportunities require engaging returning international graduates in society as citizens not just workers. In practical terms, scholarship programs could identify ways of supporting alumni involvement in volunteer work and determine the feasibility and potential impact of providing such support. An example of this is the Ford Foundation International Fellowship program that tracks alumni's community-oriented work and impact they have made at the community level and ways in which they serve the community (IIE, 2017). Scholarship programs could include university extension programs in service learning, with opportunities and requirements to participate in local meetings and policymaking, engaging in humanitarian services, and direct advocacy.

Finally, social equity invokes the issue of whose public good and whose interest, as well as who is paying the costs and who is reaping the benefits. Government operates on behalf of the community; if international education is funded by the state or through the state, then its benefits should return to the state, which is also society. Given that scholarship is an important part of public financing of international education in Vietnam, building a fairer social world whose future financing depends largely on collective benefits of education is necessary. In addition to equity policy and programs to improve access and selection for students from diverse backgrounds to undertake international education, there is a need for monitoring and compliance activities to support equity policies and create synergy between policy design and implementation (Martin, 2010). Australia, for example, requires regular statistical reporting from higher education institutions to help monitor equity efforts (Stella, 2010).

Conclusion

This chapter highlighted three concerns about social equity in Vietnamese international education from the perspectives of international graduates returning home. First, access to international education carries social advantages of wealth and academic privileges from the wider society. Provision of scholarship by the Vietnamese government, bilateral agencies, and host universities reproduces the privileged class by giving them access to international experiences. Second, acquired international education furthers the economic inequality because overseas-acquired knowledge and skills abroad provide returnees with positional advantage in the labor market. Third, returnees' lack of active engagement in community development activities limits the collective benefits of their acquired international education for social development.

Drawing on these equity issues, the chapter argued that international education has an important role in transitioning Vietnam into a modern economy and promotes "socialism", which is at the core of Vietnam's policy of international education. For international education to be effective in this role, it should be viewed as a "public good" that encompasses equity alongside socioeconomic development. If the state provides international education through government or bilateral scholarships, it should be for the benefit of society broadly not only the privileged few. This requires explicit strategies to provide opportunities for all to study abroad as well as incentives for returning graduates to directly contribute to Vietnam's development needs through employment and community development activities. It is not possible to separate the contribution of international education to society if the selection of students carries social inequity of the wider society, and if these students are not willing or able to contribute to public benefits and improve social justice.

Conceptualizing international education as a public good needs further research and questions for theory and policy beyond the case study of Vietnam presented here. The findings and discussions in this chapter are limited by inherent limitation of methods used and sample size. Nevertheless, the conceptual argument contributes to a much-needed debate and orients research to linking social and economic returns with equitable international education opportunities. The appeal for international education stakeholders to engage with the public good, and to act in the public good, is a necessary way to confront social inequality in the progress of Vietnam's transitional economy and wellbeing of its society, as with other similar developing countries that send students abroad. The broader notion of public good and the role of international education in functioning as a public good demand self-reflection by all stakeholders as part of our critiques of the present and of our ideas and actions for the future. We must be conscious of policies and practices regarding access and outcomes of international education that do not frustrate the concept of equity, at the same time, advancing collective benefits for international graduates' societies.

Note

1 Scholarship recipients accounted for 4% of the total number of Vietnamese students abroad (Thanh Nien News, 2014) according to the Ministry of Education and Training (MOET) of Vietnam.

References

Australian Department of Foreign Affairs and Trade. (2013). Australia awards. *2011 Vietnam tracer study of Australian scholarships alumni*. https://www.dfat.gov.au/sites/default/files/australia-awards-vietnam-lessons-learnt-study.pdf

Australian Department of Foreign Affairs and Trade. (2014). *Australia Awards Vietnam Annual Report 2014*. Retrieved from https://www.dfat.gov.au/sites/default/files/australia-awarsd-vietnam-annual-report-2014.pdf

Barnett, R. (2007). Recovering the civic university. In L. McIlrath & I. M. Labhrainn (Eds.), *Higher education and civic engagement: International perspectives* (pp. 25–36). Hampshire, UK: Ashgate Publishing.

Bourdieu, P. (1984). *Distinction: A social critique of the judgement of taste*. Transl. by R. Nice. London, UK: Routledge and Kegan Paul.

Campbell, A. (2010). Developing generic skills and attributes of international students: The (ir)relevance of the Australian university experience. *Journal of Higher Education Policy and Management, 32*(5), 487–497.

Chao Jr, R. (November 2019). Achieving social mobility through regional HE networks [Blog post]. *University World News*. https://www.universityworldnews.com/post.php?story=20191112141231594

Creswell, J., & Clark, V. (2011). *Designing and conducting mixed methods research*. Thousand Oaks, CA: Sage Publications.

Crossman, J., & Clark, M. (2010). International experience and graduate employability: Stakeholder perceptions on the connection. *Higher Education, 59*, 599–613.

Dang, T. T. H. (2019). Does horizontal inequality matter in Vietnam? *Social Indicators Research, 145*, 943–956.

Dassin, J. R., Marsh, R. R., & Mawer M. (2018). Introduction: Pathways for social change? In J. Dassin, R. Marsh, & M. Mawer (Eds.), *International scholarships in higher education* (pp. 3–21). Cham, Switzerland: Palgrave Macmillan.

de Wit, H., & Hunter, F. (2015). The future of internationalization of higher education in Europe. *International Higher Education*, (83), 2–3. https://doi.org/10.6017/ihe.2015.83.9073

Delanty, G. (2001). *Challenging knowledge. The university in the knowledge society*. The Society for Research into Higher education & Open University Press.

Ergin, H. (November 2019). Is international higher education just an elite club? [Blog post]. *University World News*. https://www.universityworldnews.com/post.php?story=20191104073714229

Hao, J., Wen W., & Welch, A. (2016). When sojourners return: Employment opportunities and challenges facing high-skilled Chinese returnees. *Asian and Pacific Migration Journal, 25*(1), 22–40.

Harman, G. (2005). Internationalization of Australian higher education: A critical review of literature and research. In P. Ninnes & M. Hellsten (Eds.), *Internationalising higher education: Critical explorations of pedagogy and practice*

(pp. 119–140). Hong Kong, People's Republic of China: University of Hong Kong, Comparative Education Research Centre.
Institute of International Education (IIE). (2016). Open doors. https://www.iie.org/opendoors
Jonathan, R. (2001). Higher education transformation and the public good. Kasigano higher education discussion series. *Reinserting the "Public Good" into Higher Education, 1*, 28–63.
Kallick, J., & Brown Murga, A. (2018). *Transformational leaders and social change: IFP impacts in Africa and the Middle East*. Ford Foundation International Fellowships Program Alumni Tracking Study, Report No. 4. New York, NY: Institute of International Education.
Liên Hiệp Các Hội Khoa Học và Kỹ Thuật Sơn La. (2012). Giới thiệu tóm tắt Đề án 165. [Introductory Summary of Scheme 165]. https://susta.vn/bai-viet-Gioi-thieu-tom-tt-de-an-165-165.html
Marginson, S. (2011). Higher education and the public good. *Higher Education Quarterly, 65*(4), 411–433.
Martel, M. (2019). *Leveraging higher education to promote social justice: Evidence from the IFP alumni tracking study*. Ford Foundation International Fellowships Program Alumni Tracking Study, Report No. 4. https://www.iie.org/Research-and-Insights/Publications/IFP-Report-5
Nghia, T. L. H., Giang, H. T., & Quyen, V. P. (2019). At-home international education in Vietnamese universities: Impact on graduates' employability and career prospects. *Higher Education, 78*, 817–834.
Organization of Economic Cooperation and Development. (2019). Foreign/international students enrolled. https://stats.oecd.org/Index.aspx?DataSetCode=RFOREIGN
Paige, R., Fry, G., Stallman, E., Josić, J., & Jon, J. E. (2009). Study abroad for global engagement: The long-term impact of mobility experiences. *Intercultural Education, 20*(Suppl. 1), S29–S44. doi:10.1080/14675980903370847
Perkins, D., Nguyen, X. T., Vu, T. T. A., Huynh, T. D., Pincus, J., & Saich, T. (2008). *Choosing success: The lessons of east and southeast Asia and Vietnam's future*. Asia Programs. John F. Kennedy School of Government, Cambridge: Harvard University.
Pham, L. (2018). Aspirations of Vietnamese overseas-trained graduates in their homeland. In L. Tran & S. Marginson (Eds.), *Internationalization of Vietnamese higher education* (pp. 177–200). Melbourne, Australia: Springer.
Pham, L. (2019). *International graduates returning to Vietnam. Experiences of the local economies, universities and communities*. Singapore: Springer.
Samuelson, P. (1954). The pure theory of public expenditure. *Review of Economics and Statistics, 36*(4), 387–389.
Slaughter, S., & Leslie, L. (1997). *Academic capitalism*. Baltimore, MD: John Hopkins.
Thanh Nien News. (2014). *Nearly all Vietnamese study abroad with private funds*. http://www.thanhniennews.com/education-youth/nearly-all-vietnamese-study-abroad-with-private-funds-31582.html
Thanh Nien News. (2015). Vietnamese spend $3 billion a year to study abroad: Report. http://www.thanhniennews.com/education-youth/vietnamese-spend-3-billion-a-year-to-study-abroad-report-54463.html
UNESCO. (2017). *Policy paper 30. Six ways to ensure higher education leaves no one behind*. https://unesdoc.unesco.org/ark:/48223/pf0000247862

UNESCO Institute for Statistics. (2019). http://uis.unesco.org/en/country/vn
Vallely, T., & Wilkinson, B. (2008). *Vietnamese higher education: Crisis and response.* Asia Programs. Ash Institute for Democratic Governance and Innovation, Harvard Kennedy School, Cambridge: Harvard University.
Vietnamese International Education Department (VIED). December 2016. http://icd.edu.vn
World Bank. (2019). https://www.worldbank.org/en/country/vietnam/overview

5 Enriching Australian Exchange Student Learning Experiences at Japanese Universities

Kayoko Enomoto, Richard Warner and Julia Miller

Introduction

This chapter presents a study that investigates student learning experiences during exchange study abroad from both academic readiness and cultural (dis)engagement perspectives. The first aim of the study was to help inform institutional practices to enrich exchange study abroad experiences for Australian undergraduate students in Japanese universities. Much research on international students has traditionally focused on student mobility from non-English-speaking countries to English-speaking countries. However, the 21st-century student mobility landscape has progressively changed. This calls for more research that contributes to a more geo-culturally balanced examination of global student mobility. Therefore, the second aim of our study was to help bring about more equity in research directions in global student mobility by focusing on English-speaking to non-English-speaking countries. Our study therefore investigates the experiences of 20 English-speaking Australian undergraduate students going on exchange study abroad in Japan, "a hitherto rarely explored population" (Iizuka, 2019, p. 135). The study examines how they navigate academic, linguistic and cultural challenges in a non-English-speaking, culturally non-cognate destination.

Literature Review

The need to engage internationally as a global player is vital for the 21st-century university in most developed countries. In Australia, for example, education is now the third largest export industry (Department of Foreign Affairs and Trade, 2019a), largely due to a neo-liberal shift (Scott, 2016) whereby university education has increasingly been viewed as a marketable commodity, and thus students can be seen as fee-paying customers. In such an educational environment, students would naturally expect not only a high-quality education that would maximize their learning outcomes but similarly a high-quality international experience to enhance their employability for a successful career in the increasingly globalized workplace.

This need to further internationalize universities' operational contexts has become a catalyst for increased student mobility (Byram, 2009) in the 21st century. Thus, internationalization involves "prioritizing a global outlook in the curriculum, attracting international students, and encouraging domestic students to take part in an outbound mobility experience" (Jones et al., 2016, p. 1). Nevertheless, in Australian universities, the internationalization agenda has been commonly strategized through recruiting international students largely from Asian and Middle Eastern countries (Daly, 2011), meaning that much student mobility has been neither bi-directional nor balanced. Indeed, for an English-speaking country like Australia that is situated in the Asia Pacific region, to increase the nation's Asian literacy and capability (Department of Foreign Affairs and Trade, 2019b) is paramount to its economic and political future. Thus, in 2014, the Australian Government piloted the New Colombo Plan (Department of Foreign Affairs and Trade, 2019b) to support over 1,300 students financially to undertake their studies in four Asian destinations (Hong Kong, Indonesia, Japan and Singapore). Subsequently, the New Colombo Plan has encouraged and pointed many Australian undergraduate students to a wider range of Asian countries.

Many studies on inbound international students worldwide have tended to focus primarily on academic, linguistic and cultural challenges, often from a deficit model perspective, that English as an additional language (EAL) students face in English-speaking countries such as the U.S.A., U.K. and Australia (Hanada, 2019; Hyland & Hyland, 2019; Sato & Hodge, 2015; Warner & Enomoto, 2015). A small number of studies on Australian outbound students (e.g., Forsey, Broomhall, & Davis, 2012) and English-speaking outbound students to Japan (e.g., Iino, 2006; Iizuka, 2019) do exist, but such studies have tended to focus on the effectiveness of certain approaches to teaching or learning Japanese, often in the context of short-term Japanese language programs. Therefore, within the wider context of university internationalization and global student mobility, more research is needed to examine the English-speaking students' learning experiences in linguistically and culturally non-cognate countries for a period of time longer than the traditional (one- or two-month) short-term program.

The goals of internationalization and more balanced student mobility can be enabled through study abroad programs. In fact, much literature on study abroad has shown a wide range of desirable effects, including broader life experiences (Yang, Webster, & Prosser, 2011); intercultural awareness and competencies (Hanada, 2019); developed social and communication skills, including in foreign languages (Isabelli-García, 2001); self-efficacy (Cubillos & Ilvento, 2012; Nguyen, Jeffries, & Rojas, 2018); cultural intelligence (Nguyen et al., 2018) and adaptability and resilience (Sanz & Morales-Front, 2018), leading to personal growth (Marjanović & Križman Pavlović, 2018). However, study abroad programs in higher education have not been without their shortcomings (Tran & Vu, 2018). There is scope for improvement in terms of supporting outbound English-speaking students and enhancing their study abroad experiences, especially in linguistically and culturally non-cognate countries.

Our particular study abroad focus is upon university exchange programs. The duration of such programs in Australian universities is normally six months (one semester) to twelve months (two semesters). Student participation in such programs during their university studies is one obvious way to gain international experience and enhance employability (Tran & Vu, 2018), bearing in mind that "employability is not an outcome, but a process" (Smith, Bell, Bennett, & McAlpine, 2018, p. 6). University exchange programs usually allow participating students to transfer the credits they earn in their overseas partner university to their home university, with such credits counted towards their home degree. This enables participating exchange students not to have to repeat the period of study they spent overseas upon their return. However, successfully completing university courses in non-cognate countries demands English-speaking students to navigate academic, linguistic and cultural challenges. As Hanada (2019) points out, both students' target language proficiency prior to exchange and structured pre-departure orientation can positively impact upon the development of their intercultural competence during exchange. With these findings in mind, it is crucial for universities to prepare and support outbound students prior to going on exchange in non-cognate countries to enhance the development of their intercultural competence. For prospective outbound students going on such exchange programs from Australia to non-cognate countries, there are many considerations to ponder, such as destination, duration, cost and institutional support from both home and host universities.

In addition, one major consideration is a recognition of the nexus between language learning and culture (Liddicoat, 2011). As Byram and Wagner (2018, p. 140) state, "linguistic competence needs to be enriched with deep intercultural competence". Likewise, Scarino and Liddicoat (2009, p. 15) argue that language is not merely a code, but demands interpretation and making of meanings which are in themselves social practices. Yet, cultivating intercultural competence poses more challenges when a culture is markedly distant from the student's own culture. In this study, we adopt Borghetti's (2017, p. 2) definition of intercultural competence: "an integral whole of cognitive, affective and behavioral factors that influence . . . understanding of and interaction with diversity in a broad sense and . . . [are] developed through education". This definition importantly focuses on the 'processes' involved in developing intercultural competence, rather than viewing intercultural competence as an 'outcome'. Borghetti's process-focused interpretation of intercultural competence derives from Deardorff's (2011) cyclic model of intercultural competence, comprising four process dimensions (see Figure 5.1).

By adopting this process-focused definition, the present study recognizes the intertwining nature of developing language and intercultural competence in 'the third place' (Crozet, Liddicoat, & Lo Bianco, 1999; Kramsch, 1993). This notion of the third place refers to students' interculturality at the intersection of the two cultures. The third place corresponds to Process Dimension 4 as a desired external interactional outcome, yet this outcome is not static

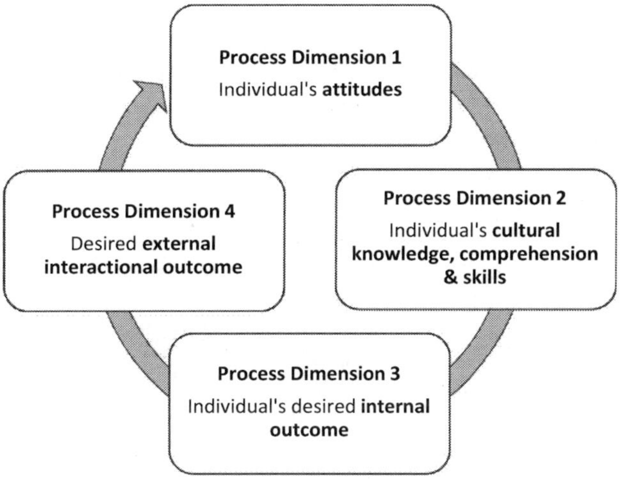

Figure 5.1 Cyclic process model of intercultural competence adapted from Deardorff (2011, p. 67).

because it again feeds into Process Dimension 1 (individual's attitudes), following this cyclic process model. As such, the methodology outlined below was employed with the aim of obtaining data that would indicate the processes involved in developing intercultural competence rather than any outcomes relating to intercultural competence. Bearing the language-culture nexus in mind, our study will investigate English-speaking Australian students' learning experiences during their Japan exchange from two perspectives: advancing Japanese language proficiency and cultivating intercultural competence.

Research Method

Our study focused on the learning experiences of 20 English-speaking Australian undergraduate students who went on study exchange to Japan between 2016 and 2018. The study utilized face-to-face semi-structured interviews to investigate how individual students navigated both language and cultural challenges while studying at Japanese universities as an English-speaking Australian exchange student. In order to ascertain both the nature and dimensions of student experiences (Richards, Ross, & Seedhouse, 2012, p. 33), we felt it requisite to spend sufficient time with individual participants involved, adopting interviews as one effective technique. As with any research methods, there are shortcomings associated with the research interview, such as the possibilities of the interviewer's (the first author in the present study) interview manner and responses influencing how the interviewee would respond (Richards et al., 2012). Nevertheless, conducting interviews individually can make the participants feel more comfortable talking about their personal experiences and expressing their own personal opinions without being heard by others. To capture the students' academic, linguistic and cultural experiences, 20 recordings of interview data were collected from their post-exchange reflections, each interview lasting for approximately 45 minutes. The time was sufficient for participants to relax and feel comfortable discussing their exchange experiences and for the interviewer to gauge the value of their responses. The interviewer was the head of the Japanese studies program at the outgoing university, but this was not seen as a limitation, as she had excellent rapport with the students, and her academic position enabled her to understand better the students' home university preparation.

The Study Overseas office at the outgoing university has a list of around 15 exchange partner Japanese universities (which varies from year to year) on their website. In terms of which Japanese university they went to, the students had to rank their preferred universities on their exchange application. Their preference was determined as a result of their researching online and obtaining information from both the Study Overseas office at the outgoing university and from their potential host universities. In so doing, they had to self-determine the type of university (public or private), Japanese language and culture/society course availability, location (urban or semi-urban) and student accommodation. Thus, there are a wide range of factors that could influence individual students' learning experiences. Nevertheless, this is not seen as a limitation, as this study focused on the exchange experience rather than language courses per se. Indeed, the focus of our study was upon the students' own overall exchange learning experiences, rather than the particular impact and responses as a result of taking different courses in varying learning environments at different Japanese universities.

Participants

All the interview participants were Japanese Studies majors and English native speakers. There were 14 female and 6 male participants whose ages ranged from 19 to 27 years. The students had no previous university exchange study experience in Japan. These students studied both Japanese language courses (taught in Japanese) and Japanese culture/society courses (taught in English) at nine different partner Japanese universities, six in urban areas and three in semi-urban areas, with four national (public) and five private universities. None of the students was studying concurrently at the same Japanese university as any other of the study participants, and they mingled in Japan with a diverse international student cohort. Eighteen students went for one full academic year and two for one semester. Participation in the study was voluntary (with a $10 gift card incentive) and had university ethics clearance. Student comments are reported anonymously, with each student referred to by number (e.g., S1, S2) to distinguish their voices.

Through the current exchange partnerships with these Japanese universities, participating students are usually able to transfer the credits they earned in their host Japanese university to their Australian university and to count such exchange credits towards their Japanese Studies major. Such a cross-institutional credit transfer arrangement is one major attraction for students to participate in university exchange programs in Japan, as they need not repeat the year of study they spent overseas.

Procedure

Closed questions were first asked in order to gain demographic information, followed by audio-recorded, semi-structured face-to-face individual interviews. The interviews were spread over a two-year period from February 2017 to March 2019, owing to differences in the students' return dates from Japan to their Australian university. During the interviews, the opening question was: 'What did it feel like to be a student at [name of university] as an exchange student?' This was followed by Guiding Prompts (1–4) to stimulate the participants to reflect upon their exchange experiences:

- Guiding Prompt 1: Academic preparation prior to exchange;
- Guiding Prompt 2: Differences in academic expectations and the necessary adaptations;
- Guiding Prompt 3: Cultural (dis)engagement and adaptation;
- Guiding Prompt 4: Advice to prospective Japan exchange students.

Results and Discussion

Overall, the participants were overwhelmingly positive in describing their exchange experiences. This positivity was clearly evident in their perception of their own language development and personal growth through their cultural experiences whilst in Japan. Based on the transcription of audio-recordings of the interviews, we were able to discern what Parker and Tritter (2006, p. 3) allude to as "a sense of respondent commonality" under each of the four guiding prompts for reflection (expanded upon below).

Guiding Prompt 1: Academic Preparation Prior to Exchange

A majority of participants considered pre-exchange academic preparation as crucial, regardless of whether they judged themselves as well prepared before going to Japan. Such perceptions concur with Hanada's (2019) results, whereby the Intercultural Developmental Inventory (IDI) score was 4.46 for students who attended a pre-departure orientation, in contrast with the IDI score of −0.91 for those who did not attend such an orientation. In our study, of the 20 students, five felt unprepared academically and another five felt reasonably prepared, whilst ten felt that they were well prepared before exchange. However, those who felt most strongly about this issue were those who felt that their own pre-exchange academic preparation was insufficient. As one student graphically commented: *it needs maturity to sort your s**t together* (S18). Many participants reflected upon the importance of this very issue of maturity with respect to academic preparation. Some of the factors for being well prepared ranged from researching the textbooks to be used in Japan in advance, via reading online course outlines in Japanese (S11) or emailing the host university for certain information (S6); studying for the placement test focusing on Kanji characters and vocabulary continuously until departure (S8); arriving in Japan early to prepare for the placement test (S11); and sitting for the Japanese Language Proficiency Test prior to exchange (S4). No single method was consistently reported, but rather students appeared to have devised their own way of preparing themselves, such as helping with Japanese classes at their former high school (S5), focusing on everyday Japanese (S14) and doing extra study before the exchange (S4).

Another dimension was the role of the home institution in guiding and supporting prospective exchange students for Japanese universities. Issues that arose centred around a lack of an accessible, structured pre-departure orientation program specifically for Japan. For instance, one student (S9) spoke of having to help other students gather information on their exchange credit transfer, including how to find people who were needed to approve courses. Similarly, another student (S15) commented that pre-exchange paperwork preparation was complicated due to lack of information and explanation (including scholarship opportunities) as to what to do or where to go or whom to see. Again, these findings are in line with those of both Hanada (2019) and Iizuka (2019), stressing the need for a specific destination-focused, well-structured pre-departure orientation program. Such a program is necessary irrespective of the student mobility direction, from English-speaking to non-English speaking destinations or vice versa.

It is true that the process of applying and preparing for exchange is complex. However, this process is part of developing life skills on the part of the students. This means that it is vital to construct a systematically structured pre-departure orientation program that clarifies who is responsible for what, when and how. Doing everything for the students does not facilitate their personal growth; they need encouragement to become resourceful in order to be able to navigate life in Japan. Thus, such an orientation program requires defining and equitably balancing both institutional and individual students' responsibilities in the process of preparing for exchange study abroad programs.

Guiding Prompt 2: Differences in Academic Expectations and the Necessary Adaptations

Students' concerns about the expected 'demands' of language learning at Japanese universities seem to have begun with the requirement to sit a placement test upon arrival. Each Japanese university had a different way of conducting placement tests to determine students' language levels. This meant that the students were not able to prepare for a particular type/format of the placement test, as some students commented: *passed it through a bit of dumb luck* (S6); *it [placement test] was terrifying* (S8); *I didn't like the selection test process as I test poorly . . . so I was put in possibly too low a class* (S4). To alleviate such worries over the placement test requirement, in future we could establish a formal exchange study abroad peer-mentoring program or a buddy system at the students' home university by matching those students who have been accepted to go on Japanese exchange with those who have already experienced one. A peer-mentor or buddy at this stage could also help promote departing students' sense of self-efficacy (Cubillos & Ilvento, 2012) and provide them with 'cultural intelligence' (Nguyen et al., 2018). Such a peer-mentoring or buddy system would also help address other dimensions of exchange study abroad, such as homework, assessments and attendance, which we will discuss below.

One particular dimension that the students had to adapt to was the small class size. A total of 14 students commented that both language and culture/society courses had much smaller class sizes, ranging from 8 to 16 students of mixed nationalities (many from Asian countries), than those they had experienced in their home university. They felt that the small class size made them engage even more with their study, particularly in language classes. They commented that they had to preview and review before and after every language class because of their increased visibility and expectation for active class participation, leading to an improvement in their grades. This positive effect of a small class size has been demonstrated elsewhere, as illustrated by Kokkelenberg, Dillon and Christy's study (2008, p. 2) in the context of a public university: "there are dis-economies of scale associated with a deterioration of student outcomes as class sizes grow larger".

In addition, all the participants commented on marked differences in teachers' academic expectations of students at Japanese universities. Such expectations included regular weekly in-class tests and strict class attendance, both of which counted towards their final grade. Moreover, students were expected to complete homework before every class. Indeed, whilst they commented that the expected weekly workload was much heavier than what they had been used to in Australia, many students recognized the advantage of such expectations: *most assessment was continuous, which meant that exams weren't stressful* (S2); *it [memorizing 5-minute speech as homework] was terrible, but it was really good* (S1). Individual participants' experiences with teachers in Japanese universities varied widely in relation to how the classes were delivered. Several students commented on how interactive the classes were. For example, some students commented: *small groups meant interactions with lecturers—you got to know the teachers well in class* (S4); *student-teacher interactions were good, and teachers really encourage student participation* (S17). In contrast, a small minority of the students had found some teachers *boring* (S12) and *strict* (S9) in their interactions. Nevertheless, a theme that resonated throughout the interviews was one of positive surprise. The largely informal nature of the teaching style was not something that they had anticipated. As one student said, *[The teacher] was a bit of a comedian, giving funny stories and awful jokes in Japanese to read, which made it easier to remember* (S10), while another student said that the teacher was caring and supportive to the point that *they almost baby you a little bit* (S6).

When asked about any difficulties faced in the classroom, 50% of the participants commented that it was a shock at first to experience Japanese as a medium of instruction: *the classes were delivered almost totally in Japanese* (S6). They did struggle to understand their teachers' instructions in Japanese in the early stages of their exchange: *I couldn't even hear Japanese—it was too fast!* (S2). However, *it was very daunting in the first few weeks, but it clicked eventually* (S15) and *in the end, it was alright. You find other ways of communicating* (S11). Thus, instruction in Japanese became less of an issue over time.

A proposed pre-departure orientation program, drawing on experiences of returnee exchange students acting as peer mentors or buddies, could explore the above-mentioned major differences in academic expectations and the necessary adaptations which emerged from this study. These issues particularly related to the placement test, class size, workload, attendance and teaching style.

Guiding Prompt 3: Cultural (Dis)engagement and Adaptation

One of the issues that emerged during the topic of cultural adaptation was related to rigid requirements for class attendance. Several students commented that absence due to sickness was considered as an unjustified absence by their teachers, with one student remarking that *absence was seen as laziness culturally* (S15). Five students who had absences due to mental health issues or religious practice reported that these were not considered to be mitigating factors for attendance exemption, resulting in a loss of attendance marks. Although they perceived this as unfair, they accepted it, given the very different cultural norms held by Australian universities (Possamai et al., 2016). However, it appeared that such negative experiences led to some sense of cultural disengagement. These findings highlight the importance of students' pre-departure preparation in terms of not only developing target language proficiency but also equally raising awareness of and sensitivity towards different cultural values and how to manage them prior to exchange study abroad.

One issue which emerged from several female participants was gender-related, particularly in relation to clothing: *I felt uncomfortable wearing shorts [on a train]—you got leered at* (S17). As a consequence, they opted to wear jeans even in summer. Likewise, two female students reported being followed in Tokyo streets and having to take evasive action. Japan is commonly perceived as a very safe destination, so for those female students, this was an aspect of life in Japan they had not anticipated but had to adapt to very quickly. None of the male participants shared this aspect of cultural adaptation. These gender-specific issues must be spelt out clearly in any pre-departure orientation program in order to prepare students to be 'street smart' and to feel more comfortable living in Japan.

Such a conceptual mismatch of what is culturally acceptable is not an unusual phenomenon. Indeed, Iizuka's (2019) study, which examined American study abroad students in Japan, revealed a similar mismatch between the students' and host families' perceptions in relation to leaving food:

> She (student) doesn't finish the food on her plate. I once told her to let me know beforehand if she would not, so that I can reduce the amount on her plate beforehand, but still . . . perhaps she doesn't really have a sense of mottainai 'regret concerning waste'.
>
> (Iizuka, 2019, p. 138)

Iizuka (2019) points out that this situation could have been avoided if the student had had pre-departure preparation to raise awareness of different cultural values. Likewise, our study revealed another example of perceptual mismatch of what is culturally acceptable. Thus, the evidence of cultural adaptation – a deepening process of intercultural competence – transpired from our findings on both attendance- and gender-related issues. Such evidence concurs with Borghetti's (2017) and Deardorff's (2011) notion of intercultural competence as a process rather than an outcome and demonstrates the development of intercultural competence, 'the third place' to which Kramsch (1993) alludes. This involves the students' learning that operating in another culture does not mean that they must fully accept that culture or become fully comfortable in that culture. Rather, students need to become culturally flexible to be open to, respect and understand different values and expectations.

Guiding Prompt 4: Advice to Prospective Japan Exchange Students

The final prompt gave students the chance to help enhance the experience of future exchange students going to Japanese universities. Several themes emerged. First, in terms of pre-departure preparation, some students strongly advocated the importance of studying Japanese as much as possible prior to going to Japan, whilst others made a strong point of suggesting to study the textbooks they would be using in advance, especially if these were different to those used at their home institution. In addition, some students, reflecting on their own experiences, strongly suggested prospective exchange students select and plan which courses to study prior to exchange and advised to *get into it as much as you can and take the courses you want to take* (S10); *plan your courses…and what you are going to do when you come back* (S12); *definitely take the JLPT [Japanese Language Proficiency Test] while in Japan . . . many exchange returnees regret not taking the test while there* (S8).

Alluding to the timing of exchange at Japanese universities, it was intensely felt by six students that *going to Japan during the 3rd year is the best . . . to get the most out of the exchange, after learning elementary Japanese grammar* (S18) and after *knowing how to learn the language* before exchange (S1). Moreover, two of these students also went on to encourage prospective students to persevere for the first semester because they found things improved significantly for them in their second semester. This perseverance factor is also borne out by the related literature (Marjanović & Križman Pavlović, 2018; Sanz & Morales-Front, 2018). In our study, one student advised that *One semester is not much time, take time to get used to the language and classes [taught in Japanese as a medium of instruction]* (S6). Several suggestions were made in order to overcome the challenges, particularly in the first semester, which included taking lots of Japanese courses, making an effort to speak the language, knowing the importance of using polite language (especially in shops) and understanding that *Japan can be overwhelming, but Japanese people are welcoming* (S17). Such perseverance-related attributes are indeed crucial for enhancing students' future employability (Tran & Vu, 2018) and support the notion of employability as a process rather than an outcome (Smith et al., 2018).

Another theme that emerged was the participants' encouragement to have a broader cultural experience (Yang et al., 2011), including *make Japanese friends* (S4, S17), *don't stay in your room* (S4) and *take extracurricular activities* (S5, S10, S15), although one student was sufficiently mindful to point out that *skipping commitments is really looked down upon, so don't overdo it* (S14). Similarly, asking for help and being resilient and independent were mentioned: *Don't expect things to be done for you . . . Don't expect the experience to be completely easy . . . experience can make you more adult* (S16). In addition, keeping in contact with friends and family was suggested as one way to build resilience while in Japan (S15, S16).

The final theme that transpired in relation to advice to future exchange students concerned mental health issues. Because the workload can be demanding, four students strongly advised looking after one's health. Two students suggested taking any necessary medication over to Japan for any pre-existing mental health condition, researching necessary paperwork and completing it for customs in advance. Notably, they warned that absence due to a mental health condition is unlikely to be understood or accepted as a justifiable reason for not meeting any class attendance requirements. Indeed, the aspect relating to mental health was not a theme we had expected to emerge, nor the fact that one in five of the participants had to cope with mental health issues in a linguistically and culturally non-cognate country. This reality stresses the significance of sensitively incorporating a mental health-related aspect into any pre-departure orientation program. Indeed, there is a body of literature on the mental health of non-English speaking international students in English-speaking countries (e.g., Forbes-Mewett, 2019; Mori, 2000). In contrast, this is not mirrored in the research direction of English-speaking to non-English speaking countries in culturally non-cognate destinations.

Conclusions and Implications

The study presented in this chapter has advocated the need for an accessible, systematically structured institutional approach to consolidating students' academic readiness and cultural awareness prior to exchange. Our findings demonstrated evidence that could inform a proposed pre-departure orientation program specific to Japan. This concurs with Hanada's (2019) findings that a structured pre-departure orientation program can have a positive impact in developing intercultural competence during undergraduate exchange programs. Drawing upon our findings, home Australian universities should systematically organize and facilitate such an orientation program. This accessible program could also benefit from a peer-mentoring element or buddy system between prospective outbound students and those who have returned from Japanese exchange. In addition, the program content should unpack the aforementioned major differences in academic expectations, such as attendance requirements and medium of instruction. Similarly, the content should explore the need for students to sensitively negotiate different cultural values beyond the classroom, such as gender and mental health issues. However, to bring about a more equitable institutional approach to supporting outbound students, such a systematic pre-departure orientation program requires making clear the distinction and the balance between institutional and individual students' responsibilities, moving towards more equitable partnerships between institution and student. If done effectively, an orientation program can better equip the students to be culturally flexible, enabling their personal growth and helping them navigate cultural dilemmas that they might face in Japan. This flexibility is all part of and central to developing intercultural competence that is, according to Borghetti (2017, p. 2), fostered through the students' "cognitive, affective and behavioral factors" that guide their understandings of and interactions with different cultural values.

It is also recommended that future studies involve interviews with home university administrators while participating students are at the host university. Findings from the students' post-departure interviews could then be shared with these administrators after the exchange experience and the administrators' feedback sought. This would have the benefit of enriching the research data and potentially improving the collaboration between the participating universities. Another option is to seek interviews with the student participants while they are on-site and then to interview them again after the exchange has concluded.

As its second aim, the present study has focused upon a more geo-culturally balanced examination of global student mobility. The particular imbalance that this study aimed to help counterbalance was in the direction from English-speaking to non-English speaking destinations, specifically the particular cultural instance of Australian undergraduate students on exchange in Japan. If one main goal of internationalization in universities in English-speaking countries is to cultivate intercultural competence through their study abroad programs, it is vital that these universities recognize the importance of bi-directionality in student mobility. Indeed, despite the strategic push for the international student dollar, true 21st-century internationalization demands a more balanced mobility between inbound and outbound students. In Australia, such a balance in student mobility could become a vehicle for increasing Australia's engagement with Asia in the 21st-century. Since one of the graduate attributes (Barrie, 2006) that many Australian universities publically stipulate is intercultural competence, it is ultimately the social responsibility of universities that this attribute is cultivated equally in all inbound and outbound students.

References

Barrie, S. (2006). Understanding what we mean by the generic attributes of graduates. *Higher Education, 51*, 215–241.

Borghetti, C. (2017). Is there really a need for assessing intercultural competence? Some ethical issues. *Journal of Intercultural Communication, 44*, 1–22.

Byram, M. (2009). The 'value' of academic mobility. In M. Byram & F. Dervin (Eds.), *Students, staff and academic mobility in higher education* (pp. 31–47). Cambridge, UK: Cambridge Scholars Publishing.

Byram, M., & Wagner, M. (2018). Making a difference: Language teaching for intercultural and international dialogue. *Foreign Language Annals, 51*(1), 140–151. doi:10.1111/flan.12319

Crozet, C., Liddicoat, A. J., & Lo Bianco, J. (1999). Intercultural competence: From language policy to language education. In J. Lo Bianco, A. J. Liddicoat, & C. Crozet (Eds.), *Striving for the third place: Intercultural competence through language education* (pp. 1–20). Melbourne, Australia: Language Australia.

Cubillos, J. H., & Ilvento, T. (2012). The impact of study abroad on students' self-efficacy perceptions. *Foreign Language Annals, 45*, 494–511.

Daly, A. (2011). Determinants of participating in Australian university student exchange programs. *Journal of Research in International Education, 10*(1), 58–70. doi:10.1177/1475240910394979

Deardorff, D. K. (2011). Assessing intercultural competence. *New Directions for Institutional Research, 149,* 65–79. doi:10.1002/ir.381

Department of Foreign Affairs and Trade. (2019a). *Trade and investment at a glance 2019.* https://dfat.gov.au/about-us/publications/trade-investment/trade-at-a-glance/trade-investment-at-a-glance-2019/Pages/default.aspx#exports

Department of Foreign Affairs and Trade. (2019b). *New Colombo Plan.* https://dfat.gov.au/people-to-people/new-colombo-plan/Pages/new-colombo-plan.aspx

Forbes-Mewett, H. (2019). *Mental health and international students: Issues, challenges and effective practice.* Melbourne, Australia: International Education Association of Australia (IEAA).

Forsey, M., Broomhall, S., & Davis, J. (2012). Broadening the mind? Australian student reflections on the experience of overseas study. *Journal of Studies in International Education, 16*(2), 128–139.

Hanada, S. (2019). A quantitative assessment of Japanese students' intercultural competence developed through study abroad programs. *Journal of International Students, 9*(4), 1015–1037. doi:10.32674/jis.v9i4.391

Hyland, K., & Hyland, F. (2019). Contexts and issues in feedback on L2 writing: An introduction. In K. Hyland, & F. Hyland (Eds.), *Feedback in second language writing: Contexts and issues* (pp. 1–22). Cambridge, UK: Cambridge University Press.

Iino, M. (2006). Norms of interaction in a Japanese homestay setting: Toward two-way flow of linguistic and cultural resources. In M. DuFon & E. Churchill (Eds.), *Language learners in study abroad contexts* (pp. 151–173). Clevedon, UK: Multilingual Matters.

Iizuka, T. (2019). Task-based needs analysis: Identifying communicative needs for study abroad students in Japan. *System, 80,* 134–142. doi:10.1016/j.system.2018.11.005

Isabelli-García, C. (2001). *Motivation and extended interaction in the study abroad context: Factors in the development of Spanish language accuracy and communication skills.* New York, NY: Edwin Mellen Press.

Jones, B., Power, A., Gray, T., Downey, G., Hall, T., & Truong, S. (2016). If you build it, they may not come: Why Australian university students do not take part in outbound mobility experiences. *Journal of University Teaching and Learning Practice, 13*(3). https://ro.uow.edu.au/jutlp/vol13/iss3/9/

Kokkelenberg, E. C., Dillon, M., & Christy, S. M. (2008). The effects of class size on student grades at a public university. *Economics of Education Review, 27*(2), 221–233.

Kramsch, C. (1993). *Context and culture in language teaching.* Oxford, UK: Oxford University Press.

Liddicoat, A. J. (2011). Language teaching and learning from an intercultural perspective. In E. Hinkel (Ed.), *Handbook of research in second language teaching and learning* (pp. 837–855). Abingdon, UK: Routledge.

Marjanović, B., & Križman Pavlović, D. (2018). Factors influencing the high school graduates' decision to study abroad: Toward a theoretical model. *Management: Journal of Contemporary Management Issues, 23*(1), 221–241. doi:10.30924/mjcmi/2018.23.1.221

Mori, S. C. (2000). Addressing the mental health concerns of international students. *Journal of Counseling & Development, 78*(2), 137–144. doi:10.1002/j.1556-6676.2000.tb02571.x

Nguyen, A. M. D., Jefferies, J., & Rojas, B. (2018). Short term, big impact? Changes in self-efficacy and cultural intelligence, and the adjustment of multicultural and monocultural students abroad. *International Journal of Intercultural Relations, 66,* 119–129. doi:10.1016/j.ijintrel.2018.08.001

Parker, A., & Tritter, J. (2006). Focus group method and methodology: Current practice and recent debate. *International Journal of Research & Method in Education, 29*(1), 23–37.

Possamai, A., Dunn, K., Hopkins, P., Amin, F., Worthington, L., & Ali, J. (2016). Muslim students' religious and cultural experiences in the micro-publics of university campuses in NSW, Australia. *Australian Geographer, 47*(3), 311–324. doi:10.1080/00049182.2016.1191136

Richards, K., Ross, S., & Seedhouse, P. (2012). *Research methods for applied language studies.* New York, NY: Routledge.

Sanz, C., & Morales-Front, A. (Eds.). (2018). *The Routledge handbook of study abroad research and practice.* Abingdon, UK: Routledge.

Sato, T., & Hodge, S. R. (2015). Japanese exchange students' academic and social struggles at an American university. *Journal of International Students, 5,* 208–227.

Scarino, A., & Liddicoat, A. (2009). *Teaching and learning languages: A guide.* Melbourne, Australia: Curriculum Corporation.

Scott, P. (2016). International higher education and the "neo-liberal turn". *International Higher Education, 84*, 16–17. doi:10.6017/ihe.2016.84.9113

Smith, M., Bell, K., Bennett, D., & McAlpine, A. (2018). *Employability in a global context: Evolving policy and practice in employability, work integrated learning, and career development learning.* Wollongong, Australia: Graduate Careers Australia.

Tran, L. T., & Vu, T. T. P. (2018). Beyond the 'normal' to the 'new possibles': Australian students' experiences in Asia and their roles in making connections with the region via the New Colombo Plan. *Higher Education Quarterly, 72*(3), 194–207. doi:10.1111/hequ.12166

Warner, R., & Enomoto, K. (2015). Embedding research skills in the curriculum design of a pathway programme for international students. In C. Nygaard, P. Bartholomew, & C. Guerin (Eds.), *Learning to research – researching to learn* (pp. 19–38). Abingdon, Oxon., UK: Libri Publishing.

Yang, M., Webster, B., & Prosser, M. (2011). Travelling a thousand miles: Hong Kong Chinese students' study abroad experience. *International Journal of Intercultural Relations, 35*(1), 69–78.

Part II

Inequality in Students' Opportunities to Gain International Experiences

6 Secondary School Student Mobility

Social and Cultural Capital Transmission through Merit-based Exchange Programs

Manca Sustarsic and Baoyan Cheng

Introduction

Since the year 2000, the number of international students worldwide has more than doubled with approximately 5.3 million international students studying abroad in 2017 compared to two million in 2000 (United Nations Educational, Scientific and Cultural Organization [UNESCO], 2019). While the number of internationally mobile students is increasing and host destinations are diversifying, International Student Mobility (ISM) primarily flows from low-income to high-income western countries, with the United States (U.S.) remaining the top host destination (Farrugia, 2014; UNESCO, 2019). This may indicate that, at the core, ISM is not equitable since it excludes those who do not possess sufficient economic capital to relocate to higher-income countries, thus further perpetuating social inequalities (Green, Gannaway, Sheppard, & Jamarani, 2014).

In recent years, an increasing number of secondary school students have decided to study abroad. In 2016, there were 82,000 international students enrolled in American secondary schools. However, not all students come to earn a high school diploma (Institute of International Education [IIE], 2017). In 2017, there were 21,005 students on short-term exchange programs and living with a host family or at an accredited boarding school (Bureau of Educational and Cultural Affairs [ECA], 2018). This figure includes students in programs sponsored by the U.S. Department of State, such as the Future Leaders Exchange (FLEX) and the Kennedy Lugar Youth Exchange and Study (YES) that are participants of this study. The FLEX and YES merit-based scholarships are an important tool of the U.S. soft diplomacy to promote mutual understanding between Americans and international students as they learn about American culture, democratic institutions and civic rights (Marklein, 2014). FLEX and YES offer adolescent students a golden opportunity which does not rely on merely economic capital to study in the U.S. for an academic year.

The purpose of this study is to explore equity issues in ISM at a secondary school level. Drawing upon Bourdieu's theory of cultural capital, this study aims to get a nuanced understanding of the FLEX and YES alumni experiences relating to the selection process, exchange and post-exchange, in general, and the impact of exchange on the alumni learning, skills, personal growth and future international mobility in particular. Both FLEX and YES programs are sponsored by the U.S. Department of State and are structured and administered in the same way. The collective context of these programs makes it logical to choose them as a single case.

Literature Review

Studies conducted in developing countries found school-related factors more closely associated with students' academic achievement than family background and socio-economic status (SES) (Buchmann & Hannum, 2001). For the privileged elite, obtaining western-based education is a way of maintaining or reinforcing their class advantage in society. Thus, ISM may result in the perpetuation of social inequality (Tran, 2016). One way to challenge this cycle is through international exchange programs, which have become increasingly accessible to students of diverse countries of origin, thanks to merit-based scholarships. Short-term ISM can still reproduce social distinction as it enables participants to seize opportunities for self-improvement, stronger career prospects and personal and social distinctions (Prazeres et al., 2017). Since FLEX and YES students come from economically less developed countries, the level of parental social and cultural capital could play a bigger role than the family's SES while setting the ground for these students to participate in the program. In other words, parents' educational and cultural backgrounds may generate significant resources that students possess even before they make the decision to study abroad (Cheng, Fan, & Liu, 2017; Green et al., 2014).

In contrast to students whose main goal is to earn an American high school diploma, exchange students come to the U.S. for cultural exchange (Farrugia, 2014). The FLEX program was established in 1993 for the U.S. to promote people-to-people diplomacy with former Soviet Union countries, and the YES program was initiated in 2002 as a way to maintain good diplomatic ties with predominantly Muslim countries (American Councils for International Education [ACIE], 2019a, b). Students who wish to become finalists of these programs undergo a rigorous selection process based on merit that includes strong academic standing, English language skills, personal traits and social skills (ECA, 2018). Once in the U.S., students are placed in a host family's district school and are exempt from paying tuition fees. The scholarship covers a round-trip flight, placement with a screened volunteer host family, activities organized by local coordinator, medical insurance and a modest monthly allowance (ACIE, 2019a). Therefore, these programs are more equitable because there is minimal financial burden placed on the participant's family compared to the self-funded exchange programs (Cheng, 2019).

A few studies on secondary school exchange alumni show that compared to their immobile peers, alumni feel better equipped with skills and traits including independence, courage to try new things and open-mindedness

(ECA, 2009; Hansel, 2008; Weichbrodt, 2014). Weichbrodt (2014) reveals that 80% of the 3,000 German alumni think that due to changes in the worldview, they feel more comfortable among different cultures. A study on the YES alumni shows that the exchange experience made them apply intercultural skills to benefit the society at home through community service (ECA, 2009). A year abroad may serve as a stepping-stone for future international mobility (Hansel, 2008). In Weichbrodt's (2014) study, 80% of the alumni returned abroad for at least six weeks, stating secondary school exchange being one of the main reasons. As a result of prior ISM, individuals may increase social and structural embeddedness that results in a greater chance of future mobility (Carlson, 2013). None of the existing alumni studies, however, examine the social and cultural capital stratification that may occur in years following the secondary school exchange program.

Social and Cultural Capital

This study uses Pierre Bourdieu's (1986) concepts of social and cultural capital to examine how different forms of capital intersect with ISM, including how resources beyond economic capital can perpetuate inequality in ISM. Bourdieu (1986) distinguishes between economic, social and cultural capital. Economic capital refers to one's access to financial and material resources and also includes parental profession and education. Bourdieu (1986) argues that social and cultural capital can be used to overcome socio-economic obstacles in the attainment of education with middle-class students having added advantage in such pursuits.

Social capital is having a connection to a network based on group membership and relationships that serve to enrich knowledge, give support and provide resources (Bourdieu, 1986). In regard to education, Coleman (1988) maintains that social capital should not be seen as a tool in the hands of merely the upper class as it is embedded within families and within communities. This type of capital refers to productive social relations that provide individual access to information, resources and support acquired through interactions with others.

Bourdieu (1986) claims that cultural capital is transmitted within the family and that it includes cultural knowledge, language proficiency, educational level and knowledge gained through education. Bourdieu divides cultural capital in three subcategories: the embodied state (e.g. attributes of the person), the objectified state (e.g. cultural goods) and the institutionalized state (e.g. academic qualifications). By way of accumulating cultural capital over generations, the middle-class reproduces its social status (Bourdieu, 1986).

ISM is influenced by one's pre-existing social and cultural capital (Armstrong & Harbon, 2010), enabling students to advance their social and economic positioning through better employment opportunities (Tran, 2016). In the context of study abroad programs, superior knowledge, skills, dispositions and qualifications can be converted to economic and symbolic capitals, granting individuals access to better education, income and status (Bourdieu, 1986). The process of capital reproduction occurs "within social groups and networks in the form of exchanges, social obligations and symbols, to define group membership, fix boundaries and create a sense of belonging" (Ball, 2003, p. 80). International students may be prone to acquire social and cultural capital in the economically advanced societies (Xiang & Shen, 2009). The combined effect of different types of capital may reproduce social inequality (Green et al., 2014).

Research Method

This qualitative study employs a phenomenological approach to explore the experiences of the FLEX and YES alumni. The basic purpose of the phenomenology is to "reduce individual experiences with a phenomenon to a description of the universal essence" (Creswell & Poth, 2018, p. 153). Semi-structured interviews with 20 alumni were conducted to address the following research questions:

- What are participants' experiences relating to the selection process, exchange and post-exchange?
- In what ways have the exchange experiences impacted FLEX and YES alumni learning, skills, personal growth and future international mobility?

Snowball technique was used to enlarge purposeful sampling. To minimize biases, a sample as diverse as possible was chosen in terms of gender, age and country. Except for one in-person interview, interviews were conducted via video call due to physical distance between the interviewees and the researcher. The interviews were audiotaped and took about 60 minutes each. The data were first transcribed and then coded to identify emerging themes across the interviews. Member checking that was utilized in the data-collection process guaranteed credibility and trustworthiness of the participants (Creswell & Poth, 2018).

One of this study's limitations is its small and limited sample that does not reflect the entire population of FLEX and YES alumni. Another limitation is that participants were self-selected. As a result, participants may be keen on emphasizing the positive experiences as they recount the impact that the exchange has had on their lives.

Participants. Ten FLEX and ten YES alumni who had participated in the exchange program from 2004 to 2017 are participants of this study (see Tables 6.1 and 6.2). The variability in the reflections 2–15 years following the exchange experience may inform our understanding of short-term versus long-term impacts of the exchange.

The mean age at the time of the interview was 22.8 years. Seven alumni represent Eastern Europe, six represent Africa, five represent Asia and two represent the Middle East. The participants were placed in 13 different states

Table 6.1 Individual Characteristics of the FLEX Alumni

Name	*Gender*	*Age at Interview*	*Home Country*	*Family SES*	*Exchange Year*	*Age at Exchange*	*Placement State*
Iryina	F	31	Ukraine	Middle	2004–2005	16	MA
Ruslan	M	28	Moldova	Lower middle	2007–2008	16	TX
Max	M	27	Moldova	Lower middle	2010–2011	17	IL
Ana	F	26	Serbia	Middle	2009–2010	16	OH
Murad	M	22	Azerbaijan	Middle	2014–2015	17	NE
Aylin	F	21	Kazakhstan	Middle	2014–2015	16	HI
Elina	F	21	Kyrgyzstan	Middle	2014–2015	16	HI
Mary	F	20	Armenia	Middle	2016–2017	18	WA
Nino	M	19	Georgia	Lower middle	2016–2017	16	OH
Tanya	F	19	Ukraine	Middle	2015–2016	15	MD

Table 6.2 Individual Characteristics of the YES Alumni

Name	*Gender*	*Age at Interview*	*Home Country*	*Family SES*	*Exchange Year*	*Age at Exchange*	*Placement State*
David	M	28	Lebanon	Lower middle	2007–2008	15	OR
Miya	F	25	Yemen	Upper middle	2010–2011	16	OK
Peter	M	24	Kenya	Middle	2011–2012	16	MI
Aisha	F	23	Kenya	Lower middle	2012–2013	16	CO
Abu	M	21	Liberia	Middle	2015–2016	17	MI
Nisha	F	21	India	Lower middle	2014–2015	17	HI
Oumar	M	20	Mali	Middle	2014–2015	16	HI
Dario	M	20	Bosnia and Herzegovina	Upper middle	2015–2016	15	MO
Adnan	M	19	Nigeria	Middle	2016–2017	16	TX
Anis	F	18	Senegal	Middle	2016–2017	15	OH

across the U.S. Half of the participants now reside in their home countries, while the other half currently work or study abroad. To protect their confidentiality, all participants are given pseudonyms.

In terms of parental SES, just over half of the participants' families belong to the middle class. Most of the middle and upper-middle-class participants' parents hold university degrees. Parents from lower-middle-class families tend to hold a high school diploma. In terms of occupation, parents who possess higher SES work in the following sectors: education, business, science and medicine. Those with lower SES hold vocational jobs. Even though families hold varying degrees of cultural and social capital, becoming a FLEX and YES finalist is perceived as a once-in-a-lifetime opportunity to study in the U.S.

Findings

Selection process. Most FLEX interviewees heard about FLEX several years before applying from alumni in their schools, relatives or acquaintances. On the contrary, most YES interviewees had no prior knowledge about YES. They learned about it from either teachers or principals who received the information from local recruitment organizations. The lack of recruitment capacity in some YES countries in Africa still does not allow for a more inclusive application process. Abu shared that due to limited internet access in Liberia, the recruitment efforts cannot cover the whole country. Anis from Senegal was picked by her principal to partake in testing as the top student of her class saying, "The head called me in her office, me and another girl. She talked about the YES program with us and I was the only one selected by her to go and compete with others."

Due to some of the participants' remote location and family's lower SES, becoming a finalist was an inconceivable opportunity. For David, who grew up in a small southern town in Lebanon, being selected among the finalists came as a surprise: "These things are only for the privileged people, and not for some random guy from the South." This story resonates with Nisha whose principal encouraged her to apply:

> As we belong to a countryside area from a lower-class family, I could never imagine to go outside of the city even. I thought I would not get selected because there were so many good students coming from all over India. Getting an opportunity like that was magic for me.

Participants need to demonstrate a high degree of motivation to complete three rounds of selection process. While some alumni argued that they were too young to have had well-developed motives, the main motivation to become an exchange student was to experience a new culture, to meet new people and to improve English language skills. Aisha from Kenya could recognize that going to an American high school would be an advantage to study abroad in university, saying: "I really wanted to create a better life for myself and I felt that the exchange would be a great opportunity for that."

At an early age, the support received by family may be essential for success. Max from Moldova explained how his parents saw studying abroad as an opportunity for his personal growth:

> There was a bit of a push from my parents. I would not understand what it meant going abroad at that moment. It was nothing that I had deeply desired. I told my parents about it. For them it was clearer that going abroad would signify something important in my development.

While most YES participants were unable to resort to outside support services since testing was done at their schools on an impromptu basis, most FLEX participants would adopt strategies to improve their chances in being selected. Tanya from Ukraine shared: "I googled some questions, because there are a lot of people who did it before. There are YouTube videos where they talk about their application experience. I knew what to expect and what to say." Aside from asking advice from alumni, it was common among younger FLEX participants to consult online forums to prepare for the application process.

The exchange. While the disparities in learning style may initially present challenges, alumni mentioned how such differences enriched their knowledge and skills. Oftentimes, learning expanded well beyond academic knowledge. Mary from Armenia made the following comment: "The knowledge that I gained from the school is not just knowledge like calculus, but it is a lot of cultural and relationship-related knowledge." Max realized why he needed the skills that he learned in school as he shared:

> I was getting annoyed with my school [back home]; it was just about grades and passing the test, you never really learn useful things for life. But my American teachers had a very talented way of showing where you can actually apply and how useful it is to learn these things.

FLEX and YES students are encouraged by the program to make full use of school resources. Participation in extracurricular activities equips them with skills that are valued in American society (e.g. leadership skills) and can serve them well in today's globalized world. Anis from Senegal joined the "Leadership for Change" club where students practiced public speech, helping her to overcome her shyness. Active participation in such clubs may also improve one's social skills. Peter from Kenya said that he had become "more outgoing and more outspoken."

Cheng (2019) notes that the international students who leave home during their adolescence "need to feel friendliness from the host society" (p. 12). Entering a foreign community can be challenging for teenage students. Iryina from Ukraine shared her observation: "You go into a new host family, new school, new community and you are 16. You speak English but it's not perfect. This teaches you to be more adaptable, flexible, to overcome some challenges." Feeling comfortable in a homestay is crucial for these students' successful adaptation abroad. One way to grow closer to a host family is to actively engage in the family's daily life. In return, Oumar from Mali felt that he became a true member of his family:

> They would always support me in everything that I was doing, playing soccer or any type of activity that I would do. They treated me like other kids in the family. They would tell me what's wrong, they would punish me from time to time, give me rewards.

When student–host relationships become close, host families may impact exchange student's personal growth. Anis' host mother encouraged her to be more confident: "When I was in my country, I was very shy. My host mom really worked with me on that. She always used to boost me." Establishing a close-knit relationship with host families proved difficult for participants who had to move multiple times. David described his experience: "I really didn't have a chance to connect to any of my host families in a way that would be long-lasting." Even though most older alumni confessed to having lost contact with American friends over the years, they would continue to keep in touch with their host families even though less frequently than younger alumni.

Most host families include exchange students in daily lives and activities, an opportunity to extend students' community network. Many participants joined families at Sunday church service. Murad from Azerbaijan volunteered at a church cafeteria recounting his experience: "Church made a lot of difference. I met many nice people there. They were really friendly and they were willing to help whenever they could." As part of the programs' goal is to expose foreign students to American values, the exchange students need to partake in community service. Most alumni got involved through their host families. Aylin from Kazakhstan found her families' community involvement inspiring:

> I was really amazed with my host parents, because they always wanted to help out. My host mom works with people with disabilities. It inspires me how nice they are. Seeing how busy and active their lifestyle is made me think that I could also live such an active lifestyle, when you see the way they live.

Being exposed to community service in the U.S., most alumni have continued to be involved in alumni chapters that engage in community projects in their home countries. The commitment to be involved in and working for change in home countries was stronger among younger alumni.

Returning home. The knowledge and skills gained during secondary school exchange may impact student's future academic and career trajectories. Due to significant personal growth, alumni felt more mature and ready for university. Miya who stayed in Yemen for her bachelor's degree thinks that she was much better prepared for university than her classmates: "The level of academic stuff that I did in the U.S., everything gave me an advantage in university." The exchange played a major role for Nino from Georgia to identify his future career. He explained his decision to study international relations: "As I communicated with people in the US, I felt that diplomacy and international relations would be something that would really interest me." For some, new knowledge and skills proved difficult to employ in their home countries. Aylin who became passionate about robotics faced gender discrimination as a woman in science in her home university. After taking a gap year, she received a scholarship to pursue a mechatronics degree in the Netherlands.

The exchange triggered the desire to return abroad, which was strongly expressed by younger alumni. Only a few interviewees have been able to secure a scholarship that enabled them to study abroad again. Oumar has earned a prestigious national scholarship for his undergraduate studies in France:

> In the U.S., I had to learn a new way of learning that was a lot easier, so I would spend less time learning things by heart. That has helped me a lot. For the last year exam in high school I came out as the top student in the whole country. I was able to get in the program that I am in now. It is really because of that that I got the scholarship.

ISM may generate profitable gains in better employment opportunities. Several alumni note that their first job required excellent English language skills, for which being in the U.S. proved advantageous. For most, the exchange has created a sense of empowerment to dream bigger and aim higher, setting them apart from their immobile peers. Ruslan from Moldova explained his experience:

> Sometimes you do not apply for things not because you are less qualified but because your horizon of opportunities is smaller. You self-exclude yourself before you are excluded by the system. FLEX challenges that. FLEX allows you to think that you can do more.

Few older interviewees decided to pursue a career at home after obtaining a graduate degree abroad. Ruslan reflects on the social pressure he felt upon his return: "When you were in a FLEX community which is more selective, more progressive and you want to be a part of that, you want to stay progressive and selective." With his successful career and active community involvement back home, Ruslan challenges the perception that staying home is a sign of failure. Older alumni who currently work abroad expressed enthusiasm to connect with companies or governments at home in sharing their knowledge and skills. Though, such opportunities are still hard to come by.

Discussion

Drawing upon Bourdieu's concepts of social and cultural capital, this study explored equity issues in secondary school student mobility through experiences of the FLEX and YES exchange program alumni. Often, the initial process of planning to study abroad commences years before the selection process. Given FLEX's longer tradition, FLEX participants were more aware of the exchange program than YES participants. It is common among younger generations to resort to various strategies to increase chances of becoming selected.

As explained by Bourdieu (1986), students who hold a higher degree of cultural and social capital "distinguish themselves from others who cannot easily mobilize these resources, both on application forms and in interviews" (p. 245). However, students from lower SES may have an opportunity to participate in these merit-based programs, as demonstrated by few participants in this study. Most participants in this study come from highly educated middle-class families, and as per findings, parents played a significant role in supporting the participants during the application process and throughout the exchange. Sullivan (2001) maintains that cultural capital transmitted within the home may influence student's academic performance with middle and upper-class students being more likely to excel academically.

As findings demonstrate, short-term impact of exchange programs can boost participants' embodied cultural capital by enhancing their personal growth, learning and skills. These changes are pertinent to adolescent students who spend a year abroad when the changes may be more profound compared to adult students. According to Ball (2003), social capital can be accumulated through active participation in various activities. In the FLEX and YES programs, students are encouraged to actively participate in host community activities, in school and host family life, which may broaden their worldview, and further expand the host national network. Thus, cultural capital sometimes appears as social capital (Weenink, 2014), for instance when students' social network includes host family, local friends, teachers, neighbors and church members, among others. Social capital may be further reproduced when alumni maintain the newly formed contacts. All participants, no matter their age, still keep in touch with American host families and others.

With the newly acquired knowledge and skills gained during the exchange, some alumni linked the immediate impact of exchange to their academic or career trajectories. In line with existing literature, this study demonstrates that even a short-term study abroad may increase a student's desire to engage in future international pursuits (ECA, 2009; Hansel, 2008; Weichbrodt, 2014). Most participants in this study come from middle-class families and may be considered privileged compared to immobile peers in their home countries. Even those who come from lower SES, upon returning home, participants felt that they became part of a privileged group of alumni. Mobility capital that is accumulated during the exchange can extend as a form of symbolic capital and a mark of distinction (Prazeres et al., 2017) in terms of individual's uniqueness, difference or distinction in social and institutional settings (Bourdieu, 1986). FLEX and YES alumni opt to study abroad at university level were limited due to high tuition fees in western countries. Murphy-Lejeune (2002) argues that the difference between internationally mobile students and their non-mobile peers lies in the accumulation of mobility capital that enables them "to enhance their skills because of the richness of the international experience gained by living abroad" (p. 51) and to become part of a "migratory elite" (Murphy-Lejeune, 2002), which speaks to the equity issues of the merit-based scholarships. In terms of long-term impact, several older alumni challenge this idea, recognizing the importance of contributing to their societies.

Implications and Conclusion

Implications of this study are three-fold as they apply to the exchange program alumni, to the program coordinators and to home community. As a result of the social and cultural capital developed from the exchange, a promising course of action could be to shift from a primary focus on learning outcomes of short-term study abroad to focus more attention on exchange alumni who, upon return, desire to engage in school or community projects that attempt to make progress in home communities. While it is commonly argued that study abroad in less-developed countries leads to a phenomenon of a "brain drain" that negatively affects the economic, technological and social progress of sending countries, strategies should be deployed by program sponsors and local governments to sustain and to reap the benefits from social and cultural capital derived from the exchange in home communities. Participation in alumni groups with opportunities to utilize the newly acquired knowledge and skills, in cooperation with local organizations, should be encouraged by program coordinators to affect change in sending countries.

The increase in ISM has expanded the array of opportunities for study abroad participants as they accumulate valuable social and cultural capital that enables them to see and experience the world in new ways. This study found that secondary school merit-based exchange programs such as FLEX and YES extend well beyond its educational and cultural exchange purposes. As articulated by the alumni, their newly developed aspirations have influenced and sometimes even transformed their life trajectories. Even short-term ISM might tap into further transmission of not only social, cultural and economic capital but also participants' symbolic and mobility capital. Finally, ISM may contribute to exchange alumni's desires to seek better academic and employment opportunities abroad, resulting in human capital flight of highly educated individuals from low-income to high-income countries, thus perpetuating the cycle of social inequality. Both local governments and organizations should be attentive to these highly educated youth to recognize and create educational and career opportunities, which may enhance the social and economic development of these countries.

References

American Councils for International Education (ACIE). (2019a). FLEX application information. *ACIE*, 2019. http://ac-see.org/new/flex-program/#sixth

American Councils for International Education (ACIE). (2019b). YES in Southeast Europe application information. *ACIE*, 2019. http://ac-see.org/new/yes-program/

American Councils for International Education (ACIE). (2019c). Who is eligible to host? *ACIE*, 2019. http://inbound.americancouncils.org/faqs/who-eligible-host
Armstrong, A. C., & Harbon, L. (2010). Developing social and cultural capital through semesters abroad. In P. L. Jeffery (Ed.), *AARE 2009 international education research conference proceedings* (ARM091561). Canberra, (29 November to 3 December 2009).
Ball, S. (2003). *Class strategies and the education market: The middle classes and social advantage.* London, UK: Routledge Falmer. doi:10.4324/9780203218952
Bourdieu, P. (1986). The forms of capital. In J. Richardson (Ed.), *Handbook of theory and research for the sociology of education* (pp. 241–258). New York, NY: Greenwood.
Buchmann, C., & Hannum, E. (2001). Education and stratification in developing countries: A review of theories and research. *Annual Review of Sociology, 27*, 77–102.
Bureau of Educational and Cultural Affairs (ECA). (August 2009). *Evaluation of the youth exchange & study program.* Final Report. New York, NY: InterMedia.
Bureau of Educational and Cultural Affairs (ECA). (2018). What is hosting? *ECA*, 2018. https://eca.state.gov/programs-initiatives/host-high-school-student
Carlson, S. (2013). Becoming a mobile student – A processual perspective on German degree student mobility. *Population, Space and Place, 19*(2), 168–180. doi:10.1002/psp.1749
Cheng, B. (2019). Sociocultural adaptation of "Parachute Kids" from Mainland China. *British Journal of Guidance and Counselling.* doi:10.1080/03069885.2019.1643006
Cheng, B., Fan, A., & Liu, M. (2017). Chinese high school students' plans in studying overseas: Who and why. *Frontiers of Education in China, 12*(3), 367–393. doi:10.1007/s11516-017-0027-0
Coleman, J. S. (1988). Social capital in the creation of human capital. *American Journal of Sociology, 94*, S95–S120.
Creswell, J. W., & Poth, C. N. (2018). *Qualitative inquiry and research design: Choosing among the five approaches (Fourth Edition).* Thousand Oaks, CA: Sage Publications.
Farrugia, C. A. (July 2014). *Charting new pathways to higher education: International secondary students in the United States.* IIE Center for Academic Mobility Research Institute of International Education. New York, USA.
Green, W., Gannaway, D., Sheppard, K., & Jamarani, S. (2014) What's in their baggage?: The cultural and social capital of Australian students preparing to study abroad. *Higher Education Research and Development, 34*(3), 1–14. doi:10.1080/07294360.2014.973381
Hansel, B. (2008). AFS Long Term Impact Study. Report 1: 20 to 25 years after the exchange experience, AFS alumni are compared with their peers. New York, NY: AFS International.
Institute of International Education (IIE). (2017). Globally mobile youth. *IIE Center for Academic Mobility Research and Impact*, August 2017. https://p.widencdn.net/xguzsn/Globally-Mobile-Youth-Trends-in-International-Secondary-Students-in-the-United-States-2013-201
Marklein, M. B. (2014). International students flock to US high schools. *USA Today*, July 8, 2014. https://www.usatoday.com/story/news/nation/2014/07/08/high-school-foreign-international-students/12296741/
Murphy-Lejeune, E. (2002). *Student mobility and narrative in Europe.* London, UK: Routledge.

Prazeres, L., Findlay, A., McCollum, D., Sander, N., Musil, E., Krisjane, Z., & Apsite-Berina, E. (2017). Distinctive and comparative places: Alternative narratives of distinction within international student mobility. *Geoforum, 80*(2017), 114–122. doi:10.1016/j.geoforum.2017.02.003

Sullivan, A. (2001). Cultural capital and educational attainment. *Sociology, 35*(4), 893–912. doi:10.1017/S0038038501008938

Tran, L. T. (2016). Mobility as 'becoming': A Bourdieuian analysis of the factors shaping international student mobility. *British Journal of Sociology of Education, 37*(8), 1268–1289. doi:10.1080/01425692.2015.1044070

United Nations Educational, Scientific and Cultural Organization (UNESCO). 2019. Education: Outbound internationally mobile students by host region. *UNESCO*, 2019. http://data.uis.unesco.org/Index.aspx?queryid=172

Weenink, D. (2014). Pupils' plans to study abroad: Social reproduction of transnational capital? In J. Gerhards, S., Hans, & S. Carlson (Eds.), *Globalisierung, Bildung, und grenzüberschreitende Mobilität* (pp. 111–126). Wiesbaden, Germany: Springer.

Weichbrodt, M. (2014). Learning mobility: High school exchange programs as a part of international mobility. *Children's Geographies, 12*(1), 9–24. doi:10.1080/14733285.2013.850852

Xiang, B., & Shen, W. (2009). International student migration and social stratification in China. *International Journal of Educational Development, 29*, 513–522. doi:10.1016/j.ijedudev.2009.04.006

7 International Baccalaureate (IB) Program and Students' Educational Opportunities in Japan

Yuko Ida

Introduction

The current expansion of International Baccalaureate (IB) education in Japan has not been extensively analyzed. Since the Japanese government developed the plan "Japan Revitalization Strategy – Japan is Back" in 2013, the presence of the IB program has grown in the country. The plan offers strategies for revitalizing the Japanese economy and increasing the number of IB schools to 200 (Kantei, 2013). In fact, the number of IB schools has increased from 29 to 71 after the implementation of the plan (IBO, 2019a). About 58% of the IB schools in Japan implemented the IB curriculum after 2013 (IBO, 2019a). Not only the government but also higher education has been preparing for the implementation of the IB program. Tamagawa University started a graduate program that focuses on the IB education in 2014, followed by University of Tsukuba in 2017. An IB education consortium was also established in May 2018 (MEXT, 2018).

The IB started in Geneva, Switzerland, in 1968 to "develop inquiring, knowledgeable and caring young people who help to create a better and more peaceful world through intercultural understanding and respect" (IBO, 2018a). IB education first started with the Diploma Program (DP) for students aged from 16 to 19 years. In 1994, the Middle Year Program (MYP) was created for those aged from 11 to 16 years, followed by the Primary Year Program (PYP) in 1997 for those aged from 3 to 12 years. The Career-related Program (CP) was developed in 2012 for those aged from 16 to 19 years (IBO, 2019b). The IB education also offers a Bilingual Diploma which is awarded to those who "complete and receive a grade 3 or higher in two languages selected from the DP course studies in language and literature" (IBO, 2020). In 2019, the number of IB World schools reached 5,175 across 157 countries (IBO, 2019c).

Benefits of the IB education identified include 21st-century skills development (Wright & Lee, 2014), cultivating students' critical mindsets and problem-solving skills (Taylor & Porath, 2006), preparing them for post-secondary education (Saavedra, Lavore & Flores-Ivish, 2016), "enhance students' international cultural awareness" (Culross & Traver, 2011, p. 236), "help students think critically" (Taylor & Porath, 2006, pp. 152–153), "provide a passport to university entrance that is recognized around the world" (Hill, 2012, p. 17), and expand school choices after graduation (Doherty, Mu, & Shield, 2009).

The major challenge of IB education identified is its high cost at the school and personal level. Resnik (2012) argues that it is a challenge for public schools with limited budgets in economically unstable countries to pay the high cost of IB affiliation. Dickson, Perry and Ledger (2017) point out that "most schools in Australia that offer any of IB programs such as PYP, MYP, and DP, are located in affluent communities of large cities, privately-funded, charge moderate to high fees, and enroll mostly students from privileged socioeconomic backgrounds" (Dickson et al., 2017, p. 66). In fact, IBDP has become "an indicator of new and emerging forms of social differentiation" (Outhwaite & Ferri, 2017, p. 413).

Considering that students' socioeconomic status (SES) has been closely related to their educational opportunity in Japan (Hara, 2011), SES may also determine students' opportunities and success in IBDP. There is a correlation between students' SES and their educational opportunity in Japan as similar cases identified in other countries. Fujihara and Ishida (2016) assert that there is "an increasing gap in access to the most advantageous educational attainment - entering high-ranking universities - determined by the social background of the student" (p. 34). Kariya (2018) also argues that the results of college entrance exams are crucially correlated to students' economic capital as well as their social and cultural capital. The literature suggests that there is a correlation between students' SES and their educational opportunities in Japan. However, not a lot of information exists on the relationship between the IB, students' SES, and educational opportunity in Japan. How proponents of the IB in Japan perceive the purpose, values, and effects of the IB education do not often appear in the existing literature written in English. This study would fill a gap in the literature and explore the following research questions: (1) How do administrators and teachers perceive the expansion of IB programs in Japan? (2) How do administrators and teachers perceive the potential impacts of IB programs on students and society in relation to equity and social justice? This research hopes to shed light on complicated relationships between students, academic programs, geographical locations, financial and human resources, accessibilities of pedagogical resources, and learning opportunities.

Literature Review

The literature review examines the relationship between neoliberalism, globalization, and knowledge economy to delve into the contexts where the expansion of IB schools is occurring.

Neoliberal policy, knowledge economy, and globalization are identified as the rationale behind the expansion of the IB schools worldwide. According to Resnik (2012), the collapse of the Soviet Union allowed capitalism and neoliberalism to emerge. The origin of neoliberalism is traced to von Hayek and Friedman, who were the ascendance of the Chicago school of political economy (Brown, 2003). Brown (2003) points out that neoliberalism is equated with radical-free markets. Puiggros (1999) argues that in order to achieve such a free market, efficiency, privatization, decentralization, and accountability are pursued. Increasing inequality is identified as one of the visible effects of neoliberalism (Brown, 2015).

Global knowledge economy appears to be a key attribute in the marketing and promotion of the IB (Cambridge, 2010). The international aura of the IB education and a promise to prepare students for the global world are identified as valuable aspects of IB education in a competitive educational market (Resnik, 2016). Besides the improvement of students' academic performance, state schools in the United States and in western Canada adopted the IB curriculum to create a "private school" aura in order to attract students from middle- and upper-class families and accommodate neoliberal parents' desire "for high academic standards" (Resnik, 2012, p. 250). Bunnell (2008) points out that "magnet schools especially searched for a unique marketing position" in the United States (p. 415).

In fact, the IBDP at Jefferson High School, Title 1 school in California, was established as a magnet program. This is because the school administrator hoped that "the IB program would draw students from more affluent neighborhoods of the districts that the school was located" (Mayer, 2008, p. 218). In the United States, IB programs are also implemented for gifted children. It is pointed out that the U.S. National Association for Gifted Children (NAGC) has disseminated several research papers and a position statement asserting the IBDP as an acceptable option for meeting the needs of gifted learners (Culross & Tarver, 2011).

Methodology

This is a qualitative study, and the primary method of data collection was through interviews. Qualitative research was selected primarily because the objective of this research was to deepen our understanding of the purpose, values, and effects of IB programs in Japan through the perceptions of its proponents. According to Creswell (2014), qualitative research is an approach to explore and understand a person or a group ascribed to a social or a human problem. Thus, the goal of this research can be achieved through qualitative research.

In order to answer my research questions, a semi-structured interview was developed which allowed for collecting in-depth data from a participant. Interview questions concerning the IB program consisted of 20 open-ended questions and lasted about 45 minutes to one hour. The questions were focused on the perceptions of professors, administrators, and teachers toward the expansion of IB programs in Japan and its potential impacts on students and society, particularly in relation to equity and social justice. Before conducting the interviews, my research proposal was approved by the Institutional Review Board (IRB) on March 14, 2019 for the ethical consideration.

Data Collection

For the recruitment, snowball sampling was used, and the total number of interviews conducted is ten. Patton (1990) discusses that this approach is used "for locating information-rich key informants or critical cases" (p. 176). Initial recruitment of the potential participants took place through the pre-existing relationships with researchers that were developed through academic conferences held in Japan and in the States. Through them, I was introduced to teachers at B international school and C international school. Then I sent them recruitment emails asking for their voluntary participation in this research.

Other participants were recommended and asked to participate in this research voluntarily. Since the purpose of this study was to explore diverse perceptions, I asked the participants to recommend not only Japanese speaking teachers but also English-speaking teachers as well. There are no personal connections with the participants, so the selection of the participants is as objective as possible. Table 7.1 shows the demographics of the participants in this study. One interview was conducted at A university and four were conducted at B international school in March 2019. The rest of the interviews were conducted at C private school in June 2019. Once their consent was obtained, interviews were conducted.

A University is a teacher college located in the central part of Japan. This school offers a graduate program that focuses on IB education. The interview was conducted in March 2019. B International School is in the central part of Japan, and four interviews were conducted in March 2019 as well.

Table 7.1 Data Sources

Name (Pseudonym)	*School*	*Date*	*Language*	*Content Area(s)*	*Years Teaching (IB)*
Teacher A	A University	Mar 20, 2019	English	History	24 (24)
Teacher B	B International	Mar 27, 2019	English	Principle	(11)
Teacher C	B International	Mar 19, 2019	English	TOK	(13)
Teacher D	B International	Mar 19, 2019	English	Music	(11)
Teacher E	B International	Mar 26, 2019	Japanese	Japanese	18 (8)
Teacher F	C Private School	June 3, 2019	Japanese	Vice Principal	30 (5)
Teacher G	C Private School	June 3, 2019	Japanese	JPN Literature	9 (6)
Teacher H	C Private School	June 3, 2019	English	English B/ TOK	10 (2.5)
Teacher I	C Private School	June 3, 2019	English	English B/ History	15 (5)
Teacher J	C Private School	June 3, 2019	Japanese	CAS	12 (4)

The school is accredited by the Council of International Schools (CIS) and is also registered as an educational organization by the prefecture in which the school is located. The school offers PYP, MYP, and DP, and all the courses are taught in English except Japanese language arts class. C Private High School is in the southern part of Japan, and five interviews were conducted in June 2019. The school offers a regular track, IBDP track, prestigious, and college/ medical school preparation track. The school offers dual-language diplomas, and most of the IB courses are taught in Japanese. The interviewees include the vice principal (Japanese speaking) and four IBDP teachers (two Japanese speaking and two English speaking).

Data Analysis

Interviews were transcribed, and data were analyzed with discourse analysis (Fairclough, 2003) and open coding in grounded theory (Corbin & Strauss, 2007). Fairclough (2003) considers discourse as "ways of representing aspects of the world – the processes, relations and structures of the material world, the 'mental world' of thoughts, feelings, beliefs and so forth, and the social world" (p. 124). Considering the research questions of this study, discourse analysis was selected as the best methodology for this study combined with grounded theory.

During the initial open-coding process, the following procedures were adapted: (a) reading the transcripts several times; (b) comparing each transcript with one another to identify similarities and differences; (c) taking memos about the key concepts that appeared repeatedly in the transcripts. Throughout the data analysis, field notes were also used. Then the data was broken up into different categories based on the themes that emerged.

Since this categorizing strategy did not capture the complex perceptions the interviewees were elaborating on during the interviews, connecting strategies introduced in Maxwell (2013) were employed in the second stage. Rather than only looking at similarities that can be categorized into groups, this connecting strategy looks at "relationships that connect statements and events within a context into a coherent whole" (Maxwell, 2013, p. 113). This approach tries to understand the data in *context* as "the strategy of reading for voice" (Brown, 1988; Gilligan, Spencer, Weinberg, & Bertsch, 2003; Maxwell, 2013, p. 112). The combined categorizing and connecting process continued until saturation occurred.

Findings and Discussions

This chapter explores three themes that emerged from open-coding and discourse analysis. The themes emerged are: (1) IB education as an opportunity; (2) Exclusive aspects of IBDP; (3) Impacts of human, financial, and pedagogical resource constraints on IB. These themes allow for deeper understanding of how the proponents of IB education in Japan perceive the purposes, effects, and values of IB education.

IB Education As an Opportunity

IB education is perceived to develop international mindedness, multiple perspectives, lay a foundation of academic knowledge and skills, cultivate confidence in students, and expand school choice after graduation. As for international mindedness, it is perceived that such *mindedness* is different from international *identity*. Teacher A cognizes the difference between IB education and education offered by the nation-state as follows:

> Teacher A: when you create a system in Japan or India then it is for the local school system so there are things like developing national identity for example. But IB doesn't have that. It has international mindedness. So that's one very important value as you know for the IB.

It is also believed that IB education is necessary for Japan to increase global competitiveness and thrive in the globalized economy. The concept of internationalization and globalization often appeared during the interviews, and Teacher H perceives that internationalization is more thought process, and globalization is more of an economical process. Teacher I acknowledges that the administrator could have used IB as a brand and believes that the administrator implemented the IBDP curriculum for the betterment of students.

IB education lays a great foundation of knowledge, develops writing skills, and expands students' college choices. At the same time, it is repeatedly mentioned that the IB education is well rounded, and students are educated not only for exams. Teacher G believes that the IB diploma is an internationally recognized accomplishment, and the high level of work in the IBDP gives students confidence. As a result, it is believed by research participants that IB is expanding school choice after graduation, allowing students to pursue post-secondary education overseas. In fact, B school has sent a graduate to a college in New York, and C school also has sent its graduates to universities in Hawaii, Taiwan, China, and Malaysia.

Finding 1 suggests that IBDP is perceived to provide opportunities for Japan and students. At the macro-level, the program is cognized to help boost the country's competitiveness in the globalized economy. At the micro-level, it is recognized that IBDP prepares students for college-level study and provides opportunities for pursuing post-secondary education overseas. The research participants' perceptions toward IBDP are aligned with the benefits of IB education identified in the literature review. Although the literature review argues that IB is used as one of schools' marketing strategies in neoliberal globalization, IBDP is largely perceived to serve for the betterment of students.

Exclusive Aspects of IBDP

It is perceived that IBDP is not for everyone academically and financially. Although the PYP and MYP are recognized to be inclusive, this is not the case with the DP. It is believed that IBDP is very academically rigorous, and students need to be well prepared to thrive in the program. Along with academic preparedness, it is perceived to be indispensable for students to possess strong motivation and self-management skills to thrive in the IBDP program. Teacher I disclosed his experience where half of his class dropped out of the IB track during their second year because they were not able to keep up with their assignments. The combination of the foundation of basic academic knowledge, motivation, and management skills is perceived to be critical. Ultimately, it is believed that students with learning disabilities will be potentially excluded from the DP.

English proficiency is also perceived to impact students' access to the IBDP and their learning performance. According to Teacher J, not only applicants' grades from middle school but also their English proficiency is taken into consideration during the screening process in the C school. In the B school where all the subjects are taught in English, it is recognized that some students struggle due to the language barriers they face throughout the learning process. Teacher D explains how he perceives the relationship between students' language environment at home and their English acquisition by introducing the school's demographic as follows:

> Teacher D: for instance . . . .uhhmm . . . I really worried about that . . . so much emphasis a little bit more on language . . . you know. . . .it's very difficult . . . because this is as you know our schools is one third Japanese-Japanese couples . . . you know parents are Japanese . . . .and another third is uhhhh . . Japanese and foreigners . . . and another third is both are foreigners . . . both parents are foreigners so . . . the English acquisition . . . it's very big challenge . . . it's very big . . .

Teacher B explains that B school provides students with a lenient option. Even if students cannot complete the IBDP, the students can graduate with a regular high school diploma.

Besides students' academic preparedness and English acquisition level, SES is perceived as a barrier to accessing the IBDP. Teacher B articulates that those who cannot pay the tuition will not be allowed to enter the B international school. Teacher E, who used to teach at a public school, believes that the tuition prevents some students from entering the school.

Finding 2 suggests that IBDP is believed to be exclusionary. The proponents perceive students' SES, academic preparedness, self-management skills, learning disabilities, and English acquisition levels in determining access and completion of the IBDP. As the literature discusses, students' SES plays a role in opening and limiting their access to the IBDP. Although the literature review argues that students can be excluded due to SES and academic ability, none of the existing literature contends that the IBDP will be potentially excluding students with learning disabilities. Moreover, the existing literature does not point out that students' academic preparedness and English acquisition will be a barrier to their accessing and completing the IBDP.

As for the necessity of students' self-management skills, Taylor and Porath (2006) point out that "workload was excessive, unmanageable, and/or detrimental to their well-being while they were in the IB Program" (p. 153). Combined with Taylor and Porath (2006), Teacher I's experience reveals that the IBDP potentially leads to negative consequences of students' dropping out of the program. This research, however, sheds light on schools' efforts to ensure students' completing secondary education by allowing them to switch their tracks from the IBDP to a regular track.

This research identifies that students' personal and SES impact their learning opportunities, and schools are making an effort to minimize the negative impacts of these factors on those who are already in the program by creating a leeway for them to complete their secondary school education.

Impacts of Human, Financial, and Pedagogical Resource Constraints on IB

How to secure and prepare teachers for IB schools is cognized as a challenging aspect of the promotion of IB programs in Japan. It is discerned that IB teachers are required to be academically highly skilled to maintain the high academic standard of the IBDP. As a result, it is believed that there is a difficulty in the succession of the IB-related job especially at public IB schools in Japan where teacher rotation is implemented in the public education system.

According to Teacher G, public school teachers are transferred to another school every few years, and there is a possibility of public IB teachers being transferred to a regular school that does not offer an IBDP. Teacher F reveals that the prefecture which C School is in determined not to have public IB schools due to a lack of financial and human resources. Besides the constraints on financial and human resources, it is also believed that the number of IB training and pedagogical resources in Japanese are still limited as well.

Besides lack of the resources, it is also believed that teachers' existing work responsibilities would be a barrier to access IB training for in-service teachers. Teacher C explains his perception as follows:

> Teacher C: they feel it's OVERWHELMING to find TIME to do all this . . . all this preparation because from my experience that they tend to be quite BUSY with their regular jobs and you know getting ready for IB and doing all the taking workshops and reading through the hundred pages of . . . .IB documents (laughing). Takes a LONG TIME and. .so . . . .

> um . . . . .a lot of them are probably just saying that our school can't do this we're TOO BUSY you know . . . .

Finding 3 suggests that constraints on human, financial, and pedagogical resources along with in-service teachers' work conditions are perceived to be barriers to the promotion of IB education in Japan. According to Mingat, Tan and Sosale (2003), not only students' personal and family characteristics but also their community characteristics and pedagogical environments, which include teachers' education and training, are key factors in their learning. This research sheds light on complicated relationships between schools' geographical locations, financial and human resources, accessibilities of pedagogical resources, and learning opportunities.

Conclusion and Implications

This study attempted to deepen our understanding of potential impacts of the expansion of the IB schools on students and society, especially in relation to equity and social justice in the country. At the macro-level, IBDP is perceived to be one of the strategies to help Japan thrive in the globalized economy. At the micro-level, it is recognized that IBDP prepares students for college-level study and provides them opportunities for pursuing post-secondary education overseas. It is also identified that students' personal and SES impact their learning opportunities, and schools are making an effort to minimize the negative impacts of these factors on those who are already in the program by creating a leeway for them to complete their secondary school education. Furthermore, this research sheds light on complicated relationships between schools' geographical locations, local governments' financial and human resources, pedagogical resources, and learning opportunities. For future research, it is recommended to examine how accessibilities of the IBDP can be ensured to students who have socioeconomic and geographical disadvantages but are academically well prepared to thrive in the IB education.

References

Brown, W. (2003). "Neoliberalism and the End of Liberal Democracy." Retrieved from http://www.lchc.ucsd.edu/cogn_150/Readings/brown.pdf

Brown, W. (2015). *Undoing the demos : neoliberalism's stealth revolution*. Cambridge, Massachusetts: The MIT Press.

Bunnell, T. (2008). The Global Growth of the International Baccalaureate Diploma Programme over the First 40 Years: A Critical Assessment. *Comparative Education, 44*(4), 409–424.

Cambridge, J. (2010). The International Baccalaureate Diploma Programme and the construction of pedagogic identity: A preliminary study. *Journal of Research in International Education, 9*(3), 199–213.

Creswell, J. W. (2014) *Research Design: Qualitative, Quantitative, and Mixed Methods Approaches*. California: Sage Publisher.

Culross, R, & Tarver, E. (2011). A Summary of Research on the International Baccalaureate Diploma Programme: Perspectives of Students, Teachers, and University Admissions Offices in the USA. *Journal of Research in International Education, 10*(3), 231–243.

Corbin, J., & Strauss, A. (2007). *Basics of qualitative research: Techniques and procedures for developing grounded theory*. Thousand Oaks, CA: Sage Publisher.

Dickson, A., Perry, L. B., & Ledger, S. (2017). How accessible is IB schooling? Evidence from Australia. *Journal of Research in International Education, 16*(1), 65–79.

Doherty, C., Mu, L., & Shield, P. (2009). Planning mobile futures: The border artistry of international baccalaureate diploma choosers. *British Journal of Sociology of Education, 30*(6), 757–771.

Fairclough, N. (2003). *Analysing discourse: Textual analysis for social research*. London, UK: Routledge.

Fujihara, S., & Ishida, H. (2016). The absolute and relative values of education and the inequality of educational opportunity: Trends in access to education in postwar Japan. *Research in Social Stratification and Mobility, 43*, 25–37.

Hara, J. (2011). An overview of social stratification and inequality study in Japan: Towards a 'mature' society perspective. *Asian Journal of Social Science, 39*(1), 9–29.

International Baccalaureate Organization [IBO]. (2018a). *Mission*. Geneva: IB. https://www.ibo.org/about-the-ib/mission/ (accessed April 29, 2018)

International Baccalaureate Organization [IBO]. (2019a). *Find an IB school*. Geneva: IB. https://www.ibo.org/about-the-ib/the-ib-by-country/j/japan/ (accessed March 12, 2019)

International Baccalaureate Organization [IBO]. (2019b). *Programmes*. Geneva: IB. https://www.ibo.org/programmes/ (accessed December 5, 2019)

International Baccalaureate Organization [IBO]. (2019c). *Facts and figures*. https://ibo.org/about- the-ib/facts-and-figures/ (accessed December 7, 2019)

International Baccalaureate Organization [IBO]. (2020) *Understanding DP assessment*. Geneva: IB. https://ibo.org/programmes/diploma-programme/assessment-and-exams/understanding-ib-assessment/ (accessed January 15, 2020)

Kantei. (2013). *Japan's revitalization strategy: Japan is back*. Tokyo: Prime Minister of Japan and His Cabinet. https://www.kantei.go.jp/jp/singi/keizaisaisei/pdf/saikou_jpn.pdf

Kariya, T. (2018). Education and social disparities in Japan. *Oxford Research Encyclopedia of Education*. https://oxfordre.com/education/abstract/10.1093/acrefore/9780190264093.001.0001/acrefore-9780190264093-e-70?rskey=2eRUQJ&result=1 (accessed April 27, 2019).

Maxwell, J. (2013). *Qualitative research design : an interactive approach* (3rd ed.). SAGE Publications.

Mayer, A. P. (2008). Expanding Opportunities for High Academic Achievement: An International Baccalaureate Diploma Program in an Urban High School. *Journal of Advanced Academics, 19*(2), 202–235.

Minister of Education, Culture, Sports, Science and Technology (MEXT) (2018) About IB education consortium. Tokyo: MEXT. Retrieved from https://ibconsortium.mext.go.jp/mission/ (accessed October 8, 2018).

Mingat, A., Tan, J., & Sosale, S. (2003). *Tools for education: Policy analysis*. Washington, DC: World Bank.
Outhwaite, D., & Ferri, G. (2017). Critical reflections on modern elite formation and social differentiation in the International Baccalaureate diploma programme in England. *Oxford Review of Education, 43*(4), 402–416.
Patton, M. (1990). *Qualitative evaluation and research methods* (2nd ed.). Newbury Park, California: Sage Publications.
Puiggrós, A. (1999). *Neoliberalism and education in the Americas*. Westview Press.
Resnik, J. (2012). The denationalization of education and the expansion of the International Baccalaureate. *Comparative Education Review, 56*(2), 248–269.
Resnik, J. (2016). The development of the International Baccalaureate in Spanish speaking countries: A global comparative approach. *Globalisation, Societies and Education, 14*(2), 298–325.
Saavedra, A., Lavore, E., & Flores-Ivich, G. (2016). The International Baccalaureate Diploma Programme in Mexico as preparation for higher education. Compare: A Journal of Comparative and International Education, *46*(3), 344–368. https://doi.org/10.1080/03057925.2014.896188
Taylor, M., & Porath, M. (2006). Reflections on the international baccalaureate program: Graduates' perspectives. *Journal of Advanced Academics, 17*(3), 149–158.
Wright, E., & Lee, M. (2014). Developing skills for youth in the 21st Century: The elite International Baccalaureate diploma programme schools in China. *International Review of Education, 60*(2), 199–216.

8 Institutional Stratification in U.S. Study Abroad Participation and Experiences

Exploring the Role of Research Institution Attendance

Melissa Whatley

Introduction

In the 2017–2018 academic year, approximately 67% of U.S. study abroad students (229,746 out of 341,751) attended a doctoral university (Institute of International Education [IIE], 2001–2018), all while representing only approximately 33% of total postsecondary enrollment (National Center for Education Statistics, 2018). Such a high percentage of study abroad students attending a single institution type suggest institutional stratification in study abroad opportunities, wherein students who attend research-focused institutions have a greater number of study abroad opportunities available to them. The study presented in this chapter interrogates such stratification using U.S. data from the University System of Georgia. Specifically, this study centers attention on the role of attendance at a research-focused institution in both study abroad participation and characteristics of a student's study abroad experience, namely location and duration of study abroad. This work draws inspiration from literature addressing the intersection between institutional and individual-level stratification in U.S. higher education. That is, this study takes as its point of departure the premise that stratification of opportunities for students is at least in part determined by the stratified organizational hierarchy of the U.S. higher education system (Bastedo & Gumport, 2003; Gumport & Bastedo, 2001; Hearn & Rosinger, 2014; Stich, 2012; Taylor & Cantwell, 2018). Taylor and Cantwell (2018) highlight a global preference for research institutions, underscoring their high status in this institutional hierarchy.

Literature Review

The role of institutional stratification in students' decisions about study abroad participation is currently an underexplored topic in international education research. While researchers have identified myriad factors, such as students' demographic characteristics, academic abilities, and beliefs (e.g., Brux & Fry, 2010; Goel, DeJong, & Schnusenberg, 2010; Lingo, 2019; Luo & Jamieson-Drake, 2015; McClure, Szelenyi, Niehaus, Anderson, & Reed, 2010; Simon & Ainsworth, 2012; Whatley, 2017a) that significantly relate to study abroad participation, very little attention has been given to how the type of institution that a student attends factors into such decision-making. However, prior work does provide consistent evidence of stratification in study abroad participation at the individual level. This line of work speaks to how student-level characteristics such as race/ethnicity, socioeconomic status, and access to social and cultural capital resources relate to study abroad participation patterns (e.g., Luo & Jamieson-Drake, 2015; Salisbury, Umbach, Paulsen, & Pascarella, 2009; Simon & Ainsworth, 2012; Whatley, 2017a). In a recent example of this line of work regarding U.S. students, Lingo (2019) presents evidence consistent with theories of embodied cultural capital and effectively maintained inequality (e.g., Lucas, 2017), finding that students whose parents hold more advanced degrees are more likely to study abroad, even when a student's intent to study abroad at the start of college is held constant. Although two studies in the U.S. study abroad literature account for institution type in their analyses, finding that students attending a liberal arts institution are consistently more likely to study abroad (Lingo, 2019; Salisbury et al., 2009), these studies draw on a data source that was intended to study liberal arts institutions specifically, and institution type is not their primary focus of inquiry. Netz (2015) includes institution type as an indicator of the international mobility opportunity structure available to students in four European countries (Austria, Germany, Switzerland, and the Netherlands), finding that enrollment at a university (compared to another institution type) exhibits a negative relationship with the likelihood of study abroad participation in Austria. Institution type was not a significant predictor of participation in other countries.

Moving beyond study abroad intent and participation, some prior work has examined students' preferences for study abroad in certain locations and for certain durations. Regarding location, Amani (2011) found that familiarity with a certain region is a motivating factor for study abroad participation among community college students. Other researchers have found evidence suggesting that certain locations attract students representing different race/ethnicity groups (McClure et al., 2010; Van Der Meid, 2003; Whatley, 2017b). For example, the Hispanic-identifying students participating in McClure et al. (2010) placed great emphasis on lack of programs in Spanish-speaking countries as a factor contributing to their non-participation in study abroad. In 2017–2018, Europe hosted over half of U.S. study abroad students, suggestive of a great number of study abroad programs in this region of the world (IIE, 2019). Regarding the duration of study abroad, Hackney, Boggs, and Borozan (2012) found that students generally expressed a preference for short-term study abroad programs. This finding is in line with the national data on study abroad participation that annually suggest a greater proportion of students participating in short-term programs (65% in the 2017–2018 academic year), defined as a summer program or a program lasting eight weeks or less (IIE, 2019).

Research Method

To address its dual purpose of examining the role of research institution attendance in both a student's decision to study abroad (purpose 1) and a student's decision about where and for how long to study abroad (purpose 2), this study draws on data from the University System of Georgia. The following subsections describe these data and how they were analyzed.

Data

The *Georgia Learning Outcomes of Students Studying Abroad Research Initiative (GLOSSARI)* dataset is composed of information from students attending public, four-year institutions in the University System of Georgia (USG) between 2001 and 2008 (see Whatley [2019] for a detailed description of how students were selected for inclusion in this dataset). The dataset follows students from their entry into the USG through their exit from the system, recording information at multiple time points. In addition to containing information about students' study abroad participation and subsequent experiences, this dataset includes a collection of variables related to student financial aid, demographic characteristics, and post-enrollment academic information (see Table 8.1). The variables included in the analyses described in the following subsection fall into two categories: those related to students' choice about where to attend college (a research or non-research institution) and those related to students' decisions about whether, where, and for how long to study abroad. Variables in the first category included gender, race/ethnicity, residency status, approximate age at enrollment, and whether a student received a non-need-based grant in the first term of enrollment (a proxy for pre-college academic achievement). Variables belonging to the second category included some of the same demographic characteristics (gender, race/ethnicity, and residency status) along with students' sources of financial support while enrolled in college (i.e., grant and loan aid amounts) and academic characteristics (grade point average [GPA], major field of study, and class standing). Research institution attendance, the predictor of interest in this study, belongs to this second category of variables.

Prior to analysis, several student groups were excluded from the sample. First, since institution type is this study's primary variable of interest, data from students missing this information were discarded (N = 5,249). Second, two student groups were omitted because of their small representation in the dataset, which precluded statistical analysis: students who studied abroad in Canada (N = 58) and students whose race/ethnicity was not recorded in the dataset (N = 1). Finally, students whose approximate age of enrollment at a

Table 8.1 Variables Included in Analyses

Variable	*Categories*
Study abroad	
Study abroad participation	Yes/no
Location of study abroad	Africa/Middle East, Asia/Pacific, Europe, Latin America/Caribbean, Multiple regions
Duration of study abroad	Less than four weeks, four to six weeks, six to eight weeks, and a semester or longer
Demographics	
Gender	Male/female
Race/ethnicity	African-American, Asian-American, Hispanic, Multiple race/ethnicities, White
Residency status	In-state, out-of-state
Approximate age at enrollment	Calculated by subtracting a student's birth year from the year that he/she enrolled at a USG institution
Financial aid	
Received non-need-based aid in first term of enrollment	Yes/no
Need-based grant aid[a]	Dollar amount
Non-need-based grant aid[a]	Dollar amount
Subsidized federal loan aid[a]	Dollar amount
Unsubsidized federal loan aid[a]	Dollar amount
Post-enrollment academic characteristics	
GPA[a]	0.0–4.0 scale
Major field of study	Business, Fine Arts/Humanities, Social Sciences, STEM, Education, Other
Class standing[a]	Freshman, Sophomore, Junior, Senior
Institution type	Research institution, non-research institution (comprehensive institutions and state colleges)

[a] In the term immediately preceding possible study abroad participation.

USG institution was lower than 16 or higher than 70 were omitted from the dataset due to concern about data errors in these students' records (N = 348). These exclusions resulted in a final sample of 29,536 students with complete data on all variables. Approximately half (48%) of students in this sample had studied abroad, and slightly more than half (61%) attended a research institution. As noted below, analyses that explored characteristics of students' study abroad experiences (location and duration) used a subset of this larger dataset that included only study abroad participants. After the elimination of data from students who participated in study abroad, but about whose experiences the dataset lacked information about destination and duration (N = 279), analyses included data from 13,838 students, of which approximately 69% (N = 9,571) attended research institutions. Five world regions (Africa/Middle East, Asia/Pacific, Europe, Latin America/Caribbean, and multiple regions) comprised destination of study abroad, while four categories (less than four weeks, four to eight weeks, eight to twelve weeks, and a semester or longer) represented study abroad duration.

Analysis

In an ideal research context, to address the relationship between research institution attendance and study abroad participation patterns, students would be randomized into research (treatment) and non-research (control) institutions, ensuring that selection into treatment is not determined by observed or unobserved student characteristics. In this situation, and in the absence of sampling error, students attending research and non-research institutions would approximate each other regarding demographic characteristics, would study similar academic fields, and would exhibit similar levels of academic achievement. This ideal situation, however, is impossible for both practical and ethical reasons. As a consequence, in the absence of randomization, alternative means of producing baseline statistical equivalency with reference to the type of institution attended are necessary. This study used both standard probit regression techniques to control for differences in individual student characteristics and propensity score modeling to account for differences in observable baseline characteristics of the students attending research and non-research institutions (Lewis, 1973; Rubin, 2005). This study specifically used propensity score weighting to balance data based on observed pre-enrollment differences among students attending research and non-research institutions. Both standard and weighted regression models took the following basic form:

$$y^* = \alpha + Research\ \beta + Demographics\ \gamma + FinAid\ \delta + AcadChars\ \theta + \varepsilon, \qquad (1)$$

where the outcome y^* is the latent probability of an individual student's study abroad participation (generally), study abroad in a specific region of the world, or study abroad for a particular duration of time, β represents the coefficient of interest (research institution attendance), and the remaining terms on the right-hand side of the equation represent vectors of variables controlling for students' demographic (e.g., gender, race/ethnicity, in-state residency status, and age at enrollment), financial aid (grant and loan amounts), and academic characteristics (GPA, major field of study, and class standing).

Propensity score-weighted models additionally included a weight derived from a student's likelihood of attending a research institution. Specifically, these models estimate average treatment effect on the treated (ATT) which estimates the effect of attending a research institution on those students who did so, using the twang (Toolkit for the Weighting of Non-equivalent Groups) package in R (Ridgeway, McCaffrey, Morral, Burgette, & Griffin, 2016). Weighting of the data occurred in two steps. The first step involved the calculation of a propensity score for each student, representing the propensity of that student toward research institution attendance. Statistically speaking, this step involved generalized boosted regression (GBR), a nonparametric regression technique that employs a data-adaptive modeling algorithm capable of estimating nonlinear relationships between an outcome variable (in this case, research institution attendance) and a large number of predictor variables (McCaffrey, Ridgeway, & Morral, 2004). This estimation method is more flexible than logit and probit models that are traditionally used in the first stage of propensity score modeling and does not require variable selection, which risks potentially biasing estimates (McCaffrey et al., 2004; Ridgeway et al., 2016). The regression trees used in a GBR model employ a recursive algorithm to estimate the relationship between predictor variables and a single outcome variable (McCaffrey et al., 2004). In the case of this study, predictor variables included all pre-enrollment student characteristics available in the dataset, namely age at enrollment, gender, race/ethnicity, residency status, and whether a student received non-need-based grant aid in their first term of enrollment, while the outcome variable was research institution attendance. Unfortunately, because this dataset was collected from the university system, it does not contain other important pre-enrollment information that might be collected while a student is still in high school, such as intended postsecondary field of study and prior academic achievement. As noted previously, receipt of non-need-based grant aid in a student's first term of enrollment at a USG institution was included in an attempt to account for this latter piece of information to the extent possible. Using GBR, regression trees iteratively partitioned data into increasingly smaller groups while selecting the partition that minimized prediction error. The generalized boosted model algorithm then collected these regression tree models, which were added together to estimate a unit's propensity score (McCaffrey et al., 2004). In this study, the maximum number of iterations was set to 10,000. Equation (2) illustrates a simplified version of these regression tree models:

$$\hat{g}(x) = g_0 + g_1(age) + g_2(gender) + g_3(race) + g_4(residency) + g_5(grant\ aid), \quad (2)$$

where the outcome is the estimate of propensity toward research institution attendance ($\hat{g}(x)$), $g_1(age)$ is the first regression tree, with a split on age, $g_2(gender)$ is the second regression tree, with a split on gender, g_3 splits on race/ethnicity, g_4 splits on residency status (in- or out-of-state), and g_5 splits on the receipt of non-need-based grant aid in the first semester. The splits represented in each term on the right-hand side of (2) may be many and may interact with one another (e.g., a split into three or four age groups, a split on both gender and age), depending on which iterations provide the best fit for the data.

Second, once calculated, each student's estimated propensity score, $\hat{g}(x)$, was used as a balancing score to weight the data. In assuming that $\hat{g}(x)$ approximates a student's empirical propensity toward treatment ($e(x)$), the assumption is that analyses approach the conditions of a true randomized experiment. This assumption ignores the existence of unobservable characteristics (e.g., academic motivation) and omitted factors (e.g., pre-college academic ability) that affect selection into the research institution treatment condition (Rosenbaum & Rubin, 1983).

Individual students' weights were calculated as in equation (3) using the propensity scores estimated as in equation (2):

$$w\left(x\right)=K\frac{f(z=1\,|\,x)}{f(z=0\,|\,x)}=K\frac{\hat{g}\left(x\right)}{1-\hat{g}\left(x\right)}, \tag{3}$$

where $w\left(x\right)$ represents a student's likelihood of being included in the treatment condition and the normalizing constant K cancels out in analysis (Ridgeway et al., 2016). When estimating ATT, this weight is equal to 1 for students attending research institutions and ranges in value for students attending non-research institutions, depending on their propensity toward research institution attendance.

Table 8.2 displays the balance of treatment and control groups before and after the application of propensity score weights for all students in the sample. In this table, the first column (Mean Research) represents the mean values of variables among students attending research-intensive institutions. The second column (mean non-research (raw)) presents mean values among students attending non-research-intensive institutions prior to weighting, while the third column (mean non-research (weighted)) presents these same mean values after weighting. Significance levels correspond to comparisons between research and non-research attendees. This table clearly shows that significant differences existed between the research and non-research student groups prior to weighting for almost all of the variables taken into consideration

Table 8.2 Balance of Treatment and Control Groups (All Students)

Variable	*Mean Research*	*Mean Non-Research (Raw)*	*Mean Non-Research (Weighted)*
Age at enrollment	19.704	21.590***	19.701
Non-need-based aid	0.378	0.266***	0.379
Male	0.411	0.300***	0.409
Asian-American	0.071	0.020***	0.070
African-American	0.089	0.223***	0.091
Hispanic	0.024	0.022	0.026
American-Indian	0.002	0.003+	0.002
Multiple races/ ethnicities	0.025	0.020*	0.025
In-state resident	0.869	0.930***	0.876
Sample size	18,074	11,462	11,462

Note: $^{+}$p < .10, *p < .05, ***p <. 001.

Table 8.3 Balance of Treatment and Control Groups (Study Abroad Students)

Variable	*Mean Research*	*Mean Non-Research (Raw)*	*Mean Non-Research (Weighted)*
Age at enrollment	19.467	20.890***	19.462
Non-need-based aid	0.584	0.472***	0.592
Male	0.371	0.288***	0.367
Asian-American	0.059	0.017***	0.059
African-American	0.036	0.126***	0.037
Hispanic	0.026	0.031^{+}	0.026
American-Indian	0.002	0.004*	0.002
Multiple races/ ethnicities	0.023	0.027	0.022
In-state resident	0.858	0.936***	0.862
Sample size	9,571	4,267	4,267

Note: $^{+}p < .10$, $^{*}p < .05$, $^{***}p < .001$.

(indeed, all except for Hispanic race/ethnicity). These significant differences are not present after data are weighted.

Analyses corresponding to location and duration of students' study abroad experiences also made use of propensity score weighting to estimate ATT, this time calculating weights using the reduced sample of only study abroad students, as described previously. These analyses were identical to those just described except that a multinomial logistic rather than a probit regression model was used to estimate the final model (that represented in equation (1)). Standard multinomial models (rather than propensity-score weighted models) were not estimated. A multinomial model was used because both location and duration outcomes were multiple rather than binary in nature (i.e., five study abroad destinations and four possible durations). Table 8.3 displays the balance of treatment and control groups before and after weighting using the study abroad students' data subset. Again, significant differences between the treatment and control groups are present without weighting but disappear when data are weighted.

Results

Descriptive Statistics

Table 8.4 displays the summary statistics corresponding to the entire data subset and the dataset disaggregated by institution type (research or non-research institution). As already noted, approximately half (48%) of students in the dataset studied abroad and a little over half (61%) attended a research institution. A greater percentage of students attending research institutions (54%) studied abroad compared to their non-research-institution counterparts (38%), reflecting the national trends highlighted previously in this chapter.

Table 8.4 General Descriptive Statistics

Variable	*All Institutions*		*Research Institutions*		*Non-Research Institutions*	
	Mean	*SD*	*Mean*	*SD*	*Mean*	*SD*
Study abroad	0.48	0.50	0.54	0.50	0.38	0.48
Research university	0.61	0.49				
Male	0.37	0.48	0.41	0.49	0.30	0.46
Asian-American	0.05	0.22	0.07	0.26	0.02	0.14
African-American	0.14	0.35	0.09	0.28	0.22	0.42
Hispanic	0.02	0.15	0.02	0.15	0.02	0.15
American-Indian	0.00	0.05	0.00	0.04	0.00	0.06
Multiple races/eth.	0.02	0.15	0.02	0.16	0.02	0.14
White	0.76	0.43	0.79	0.41	0.71	0.45
In-state resident	0.89	0.31	0.87	0.34	0.93	0.25
Age at enrollment	20.44	4.09	19.70	2.43	21.59	5.63
First non-need aid	0.33	0.47	0.38	0.48	0.27	0.44
Need-based grant	138.19	500.35	109.99	466.51	182.67	546.57
Non-need grant	1,023.23	1,489.97	1,348.68	1,678.40	510.03	921.05
Sub. loan amount	1,559.93	3,562.35	1,236.72	3,132.44	2,069.60	4,099.45
Unsub. loan amount	1,299.81	3,086.01	1,150.95	2,834.60	1,534.53	3,432.42
GPA	3.18	0.60	3.24	0.56	3.08	0.65
Major: Business	0.14	0.35	0.13	0.34	0.15	0.36
Major: FA/Humanit.	0.12	0.33	0.08	0.26	0.19	0.39
Major: Soc. Sciences	0.13	0.34	0.14	0.35	0.12	0.32
Major: STEM	0.17	0.38	0.23	0.42	0.08	0.27
Major: Education	0.08	0.28	0.06	0.23	0.13	0.33
Major: Other	0.34	0.47	0.36	0.48	0.30	0.46
Freshman	0.10	0.30	0.06	0.24	0.16	0.37
Sophomore	0.29	0.45	0.28	0.45	0.30	0.46
Junior	0.38	0.48	0.42	0.49	0.30	0.46
Senior	0.23	0.42	0.24	0.42	0.23	0.42
Total Obs	29,536		18,074		11,462	

Table 8.5 provides similar information about students' study abroad experiences, namely location and duration of study abroad. Students overwhelmingly studied in European destinations (66%), a finding that was true for students at both research institutions (67%) and non-research institutions (64%). Students at both institution types participated in study abroad in Africa or the Middle East at similar rates (approximately 4%). However, differences between students at research and non-research institutions emerged for other regions of the world, including Asia and the Pacific, a more visited destination among

Table 8.5 Descriptive Statistics for Location and Duration of Study Abroad

	All	*Research*	*Non-Research*
Africa/Middle East	4%	4%	3%
Asia/Pacific	12%	14%	6%
Europe	66%	67%	64%
Latin America/Caribbean	16%	12%	26%
Multiple regions	2%	3%	0%
Less than four weeks	22%	14%	41%
Four to eight weeks	52%	51%	54%
Eight to twelve weeks	16%	22%	2%
A semester or longer	10%	13%	3%
Total Obs	13,838	9,571	4,267

students at research institutions (14%) compared to non-research institutions (6%). Similarly, students attending research institutions studied abroad in multiple regions at a higher rate (3%) compared to their non-research institution counterparts (effectively 0%). (Note that study abroad in multiple regions does not necessarily mean that a student studied abroad multiple times. Rather, a student may have participated in a program that included travel to two neighboring regions of the world, such as Europe and North Africa.) In contrast, students enrolled at non-research institutions studied in a Latin American or Caribbean destination at a higher rate compared to their research institution counterparts (26% compared to 12%).

Turning to the duration of study abroad, in general, students at research institutions were more likely to study abroad for longer amounts of time. That is, a full 35% of students enrolled at research institutions studied abroad for eight weeks or longer, while only 5% of students enrolled at non-research institutions did so. In contrast, students at non-research institutions consistently participated in study abroad for shorter amounts of time. Almost all of these students (95%) studied abroad for eight weeks or less. The corresponding percentage of students attending research institutions and participating in shorter programs is still substantial (65%), but considerably smaller.

Regression Results

Table 8.6 displays average marginal effects corresponding to β in the regression analyses predicting study abroad participation. These analyses controlled for the second, post-enrollment group of variables mentioned previously (e.g., financial aid amounts, gender, race/ethnicity), but the marginal effects corresponding to these control variables are not listed in the table due to space constraints. The first model in Table 8.6 is a standard regression model predicting study abroad participation while the second uses propensity score weighting. These models both indicate that the relationship between research institution attendance and study abroad participation is a negative one.

Table 8.6 Marginal Effects for Regression Models Predicting Study Abroad (All Students)

	Standard Regression	*Weighted Regression*
Research institution	−0.054***	−0.079***
	(0.009)	(0.009)
Sample size	29,536	29,536
Chi-square	19,369.35	4,194.46
Pseudo R^2	0.47	0.48
Control variables?	Yes	Yes

Note: Standard errors in parentheses, ***p < .001.

Table 8.7 Marginal Effects for Weighted Regression Models Predicting Location of Study Abroad (Study Abroad Students)

	Africa/ Middle East	*Asia/Pacific*	*Europe*	*Latin America/ Caribbean*	*Multiple Regions*
Research Institution	0.017*** (0.004)	0.064*** (0.008)	−0.003 (0.012)	−0.107*** (0.009)	0.030*** (0.006)

Note: Model includes control variables, Standard errors in parentheses, ***p < .001, Multinomial logistic regression model: N = 13,838; Log pseudolikelihood = −17,644.046; Pseudo-R^2 = 0.0538.

Specifically, in the weighted model, attendance at a research institution was associated with an approximate 8% decrease in the likelihood of study abroad.

Average marginal effects corresponding to the weighted multinomial logistic regression model predicting study abroad destination are displayed in Table 8.7. Like the models in Table 8.6, this model controlled for post-enrollment variables. In line with the summary statistics in Table 8.5, these results indicated that attendance at a research institution positively predicted study abroad in Asia or the Pacific ($p<.001$) and multiple regions ($p<.001$). Specifically, research institution attendance was associated with approximate 6% and 3% increases in the likelihood of study abroad in these two destinations, respectively. Research institution attendance was also significantly positively related to study abroad in Africa or the Middle East, associated with an approximate 2% ($p<.001$) increase in the likelihood of study abroad in this region of the world. On the other hand, attendance at a research institution was significantly and negatively related to study abroad in Latin America or the Caribbean, associated with an approximate 12% decrease in the likelihood of study abroad in this region ($p < .001$). Students attending research and non-research institutions were equally as likely to study abroad in a European destination.

Table 8.8 Marginal Effects for Weighted Regression Models Predicting Duration of Study Abroad (Study Abroad Students)

	Less than Four Weeks	*Four to Eight Weeks*	*Eight to Twelve Weeks*	*Semester*$^+$
Research institution	−0.230***	−0.075***	0.213***	0.093***
	(0.010)	(0.013)	(0.011)	(0.007)

Note: Model includes control variables. Standard errors in parentheses, ***p < .001, multinomial logistic regression model: N = 13,819; Log pseudolikelihood = −18,881.920; Pseudo-R^2 = 0.1327.

Table 8.8 displays marginal effects corresponding to the weighted multinomial regression model predicting study abroad duration. As the descriptive statistics in Table 8.5 suggest, these models demonstrated that students attending research institutions were less likely to study abroad for shorter amounts of time and more likely to study abroad for longer amounts of time. Specifically, attendance at a research institution was associated with approximately 23% and 8% decreases in the likelihood of study abroad for less than four weeks and four to eight weeks ($p < .001$ in both cases), respectively, while research institution attendance was associated with approximately 21% and 9% increases in the likelihood of study abroad for eight to twelve weeks and a semester or longer ($p < .001$ in both cases).

Discussion and Conclusions

This study provides insight into the relationship between research institution attendance and study abroad participation. Results suggested that, while research institutions report more students participating in study abroad generally, once student characteristics are taken into account, attending such an institution is significantly and negatively related to study abroad participation. While this result may at first seem counter-intuitive, it is in line with what Netz (2015) found for Austrian students. Netz (2015) suggests that differential availability of advising resources or study abroad scholarships might explain this negative relationship. It is also possible that post-enrollment academic pathways explain why students attending research-focused institutions were less likely to study abroad. A second look at the descriptive statistics summarized in Table 8.4 reveals that discrepancies exist in the distribution of students among majors when comparing research and non-research institutions. These differences are clearest for fields in the Fine Arts and Humanities, Education, and the STEM fields. Specifically, greater percentages of students attending non-research institutions majored in areas in the Fine Arts/Humanities or Education while STEM majors were overrepresented at research institutions. Although the results of this study do not indicate that STEM majors are less likely to study abroad, prior research (e.g., Niehaus & Inkelas, 2016) indicates an overall negative relationship between a STEM major and study abroad participation. This finding is in line with national trends in the U.S., wherein STEM majors only recently participate in study abroad at levels comparable to students in other fields of study (IIE, 2019).

Institutionally stratified study abroad participation was most clearly evident in this study's results not in the findings related to participation itself but in the characteristics of students' international programs. Regarding location, results indicated that students enrolled at research institutions were more likely to study abroad in Africa/the Middle East, Asia/the Pacific, and multiple regions of the world compared to their non-research institution counterparts. In contrast, they were less likely to study abroad in a Latin American or Caribbean destination. These results suggest that students attending research institutions are able to access study abroad programs in a wider variety of regions of the world, while those studying at non-research institutions are mostly limited to only a few regions. Indeed, the two regions where non-research institution students were just as or more likely to study abroad are also the two most popular regions for study abroad among U.S. students generally (IIE, 2019). Inequalities in study abroad experiences are even more evident when considering the duration of study abroad. Indeed, longer study abroad programs appear to be the domain of research institutions, while students at non-research institutions appear to be mostly limited to study abroad programs of shorter durations. It is important to note here that while many in the field of international education might value longer study abroad programs over shorter ones, believing that they result in better student outcomes, recent research indicates that rather than length, elements of study abroad program design are what contribute to student outcome gains (e.g., Mapp, 2012; Tarrant & Lyons, 2011; Whatley, Landon, Tarrant, & Rubin, 2020). At the same time, from a stratification standpoint, it is a lack of opportunity to study abroad for a longer duration at non-research institutions that is troubling.

Implications

This study contributes to our knowledge of stratification in study abroad participation in two ways. First, it systematically examines the institutional stratification, defined as research or non-research institution attendance, a topic not explored in prior literature. Second, it examines this stratification not only in study abroad participation but also in characteristics of students' abroad experiences, namely location and duration of study abroad. However, it is limited in two ways that provide fruitful directions for future research. First, the GLOSSARI dataset used for this study corresponds only to students attending public institutions in a single state (Georgia) between 2001 and 2008. Future work is needed to extend this study to students attending other institution types (indeed, Di Pietro [2015] finds that, in Italy, students attending private institutions are more likely to study abroad compared to those attending public institutions), living in other states, and, perhaps more importantly, to examine institutional stratification regarding study abroad in more recent years. Second, while the propensity score modeling approach used in this study was able to account for systematic differences among students attending research and non-research institutions regarding observed student characteristics, this analytic approach is unable to account for unobserved differences among these student groups (e.g., a student's motivation for attending higher education, intended field of study prior to enrollment in postsecondary education). Moreover, in predicting study abroad participation, additional variables not available in the GLOSSARI that correspond to opportunity structures at individual institutions (e.g., number of study abroad programs, faculty/staff roles dedicated to international education) are important to consider (Netz, 2015). Additional research is needed to address these limitations.

The evidence of institutional stratification in study abroad opportunity presented in this chapter may not be entirely surprising to international educators, but it should bring renewed attention to international education's contribution to the ways in which the organization of U.S. higher education privileges some students over others. Such stratification should be more prominent in conversations among international educators who, after all, are those with the means to attenuate some of its effects on students.

References

Amani, M. (2011). *Study abroad decision and participation at community colleges: Influential factors and challenges from the voices of students and coordinators* (Unpublished doctoral dissertation). George Washington University, Washington, DC.

Bastedo, M. N., & Gumport, P. J. (2003). Access to what? Mission differentiation and academic stratification in U.S. public higher education. *Higher Education, 46*, 341–359.

Brux, J., & Fry, B. (2010). Multicultural students in study abroad: Their interests, their issues, and their constraints. *Journal of Studies in International Education, 14*(5), 508–527.

Di Pietro, G. (2015). Do study abroad programs enhance the employability of graduates? *Education Finance and Policy, 10*(2), 223–243.

Goel, L., De Jong, P., & Schnusenberg, O. (2010). Toward a comprehensive framework of study abroad intentions and behaviors. *Journal of Teaching in International Business, 21*(4), 248–265.

Gumport, P. J., & Bastedo, M. N. (2001). Academic stratification and endemic conflict: Remedial education policy at the City University of New York. *Review of Higher Education, 24*, 333–349.

Hackney, K., Boggs, D., & Borozan, A. (2012). An empirical study of student willingness to study abroad. *Journal of Teaching in International Business, 23*(2), 123–144.

Hearn, J. C., & Rosinger, K. O. (2014). Socioeconomic diversity in selective private colleges: An organizational analysis. *The Review of Higher Education, 38*, 71–104.

IIE. (2001–2018). U.S. Study Abroad at All Institutions, 2000/01–2017/18. *Open doors report on international educational exchange*. http://www.iie.org/opendoors

IIE. (2019). *Open doors 2018: Report on international educational exchange*. http://www.iie.org/Research-and-Publications/Open-Doors

Lewis, D. (1973). Causation. *The Journal of Philosophy, 70*, 556–567.

Lingo, M. D. (2019). Stratification in study abroad participation after accounting for student intent. *Research in Higher Education, 60*, 1142–1170.

Lucas, S. (2017). An archaeology of effectively maintained inequality theory. *American Behavioral Scientist, 61*, 8–29.

Luo, J., & Jamieson-Drake, D. (2015). Predictors of study abroad intent, participation, and college outcomes. *Research in Higher Education, 56*(1), 29–56.

Mapp, S. C. (2012). Effect of short-term study abroad programs on students' cultural adaptability. *Journal of Social Work Education, 48*(4), 727–737.

McCaffrey, D. F., Ridgeway, G., & Morral, A. R. (2004). Propensity score estimation with boosted regression for evaluating causal effects in observational studies. *Psychological Methods, 9*(4), 403–444.

McClure, K. R., Szelenyi, K., Niehaus, E., Anderson, A. A., & Reed, J. (2010). "We just don't have the possibility yet": US Latina/o narratives on study abroad. *Journal of Student Affairs Research and Practice, 47*(3), 363–382.

National Center for Education Statistics. (2018). *Digest of education statistics*. https://nces.ed.gov/programs/digest/

Netz, N. (2015). What deters students from studying abroad? Evidence from four European countries and its implications for higher education policy. *Higher Education Policy, 28*, 151–174.

Niehaus, E., & Inkelas, K. K. (2016). Understanding STEM majors' intent to study abroad. *College Student Affairs Journal, 34*, 70–84.

Ridgeway, G., McCaffrey, D., Morral, A., Burgette, L., & Griffin, B. A. (2016). *Toolkit for weighting and analysis of nonequivalent groups: A tutorial for the twang package*. R vignette. RAND.

Rubin, D. B. (2005). Causal inference using potential outcomes. *Journal of the American Statistical Association, 100*, 322–331.

Salisbury, M. H., Umbach, P. D., Paulsen, M. B., & Pascarella, E. T. (2009). Going global: Understanding the choice process of the intent to study abroad. *Research in Higher Education, 50*(2), 119–143.

Simon, J., & Ainsworth, J. W. (2012). Race and socioeconomic status differences in study abroad participation: The role of habitus, social networks, and cultural capital. *ISRN Education*, 2012. https://www.hindawi.com/journals/isrn/2012/413896/

Stich, A. E. (2012). *Access to inequality: Reconsidering class, knowledge, and capital in higher education*. Plymouth, UK: Lexington Books.

Tarrant, M., & Lyons, K. (2011). The effect of short-term educational travel programs on environmental citizenship. *Environmental Education Research, 18*, 403–416.

Taylor, B. J., & Cantwell, B. (2018). Unequal higher education in the United States: Growing participation and shrinking opportunities. *Social Sciences, 7*, 167.

Van Der Meid, J. S. (2003). Asian Americans: Factors influencing the decision to study abroad. *Frontiers: The Interdisciplinary Journal of Study Abroad, 9*(4), 71–110.

Whatley, M. (2017a). Financing study abroad: An exploration of the influence of financial factors on student study abroad patterns. *Journal of Studies in International Education, 21*(5), 431–449.

Whatley, M. (2017b). The role of heritage seeking in the study abroad destination decision-making of minority students. *NAFSA Research Symposium Series, 1*, 18–30.

Whatley, M., Landon, A. C., Tarrant, M. A., & Rubin, D. (2020). Program design and the development of students' global perspectives in short-term study abroad. *Journal of Studies in International Education*. doi:10.1177/1028315320906156

Part III

Promoting Diversity and Exploring Alternatives to Study Abroad

9 Mapping the Dimensions of Inclusive Internationalization

Eva Janebová and Christopher J. Johnstone

Introduction

Comprehensive internationalization is globally accepted as a higher education strategy. A recent survey by the International Association of Universities, for example, found that over 90% of institutions surveyed included internationalization in their strategic plan (Marioni, 2019). Decades of research and practice have informed internationalization strategy and have led to a relative agreement on the institutional and sectoral focus. For example, Knight's (2004) original definition of comprehensive internationalization has been cited over 2,500 times and is often the preferred approach for institutions attempting to engage globally (Hudzik, 2011). Critical scholars of internationalization, however, have identified that there is no single narrative of internationalization and homogeneity should not be assumed. Careful analysis is required.

Using a social cartographic analytic approach, Stein, Andreotti, Bruce, and Suša (2016) identified four narratives of institutionalization and attempted to map them through a comprehensive literature review. The authors identified four internationalization rationales: (1) internationalization for the global economy (i.e., strategies that align with neoliberal goals of developing global employees); (2) internationalization for the public good (that which focuses on liberal traditions and a presumed global public good); (3) anti-oppressive internationalization; and (4) relational translocalism. The social cartography approach that Stein and colleagues used assists in identifying the pluralism in the perspectives around internationalization and helps readers see that internationalization is complex and multifaceted.

In this chapter, we seek to similarly map how the term 'inclusive internationalization' has been framed by organizations and scholars. Inclusive internationalization is a subfield of internationalization itself that is relatively new as a concept, hence is lacking overall theory. The term inclusive internationalization, or inclusivity in internationalization, emerged from the perceived inadequacy of internationalization to engage different stakeholders in its processes. Further, inclusive internationalization has been framed as a reform effort to internationalization foci that, according to some scholars, are dangerously centered in neoliberal economic goals.

In the following paragraphs, we present a preliminary mapping of inclusiveness in higher education and how it is framed in contemporary literature. We present these categories as a heuristic for further engagement, understanding that 'inclusion' is a socially desirable term that can be leveraged by almost any organization for any purpose. Similar to Stein and colleagues, we seek to step away from the comfort of the words like 'inclusive' and 'all' in order to understand the motivations, parameters, and intended outcomes of inclusive internationalization. In order to do so, we present a thematic mapping of three dimensions of inclusive internationalization found in the literature: (1) theoretical dimensions; (2) representational dimensions; and (3) participatory dimensions. Each of these will be examined in the paragraphs below.

Theoretical Dimensions

Theoretical understandings of inclusive internationalization are informed by two main viewpoints: (1) a philosophical linkage to the liberal and public good aims of higher education; and (2) a critical epistemological stance on internationalization. The first theoretical conceptualization of inclusive internationalization is through a lens of liberal education and the public good. Scholars who frame inclusiveness for internationalization in this way leverage inclusive narratives as a point of defense against neoliberal conceptualizations of internationalization. Through seeking a more inclusive internationalization, these scholars appear to be seeking a return to the public good narratives of higher education with internationalization at the core, which is closer to the original rationales of international understanding and peacemaking that shaped international education in the first half of the 20th century.

Hence inclusive internationalization represents an opportunity for internationalization to embrace the public mission of higher education and counter-interpretations that have primarily focused on creating competitive advantage, workforce development, personal gain, and global capitalism. Recent trends in internationalization reporting indicate a growing managerialism, with internationalization goals dictated by rankings and other metrics. Institutions, in the neoliberal era, appear to internationalize for the purposes of higher ranking, more publications that may lead to such rankings or more income through international students.

However, the influence of finances in relation to internationalization varies widely across countries. According to the European Association of International Education (EAIE) 2019 Barometer, at the European level, financial benefits range from 42% of institutions in the UK, to 6% of Dutch and German, and to as low as 2% of respondents in Kazakhstan. In Europe, 12% of the European Higher Education Area selected financial dimensions as a top priority for internationalization (EAIE, 2019a). In the U.S., organizations like NAFSA, the Association of International Educators, have long focused on the financial implications of internationalization, specifically from international student enrollment as a rationale for internationalization (NAFSA, 2016).

Because of concerns regarding the monetization of internationalization and its broader neoliberal goals, DeLaquil (2019) and deWit and Jones (2018) argued for an inclusive internationalization by drawing upon arguments of university social responsibility, with internationalization as a way of universities 'realigning with the original purpose and mission of higher education' (p. 6). DeLaquil notes that a more inclusive mission of internationalization focuses, at its best, on global issues like 'refugee cris(e)s, climate change, ongoing war, rising nationalism and xenophobia, religious extremism, poverty, and food insecurity (p. 6).' Streitwieser, Loo, Ohorodnik, and Leong (2018) call such a mission-focused approach a 'humanistic' orientation of internationalization. Brandenburg and de Wit (2015) note that such orientations are more common in non-western institutions than those of the U.S. or Europe, which may be the impetus for new conceptualizations of inclusive internationalization emerging from these countries.

The liberal theoretical orientation for inclusive internationalization examines the meaning and purpose of internationalization itself. Stein et al. (2016) framed this orientation as 'internationalization for the public good' (p. 14). Scholars who engage with such terminology often frame inclusion as a purpose-driven activity, one that specifically aligns with liberal education and public good aspects of higher education's mission. Questions about who are included or excluded in relation to internationalization are not answered by liberal inclusion. Rather, a broad focus on the 'public' that is served by higher education, and ideally internationalization, informs this conceptualization of inclusive internationalization.

A second group of scholars are those who have a socio-philosophical orientation toward inclusive internationalization and view this concept through a critical lens of social justice. Such scholars often use the terminology of 'inclusiveness' to highlight the shortcomings of internationalization and how it perpetuates injustices and disparities. Whereas liberal arguments about inclusion note an absence of the public good in internationalization, these critical arguments focus on the substance of the injustices that internationalization perpetuates.

Wiebke Frieß and Anna Mucha (2020), for example, describe how internationalization and internationalization at home (IaH) set up false dichotomies among international and domestic students in the name of inclusion, ignoring intersectionality within both groups and 'othering' internationally mobile students. Patel and Lynch (2013) critique internationalization and its focus on intercultural communication for its neutrality or avoidance of social justice issues. The authors substitute 'glocalization' as a way of engaging within and across institutions because glocalization "obligates learners and teachers to consider action that will demonstrate a deep understanding and recognition of the benefits, differences, and similarities among diverse cultures" (p. 228).

This critical lens brings a valuable perspective to conceptualizations of international education, in reminding scholars that international education might in fact be intentionally or unintentionally magnifying embedded inequities in institutions and reproducing social disparities. In the end, some

U.S. scholars are moving away from the terminology of 'inclusion' because it denotes nothing more than a 'rearrangement' of imaginary furniture in a system that is exclusionary and masks its dominance in welcoming statements and re-arranging of programming. New thinking around pluralism is emerging to replace 'inclusion' (Carlson, 2016) for scholars with critical orientations. In this regard, inclusive internationalization with a critical lens may be better termed negatively, in the way scholar Ibram Kendi (2019) uses the term 'anti-' to clarify political intentions, such as anti-racism. In the case of inclusive internationalization, a more appropriate terminology for critical scholars may be 'anti-repressive internationalization'.

For both liberal and critical thinkers, internationalization and inclusive internationalization are strategies that should be guided by a purpose. The first purpose reviewed in this section is a liberal purpose, focused on the common good. The second is a critical purpose, which attends to injustices caused by the process of internationalization itself. These perspectives are not necessarily novel, but due to a lack of awareness about issues linked to inclusion and diversity in universities (Clayes-Kulik, Jorgenson, & Stober, 2019), they are probably not taken into account in the conceptualization of internationalization strategies at the institutional level.

For this reason, readers may consider inclusive internationalization grounded in either liberal tradition of the public good or as a mechanism for addressing social injustices. In the former example, inclusiveness may be a strategy for broadening the social impact of internationalization. For the latter, inclusiveness may be linked with the critique of inequitable practices. The use of the word inclusion is less frequent in critical discourse and, for some, is even argued as inappropriate (see Carlson, 2016). However, there is a potential connection to the term when theoretically linked to concepts like pluralism and epistemic justice.

The theoretical dimensions of inclusive internationalization address the conceptual nature of this phenomenon. When speaking of internationalization, Stein et al. (2016) called the philosophical and strategic dimensions of internationalization "articulations." According to the authors, there have long been public good and anti-oppressive articulations of internationalization as well as neoliberal and economic-based articulations. Our hope in this section was to add appropriate pieces around inclusion as they fit within these articulations (what we call the theoretical dimensions of inclusive internationalization).

Representational Dimensions

In this section, we will describe representational dimensions that focus on leadership and the drivers of internationalization. Scholars who focus on representational dimensions examine the role of the various actors that lead and enact internationalization at the institutional and cross-institutional level. Calls for inclusiveness seek to increase representation in decision-making and activities of internationalization. In this case, representation differs from participation (Hickey, Sen, & Bukenya, 2015) because represented people have the political power to influence the direction of agendas, the flows of resources, and outcomes of internationalization.

Increasing representation for the purposes of inclusion can be a tenuous process, where actors negotiate on prioritized activities, resource flows, and timelines for engagement. The concept of representation is critical to inclusion because it allows for negotiated leadership in creating a vision of internationalization. It primarily occurs at the institutional level. For example, a case study of inclusive internationalization at Bradford College (U.S.) critiqued internationalization efforts in most institutions as doing little more than following a prescribed set of activities. Freysinger (1993) argued, however, that in order for internationalization to be inclusive, a wider number of stakeholders must drive its mission and focus at institutions. "The preparation and discussion phase must be inclusive," argued Freysinger, "involving all interested and affected personnel and allowing input from all concerned, as well as adequate time and opportunity for review and amendment" (p. 187).

Hudzik (2015) refers to internationalization leadership in similar ways, highlighting what he perceives as the necessary levels of engagement for inclusive internationalization. According to Hudzik, Leadership is needed from the top (presidents, vice-chancellors, provosts, deans); from the middle (directors and chairs); and from the base (influential faculty, staff, and students). Effective leadership for internationalization is neither solely top-down nor solely bottom-up; rather, it is both. Top-down leadership sets institutional tone, reaffirms institutional values, and coordinates overarching priorities, but the work and creativity of internationalization depend on the faculty, key staff, and academic and support units (p. 6).

Representation in internationalization becomes more inclusive when stakeholders hold the power to sway the direction of it. One mechanism for doing this is through collective bargaining by populations that may hold less power at institutions than formal leaders. For example, in Europe, many students have advocated for their own engagement in international education. The involvement of student organizations like Erasmus Student Network (ESN) and the European Student's Unions has ensured that students' concerns are represented in policy discussions (EAIE, 2019b; Green, 2019). In Finland, students are an integral part of decision-making processes at both the institutional and governmental level (Lehikoinen, 2019). Brooks (2019) advocates for representation of various campus-based units that can speak to diverse stakeholders' interests in internationalization. These individuals and teams may be positioned at different levels in academic or non-academic departments across the institutional structure, but Brooks argues that teams should be representationally a part of internationalization leadership. For example, there are centers providing support to students with educational needs, multicultural centers for underrepresented students, gender and sexuality-based initiatives, offices for international students, and so on may advocate for stakeholders' interests if represented in internationalization leadership.

Diversity Abroad (2018), the U.S.-based research and practice organization, describes inclusive internationalization as that which has representational leadership in both internationalization and diversity units on campus as listed above. The organization draws on a representational definition of inclusion as one in which "individuals can access information and resources, are involved in work groups, and have the ability to influence decision-making processes" (Mor Barak & Cherin, 1998, p. 12). In this case, this means a collaborative relationship between Chief Diversity Officers (CDOs) and Senior International Officers (SIOs) in internationalization strategy development. Diversity Abroad stated that there is a "need for conversations around definitions: institutions need to define diversity in a holistic sense and highlight shared values around intercultural competency shared between CDO and SIO through collaborative work and projects" (p. 23). Johnstone (2014) also advocates the importance of CDO and SIO and collaboration and strategic planning for internationalization.

In the European context, the Academic Cooperation Association (ACA, 2019) focuses on higher education stakeholders (staff, academics, community outreach personnel) as the agents responsible for promoting inclusion at home and abroad in university programs. International education research and scholarship have long identified the central role of leadership in fostering the comprehensive institutionalization of internationalization (see Hudzik, 2011). Early scholars like Mestenhauser and Ellingboe (2008) identified that internationalization of curriculum starts with academics building their international competences in order to provide an internationalized higher education classroom experience. Similarly, Claeys-Kulik, Jorgenson, and Stober (2019) warn that central commitments to diversity and inclusion do not always translate to action due to the lack of awareness among faculty, pointing out that representation may need to be coupled with faculty development efforts

A recent addition to this conversation calls for a holistic approach and cross-sector collaboration of all actors across higher education institutions, including underrepresented groups, authorities, and other sectors. ACA also calls for a multi-layer strategy to consider broadening the understanding of inclusion in internationalization to ensure that internationalization does not further marginalize students and staff who already face discrimination or neglect at higher education institutions (ACA, 2019). One way of ensuring greater inclusion is through representational forums to allow for negotiation of direction, resources, and approaches.

Representation may also occur at the level of cross-border partnerships. Internationalization has been critiqued as a hegemonic process that bestows unequal benefits on partners who hold more or less power. Often, this hegemony is found in international partnerships between Global North and South partners. However, scholars are developing analytic tools to help identify and potentially rectify these relationships. One example is Chrystal George Mwangi's (2017) reciprocal model of international partnerships that examines how reciprocity and representation of North-South partnerships can be identified. In practice, the EAIE officials have repeatedly voiced their concerns over the dominance of scholars from specific countries such as Western Europe in shaping the discourse of international education in Europe.

An additional case example of representational inclusive internationalization is the Finnish education strategy 'Vision for Higher Education and Research in 2030.' The strategy sets up two joint actions to achieve their strategy: (1) the establishment of Tam Finland Knowledge (TFK) network consisting of higher education experts situated in eight different countries to guide policy and action and (2) an Internationalization Forum which is a network of national entities dealing with international activities in the field of higher education including students organizations, rectors' conferences, international offices, research and innovation liaison offices, students and researcher mobility actors, national agencies, and scholarship offices such as Fulbright Finland (Lehikoinen, 2019).

Representational approaches to inclusive internationalization focus on leadership within internationalization. An underlying assumption is that if leadership of internationalization is diverse and involves a wide range of stakeholders in decision-making and crafting strategy, the end result will be a more inclusive form of internationalization. It is unclear whether increasing representation would lead to more liberal or justice-oriented forms of internationalization, but outcomes may not be the end goal of this dimension of inclusive internationalization. Rather, representational politics and decision-making for internationalization represent a process to promote inclusion. Ainscow and Miles (2008), inclusive education scholars, note that inclusion is not an outcome, but a process that is constantly revised and revisited. Representational dimensions of inclusive internationalization appear to align Ainscow and Miles' assertion and provide a process for institutions and sectors to consider regarding inclusivity.

Participatory Dimensions

Participatory dimensions are the final dimension of inclusive internationalization that we will address in this chapter. These dimensions primarily focus on who participates in internationalization and how. For this section, we identify two broad approaches – accommodation and accessibility. Accommodations are individualized adjustments to standard programs or program requirements that are allowable for particular students. Accommodations provide a way for a wider variety of participants to experience internationalization. It is a common practice in higher education settings for accommodations to be made for students because of their disability status, religion, financial status, etc. Accommodations are allowances for students, faculty, or staff that are designed to promote inclusion by removing individual barriers. Accessibility, on the other hand, is a systems-based approach that attempts to change systems to be more responsive to the diverse or plural populations from the beginning (Johnstone & Edwards, 2020). Both accommodations and accessibility are designed to promote inclusion for participants of internationalization activities.

A frequently cited approach to inclusive internationalization is IaH. IaH has often been portrayed as an accommodation because it allows students to be participants in internationalization if they are unable to participate in mobility-focused internationalization activities (such as international travel). Such accommodation is frequently framed as a better way of including these students in the overall strategy of internationalization. For example, in a critical study of IaH, Frieß and Mucha (2020) cited one reason for the growth of IaH in Europe as an accommodation:

> the majority of students to date lack opportunities to make an exchange visit to another university; despite the Erasmus program being established in the late 1980s, the goal of enabling at least one in ten students to participate in an exchange program inside another European country has not been achieved
>
> (p. 55)

For example, under the banner of IaH, Europe's Social Erasmus program is framing local voluntary experiences into typical mobility narratives as a way of accommodating students with mobility barriers. The program encourages international students and local students to get engaged in volunteering in their local communities. Accommodations, in general, support individuals or populations to access programming without changing the programming itself. Challenges exist for accommodative inclusion because there could be a potentially never-ending list of accommodations that need to be made (see Claeys-Kulik et al., 2019, European Union, 2019), yet accommodations exist because there is also institutional and sectoral difficulty in creating all encompassing programming that allows for equitable and diverse intersectional participation (ACA, 2019). In short, accommodations can enhance inclusion when the parameters of programming exclude.

Accommodations can also enhance inclusion for academic staff. Jons (2011), for example, emphasized the need to make time accommodations for researchers with family obligations. She suggests creating shorter mobility visits for staff with care-giver responsibilities, provided that their impact is not compromised by these shorter mobility periods. Jons (2011) also suggested that institutions target less costly destinations for academics of lower income countries, allowing for individual changes to broad-based internationalization portfolios. Further, Jons suggested opting for online joint teaching initiatives rather than physical mobility to open up international collaborations. Similarly, European Commission launched in 2018, the Erasmus+ Virtual Exchange, establishing technology-enabled intercultural learning opportunities for academic staff with travel constraints (O'Dowd & Beaven, 2019).

Johnstone and Edwards (2020) conducted case studies of six U.S. higher education institutions and found that accommodations were a popular approach to support mobility for students with disabilities in the U.S. and that accommodations or allowances for individual students were framed as inclusion. While accommodations provide a way for a wider range of participants to experience internationalization, it must be emphasized that these often operate in silos with different budgets, accountable to different directors or vice-rectors. Accommodations often require an acknowledgement of intersectional barriers and require cross-sectoral contributions, cross-fertilization, and collaborations across the institution (ACA, 2019; Claeys-Kulik et al., 2019), demonstrating the importance of both representational and participatory dimensions of inclusive internationalization.

In the paragraphs above, IaH was framed as an accommodation because it provides an alternative option to mobility for individual students who are unable to participate in study abroad or other internationalization activities. We argue here, however, that IaH is also a mechanism to change the curricular systems in order to make internationalization accessible to all students. Hence it is also an accessibility approach. In this broader conceptualization, IaH promotes system-wide change for plural students to participate in internationalization. This acknowledges that curriculum and strategy must adapt and adjust so that all stakeholders can meaningfully participate without accommodations. Where accommodations support individuals, the accessibility approach adjusts systems.

In the paragraphs below, we highlight a second participatory dimension to inclusive internationalization – accessibility. For example, Beelen and Jones (2015) define IaH as the purposeful integration of international and intercultural dimensions into the formal and informal curriculum for all students within domestic learning environments. The definition stresses intentional inclusion of international and intercultural aspects into the existing curricula in a purposeful way. This implies that adding or infusing random internationalized elements or elective courses would not be sufficient to provide all students with international competences. It emphasizes the role and impact of IaH for all students in all programs (p. 69).

The focus on all students participating in inclusive internationalization through curricular or programmatic design is a central tenet of accessible, inclusive internationalization. Frieß and Mucha (2020) take the accessible curriculum argument a step further by incorporating belongingness and recognition principles into the design of IaH and renaming it 'transculturality'. The authors explain that:

> The prefix trans (across, beyond, through) emphasizes the crossing of (constructed) boundaries. In a world shaped by movement (migration, globalization, digitalization), cultures are marked by infiltrations and interconnectedness and can no longer be characterized as homogeneous, separated entities. (p. 64).

In this case, Frieß and Mucha frame internationalization in a way that Stein et al. (2016) would consider 'translocal' – one that creates educational accessible spaces that are plural and representationally informed.

Recent themes from an EAIE conference on inclusive internationalization call for conceptualizations of diversity that are comprehensive. European institutions have begun to acknowledge participant complexity and intersectionality and also recognize that accommodation models may isolate and stigmatize individuals or groups. An accessibility focus, therefore, places focus on the deficits of institutions in creating an array of programming for diverse stakeholders. The commitment to connect inclusion and internationalization is apparent in the recent Erasmus+ Programme (2021–2027) which included a significant increase in the budget. The intended budget is designed to expand the access to internationalization of higher education activities and requires national and institutional actors to consider and act upon the issue more profoundly and holistically, rather than a program that considers marginalized populations as an after-thought or as 'special' participants in programs (European Parliament, n.d.). How this will turn out in the real-live institutional contexts will depend on an in-depth understanding of the complexity of the phenomenon by the stakeholders enacting the internationalization agendas.

Johnstone and Edwards' (2020) above-mentioned study identified few programs that focused on shifting the curriculum to benefit all students, but there were case examples of institutions that were attempting to move from accommodations to accessibility approaches in relation to students with disabilities. The study provided a summation of how both accommodations and accessibility can promote inclusive internationalization, and argues that the latter approach requires significantly more institutional commitment and in-depth open conversations of various stakeholders:

> The creation of a culture of accessibility... will require stronger facilitation skills and a design focus on accessibility. Such a focus requires intentional planning between multiple stakeholders. As opportunities for new program options become available, accessibility can be part of the planning from the start. Experts on disability (students themselves and disability services offices), academic content (faculty), and study abroad sites (external partners) can all be part of these conversations. Conversations may be informed by national laws or even international conventions, but at the end of the day are heavily reliant on the agreement of multiple stakeholders to set a tone and approach for programs. Rather than planning programs first and sorting out accommodations on an as-needed basis, the future of inclusion in study abroad (or internationalization in general) may rely on a commitment to accessibility. Institutional models exist for such accessibility planning, but are not as common as programs that are reliant on solely accommodations. A tangible next step in this process is for professional organizations and institutions themselves to learn from models that exist and begin to develop an 'accessibility discourse' (Darcy, 2010) and approach to their programs.
>
> (p. 15)

Although Johnstone and Edwards (2020) focused on one specific population, the construction of inclusive internationalization through both accommodations and accessibility is applicable across multiple stakeholder groups. In this way, scholars who focus on the participatory aspects of internationalization do not necessarily comment on internationalization's theorization, but who participates and how. In order to facilitate such participation through accommodations and accessibility, there are larger linkages to representational dimensions of inclusive internationalization.

Conclusions

In this chapter, we reviewed three dimensions of inclusive internationalization using, as a starting point, the commonly agreed framing of internationalization as a comprehensive process and providing a critical perspective that emphasized the complexities and tensions in inclusive education.

In the first dimension of theoretical inclusive internationalization, we debated the diverse (sometimes contradictory) rationales that underpin the culture and shape of national and institutional approaches to internationalization, highlighting the shortcomings of international education in terms of the perpetuation of neoliberal ideals, competition, disparities, and injustices. We focused on what scholars advocate that inclusive internationalization should be. We identified two key themes of inclusivity: a strategy for anchoring internationalization to the liberal traditions of public service by higher education institutions (De Laquil, 2019) and the concept of inclusiveness as a way of critiquing internationalization itself (Frieß & Mucha, 2020).

The second dimensions, the representational dimensions of inclusive internationalization, related to internationalization leadership and participation. This section provided an insight into who is at the core of the decision-making process and focused on the need for wide engagement and cross-sectoral collaborations. Together with scholars who discuss internationalization representationally (Green, 2019; Hudzik, 2015; Mwangi, 2017), we frame inclusiveness as diverse leadership that drives the agendas of internationalization, whether that be within institutions or between partners in disparate geographies and economic circumstances.

Finally, we reviewed the participatory dimensions, which focus on inclusion *within* the approaches to internationalization programming. Two main ways of achieving inclusiveness in participation are through accommodations to participants that have mobility constraints and to make curricular systems more accessible. The former focuses on individual allowances while the latter is a systemic change approach (Johnstone & Edwards, 2020). We have argued that IaH can enable institutions to incorporate either or both approaches in its internationalization response, and we have emphasized that cross-sectional communication and collaboration are critical.

Readers of this book are most likely interested in the participatory dimensions of inclusive internationalization, but we argue that all three dimensions are interwoven. Without a theoretical or philosophical model of inclusive internationalization, representational leadership that includes a wider number of stakeholders to lead the development and implementation of strategy could be problematic. Further, without plural, representative leadership for internationalization, participation is unlikely to be inclusive.

In this chapter, we have reframed the key scholarship of De Wit and Jones (2018) by conceptualizing three key dimensions of internationalization – philosophical, representational, and participatory. These dimensions are aligned with the calls from De Witt and Jones to: (1) incorporate IaH as essential to Internationalization for All; (2) recognize, value, and utilize classroom diversity, bringing alternative perspectives to study programs – from international students, those returning from mobility experiences, and students from diverse communities in the local population; (3) involve the whole institution in delivering inclusive internationalization; (4) bridge the local and the global in research, education, and service; (5) focus on regional as well as global partnerships to help deliver an inclusive internationalization agenda (de Wit & Jones, 2018, p. 16). The multidimensionality of inclusive internationalization requires constant framing and reframing of its definitional boundaries. Based on this review of its dimensions, we conclude that inclusive internationalization is a collaborative cross-sectional process encompassing plural voices at the institution and an interconnected world. We further contend that the aim of inclusive internationalization is to leverage internationalization to address injustice and enhance interconnectedness to the benefit of its diverse societies and natural world. We invite readers to critique, reframe, and reimagine this definition as the dimensions, boundaries, and participants of internationalization change and shift in the coming decades.

References

Academic Cooperation Association. (2019). *Internationalisation for all? Wider inclusion in the internationalisation of higher education: ACA reflection paper.* Brussels: Author. http://www.aca-secretariat.be/fileadmin/aca_docs/event_presentations/ACA-2019-April_Reflection_Paper_Inclusion.pdf

Ainscow, M., & Miles, S. (2008). Making education for all inclusive: Where next?. *Prospects, 38*(1), 15–34.

Beelen, J., & Jones, E. (2015). Redefining internationalization at home. In A. Curaj, L. Matei, R. Pricopie, J. Salmi, and P. Scott (Eds.) *The European higher education area* (pp. 59–72). Springer: Cham, Switzerland.

Brandenburg, U., & De Wit, H. (2015). The end of internationalization. *International Higher Education,* (62).

Brooks, R. (2019). Diversity and European higher education students: National perspectives in a global age. In L. E. Rumbley (Ed.), *Encompassing all voices* (pp. 11–14). Amsterdam, The Netherlands: European Association for International Education.

Carlson, J. (2016). Against being inclusive. *Liberal Education, 101/102 (4/1).* https://www.aacu.org/liberaleducation/2015-2016/fall-winter/carlson

Claeys-Kulik, A., & Estermann, T. (2015). DEFINE thematic report: Performance-based funding of universities in Europe. Brussels, Belgium: European University Association. https://eua.eu/downloads/publications/define%20thematic%20report%20performance-based%20funding%20of%20universities%20in%20europe.pdf

Clayes-Kulik, A. L., Jorgenson, T. E., & Stober, H. (2019). *Diversity, equity, and inclusion in European higher education institutions: Results from the INVITED project.* Brussels, Belgium: European University Network.

Darcy, S. (2010). Inherent complexity: Disability, accessible tourism and accommodation information preferences. *Tourism Management, 31*, 816–826.

de Wit, H., & Jones, E. (2018). Inclusive internationalization: Improving access and equity. *International Higher Education, 94*(16–18).

DeLaquil, T. (2019). Inclusive internationalization as innovative internationalization. Purpose-driven higher education against inequity in society. In R. Schendel, H. de Wit, & T. DeLaquil (Eds.), *Inclusive and innovative internationalization of higher education: Proceedings of WES-CIHE Summer Institute* (pp. 5–8). Boston, MA: Boston College.

European Association for International Education. (2019a). *The EAIE barometer: Internationalization in Europe: Money Matters.* Amsterdam, The Netherlands.

European Association for International Education. (2019b). *The EAIE barometer 2019: Signposts of success.* Amsterdam, The Netherlands: Author.

European Commission. (n.d.). *The European principle of social rights in 20 principles.* Brussels, Belgium: Author. https://ec.europa.eu/commission/priorities/deeper-and-fairer-economic-and-monetary-union/european-pillar-social-rights/european-pillar-social-rights-20-principles_en

European Parliament. (n.d.). *Erasmus+ 2021–2027: More people to experience learning exchanges in Europe.* https://www.europarl.europa.eu/news/en/press-room/20190321IPR32121/erasmus-2021-2027-more-people-to-experience-learning-exchanges-in-europe

European Union. (2019). *Erasmus plus mobility guide.* Brussels, Belgium: Author. https://ec.europa.eu/programmes/erasmus-plus/sites/erasmusplus2/files/erasmus-plus-programme-guide-2019_en_1.pdf

Freysinger, R. C. (1993). Towards total internationalisation: Comprehensive institutional reform and global studies—The case of Bradford College'. *The Journal of General Education, 42(3)*, 177–190.

Frieß, W., & Mucha, A. (2020). International students as learning space inventory? On the functional production of difference in the context of the university strategy Internationalization at Home: A post-structural analysis. In W. Frieß, A. Mucha, & D. Rastetter (2020), *Diversity management und siene kontexte: Celebrate diversity?!* (pp. 55–68). Opalden, Germany: Verlag Barbara Burdich.

Green, W. (2019). Engaging students in international education: Rethinking students engagement in a globalized world. *Journal of Studies in International Education, 23*(1), 3–9.

Hickey, S., Sen, K., & Bukenya, B. (2015). *The politics of inclusive development: Interrogating the evidence.* Oxford: Oxford University Press.

Hudzik, J. K. (2011). *Comprehensive internationalization: From concept to action.* Washington, DC: NAFSA: Association of International Educators.

Hudzik, J. K. (2015). Integrating institutional policies and leadership for 21st century internationalization. *International Higher Education*, (83), 5–7.

Johnstone, C. (2014). Five (more) reasons why international and diversity offices should collaborate in universities. *Association of International Education Administrators Issue Brief.* https://www.aieaworld.org/assets/docs/Issue_Briefs/issue%20brief-johnstone%202014%20november%205.pdf

Johnstone, C., & Edwards, P. (2020). Accommodations, accessibility, and culture: Increasing access to study abroad for students with disabilities. *Journal of Studies in International Education*, 24(4), 424–439.

Jons, H. (2011). Transnational academic mobility and gender. *Globalisation, Societies and Education, 9*(2), 183–209. https://www.researchgate.net/publication/233303932_Transnational_academic_mobility_and_gender

Kendi, I. X. (2019). *How to be an anti-racist.* New York, NY: Random House.

Knight, J. (2004). Internationalization remodeled: Definition, approaches, and rationales. *Journal of studies in international education, 8*(1), 5–31.

Lee, A. & Williams, R. (2017). *Engaging dissonance: Developing mindful global citizenship in higher education.* Bingley, UK: Emerald.

Lehikoinen, A. (2019). Encompassing all voices: Finland's new challenges and opportunities. In L. E. Rumbley (Ed.), *Encompassing all voices* (pp. 15–19). Amsterdam, The Netherlands: European Association for International Education.

Marinoni, G., & de Wit, H. (2019). Is Strategic Internationalization a Reality? *International Higher Education*, (98), 12–13.

Mor Barak, M. E., Cherin, D. A., & Berkman, S. (1998). Organizational and personal dimensions in diversity climate: Ethnic and gender differences in employee perceptions. *The Journal of Applied Behavioral Science, 34*(1), 82–104.

Mwangi, C. A. G. (2017). Partner positioning: Examining international higher education partnerships through a mutuality lens. *The Review of Higher Education, 41*(1), 33–60.

NAFSA. (2016). *Bringing global diversity to U.S. campuses - An economic and national security imperative.* NAFSA International Student Economic Value Tool. http://www.nafsa.org/Policy_and_Advocacy/Policy_Resources/Policy_Recommendations/Bringing_Global_Diversity_to_U_S__Campuses_An_Economic_and_National_Security_Imperative/

O'Dowd, R., & Beaven, A. (2019). Examining the impact of virtual exchange. *FORUM: The EAIE Member Magazine.* Winter, 16.

Patel, F., & Lynch, H. (2013). Glocalization as an alternative to internationalization in higher education: Embedding positive glocal learning perspectives. *International Journal of Teaching and Learning in Higher Education, 25*(2), 223–230.

Stein, S., Andreotti, V., Bruce, J., & Suša, R. (2016). Towards different conversations about the internationalization of higher education. *Comparative and International Education/Éducation comparée et internationale, 45*(1), 2.

Streitwieser, B., Loo, B., Ohorodnik, M., & Jeong, J. (2019). Access for refugees into higher education: A review of interventions in North America and Europe. *Journal of Studies in International Education, 23*(4), 473–496.

10 Creating a Campus Global Learning Ecosystem by Employing Internationalization at Home Strategies

Melissa K. Mace

Introduction

Not all students who desire a study abroad experience have the ability to do so. In fact, there are documented reasons why many students restrict studies to their home campus. Financial limitations, stringent programs of study that significantly restrict time and access to study abroad opportunities, and fear of traveling abroad are all possible barriers (Anderson & Lawton, 2011; Soria & Troisi, 2014).

Therefore, a case can be made for building a robust global learning ecosystem on campus to bridge the global competencies gap between students who study abroad and those who do not. Even though many colleges and universities tout graduates who are prepared for personal and professional lives within a global context, evidence is to the contrary. Study abroad has long been considered the most effective educational tool for elevating the global competencies of college-going and college-graduating students. Is it, however? According to the most recent Open Doors (http://iie.org/opendoors) data, one in ten undergraduate students will participate in a study abroad experience before graduating, leaving 90% of students with global education deficits. In addition, not all who study abroad gain those essential competencies (Anderson & Lawton, 2011) implied on resumes.

But what exactly are those competencies? Soria and Troisi (2014) define the global, international, and intercultural competencies (GII) "to include knowledge about several dimensions of global and international cultures; appreciation of cultural, racial, and ethnic diversity; understanding of the complexities of issues in a global context; and comfort in working with people from other cultures" (p. 262). Two of the most widely utilized tools for measuring students' development of competencies are the Intercultural Development Inventory (IDI) (https://idiinventory.com/) and the Global Perspective Inventory (GPI) (http://www.gpi.hs.iastate.edu/). The IDI places students along a continuum of intercultural development that moves from denial, polarization, minimization, acceptance, and adaptation, while the GPI measures knowing, knowledge, identity, affect, social responsibility, social interactions, community, and intercultural wonderment depending on which GPI assessment form is utilized. Each tool has its merits and offers institutions insights into how to develop, coordinate, and employ curricular and co-curricular global education experiences for all students.

Literature Review

Internationalization at Home (IaH) is an umbrella term encompassing those global education experiences that occur on campus and in the home country. An updated definition by Beelen and Jones (2015) states "Internationalization at Home is the purposeful integration of international and intercultural dimensions into the formal and informal curriculum for all students within the domestic learning environments" (p. 69); in other words, creating a global learning ecosystem on campus.

Developing a global learning ecosystem that ensures more students graduate with the necessary skill sets to thrive in a global market requires focused energy on behalf of the university, which may be why so few institutions have engaged in such an arduous undertaking. As noted in the definition above and explored in this chapter, there is both a curricular and co-curricular dimension to IaH. Mace and Pearl (2019) developed and validated the *Institutional Assessment Rubric on Comprehensive Internationalization in Higher Education* (IARCIHE), a tool to assess institution-wide internationalization. The six major areas of the rubric focus primarily on IaH priorities, consisting of (1) articulated institutional commitment, (2) administrative leadership, structure, and staffing, (3) curriculum, co-curriculum, and learning outcomes, (4) faculty policies and practices, (5) student mobility, and (6) collaboration and partnerships (ACE, 2017; Mace & Pearl, 2019). Jones (2013) determined that there are ten essential components in educating globally competent graduates:

> (1) rationale and strategy for internationalization, (2) governance, leadership and management, (3) internationalization of the formal curriculum for all students, (4) international campus culture and informal curriculum, (5) student diversity, (6) guidance and support for the students outside the classroom, (7) staff development, recognition and reward – all staff, (8) broad and deep international partnerships, (9) resources [that] follow strategy, and 10)monitoring, reflection, evaluation and review
>
> (p. 166)

Soria and Troisi (2014) conducted a large-scale quantitative study with a response rate of 38.1% or 81,135. One purpose of the study was to determine how students who participate in IaH activities on campus including in the classroom, co-curricular activities, and interaction with international students compare to students who study abroad with respect to global competencies. Their findings suggest that IaH efforts can be successful at bridging the divide between students who study abroad and students who do not. However, certain types of activities are more successful than others depending on if the institution's focus is international competencies or intercultural competencies. One finding offered by the researchers regarding international versus intercultural students who followed global media was positively associated with the international competencies but negatively associated with intercultural competencies. Thus, institutional leaders must have a firm grasp on the competencies and how they are instilled.

Administration and the Big Picture

Institution senior administrators determine the global education drivers (mission, vision, strategic plan) for how the campus goes about developing graduates with global competencies. The clearer the articulated expectations, the better understanding the campus community has regarding roles and responsibilities (Mace & Pearl, 2019). The challenge, however, has not been in setting goals around internationalization and global education outcomes; it has been in the implementation of those strategic plans (Childress, 2009; Mace & Pearl, 2019). Disparate to-do lists (Hudzik, 2011) have been the norm, with few institutions able to achieve the goal of global competencies outcomes for graduating students. Likely because of what Childress' 2009 study determined; high level leaders, such as college and university presidents, are essential in the development of internationalization plans.

According to the IARCIHE tool (Mace & Pearl, 2019), institutions with sustained internationalization frameworks, necessary for developing the GII competencies, would likely possess some or all of the following: a mission or vision statement articulating global education as a priority; a strategic plan that references global education or internationalization and requires outcomes; a university-wide committee or task force on global education; appropriate budget allocations; and assessment mechanisms. In addition, an institutional leadership and staffing structure that optimizes coordination and oversight would be in place and led by a senior internationalization officer (SIO) (ACE, 2017; Mace & Pearl, 2019).

Global education structure and staffing are as varied as the number of campuses engaged with any form of internationalization ranging from the most basic extra duty assigned to staff with few international students to the more complex global education centers on campuses serving thousands of students and scholars. ACE's (2017) study noticed an increasing trend toward the leadership of internationalization efforts through a single office and administrator(s). While a single office and administratively led efforts may be key in progressing internationalization, Choi, Khamalah, Kim, and Burg's (2014) study is cautionary regarding the need to be inclusive of faculty voices. They conducted a single-campus case study around "internationalization activities, rationale, processes and challenges" (p. 7) of a Midwest regional university through the faculty lens. Their goal was to examine how faculty members perceived their role in the campus internationalization process. Using a 25-question survey with both closed and open-ended questions, they surveyed 450 faculty members, associate teaching staff, administrators, and professional staff, of which 139 responded. Over 75% of the respondents felt that internationalization was either important or very important in educating students but faculty members were more likely to engage if they had a connection in another country. The survey results revealed an important result that personal or professional affiliations abroad is key to faculty engagement in internationalization. Based on their research, Choi et al. (2014) also drew the conclusion that bringing faculty and staff together in unison on how and why internationalization is accomplished is imperative to overall institutionalization of CI.

Faculty and the Classroom

Internationalization of the Curriculum has been defined by Leask (2009) as "the incorporation of an international and intercultural dimension into the content of the curriculum as well as the teaching and learning arrangements and support services of a program of study" (p. 209). This could also be thought of as the formal learning content outlined on the syllabus as well as the classroom dynamics, student and faculty demographics, and how they are intertwined to provide a more global learning environment. However, there are many challenges around working with faculty to internationalize the curriculum.

One such challenge, around widespread faculty inclusion in overarching comprehensive internationalization efforts, exists because institutions do not adequately prepare faculty for internationalization of the classroom, curriculum, and campus. The American Council on Education (2017) found that while professional development opportunities are on the rise with respect to internationalization, training faculty is a low priority. A lack of personal experiences and exposure to international perspectives may cause hesitation or even a negative disposition toward creating a more globally focused course (Childress, 2018). Mertova and Green (2010) conducted a qualitative case study including 115 interviews with senior academic faculty leaders including deans, chairs, and research directors. Their analysis of the data unveiled a pervasive lack of clarity about the institution's expectancies for how the curriculum would be internationalized. In a subsequent study, Green and Mertova (2016) defined two orientations of faculty perceptions when considering internationalization of the curriculum, transformalist and transnationalism, and found that faculty tended to gravitate toward one or the other end of the spectrum, with few situated along the spectrum. The transformalist tended to view pedagogy informed by the context of globalization within higher education while the transaction list tended to view internationalization as an economic endeavor. Finally, Green and Mertova (2016) conducted a single-campus qualitative study involving faculty from a wide range of disciplines. For this particular research, they focused only on the subset of faculty who scored the lowest when it came to understanding internationalization and the impact it had on their course content and their teaching. What they found was that how faculty members comprehend and apply the concept of internationalization to the curriculum is shaped by their underlying belief structure of their roles and responsibilities as educators.

Korhonen and Weil (2015) conducted a study to assess faculty perceptions of themselves, self-conception, with regard to internationalization. In this qualitative, narrative role-playing method of research, Korhonen and Weil (2015) sampled doctoral and post-doctoral university faculty members from Finland, Switzerland, and Germany. Their research unmasked the ways faculty members made sense of themselves as professors in an internationalizing environment. Korhonen and Weil (2015) identified five themes from the data collected: (1) "*teachership*" (p. 204) or the development of faculty personally and in their pedagogy; (2) "*directing values*" (p. 205) or faculty members' perceptions of international students and scholars; (3) "*diversified teaching and learning environment*" (p. 205); (4) "*curriculum enhancement*" (p. 205) or incorporating internationalization into the curriculum; and (5) "*organisation and structure*" (p. 205) or institutional support of internationalization. When institutional leaders seek to internationalize the university, the impact of the faculty member and classroom is not always given its just consideration. Korhonen and Weil suggest (2015) broader consideration of the effects of such decisions and support faculty appropriately with quality faculty development.

In addition to providing important training to faculty members, recruiting and retaining international faculty members is an important part of internationalizing the campus environment, but one that is frequently discounted. Philipsen (2010) analyzed data pulled from a 2008 qualitative research study on female faculty in the United States she conducted on the challenges of being female and faculty (Philipsen, 2008) and focused on data collected on a sub-group of participants: international faculty working on campuses across institution types in the United States. Philipsen (2010) derived her study from her earlier larger study which consisted of interviews and sought to gain understanding of female faculty experiences. Of the original 44 female faculty members, eight were immigrant scholars, and they were the focus of Philipsen's (2010) research. While this subset of women shared common ground with their American colleagues, they also faced special challenges that should not go overlooked by administrators. Isolation, marginalization, legal challenges, and sacrifice are notable among Philipsen's findings. As important, however, was their strength and perseverance that made them such good scholars and mentors to international students.

While international faculty members may bring a different perspective to the classroom, they can also bring unique challenges. Ewy, Geringer, and Taylor (2015) conducted a quantitative study of undergraduate business students at a large U.S. Western university on their perceptions and attitudes toward foreign-accented faculty. The survey found that business students with greater international exposure, through traveling or living abroad, were less likely to take issue with any obstacles around communicating with faculty members with a native language other than English. In addition, and equally important, is the finding that foreign-accented faculty members who made a conscious effort to transcend language barriers were perceived more favorably.

Aktas, Pitts, Richards, and Silova (2017) conducted a consensual qualitative research analysis of data collected through an inductive and analytical approach by examining the mission statements and curricula of global citizenship programs of 24 universities where a recognition or credential of some fashion was noted on the student academic transcript. The researchers' goal was to ascertain how universities institutionalize global citizenship in their curricula. Aktas et al. (2017) gleaned that while there were major differences between global citizenship programs, four common characteristics existed: "requirements for international travel, language proficiency, engagement/service learning, and curriculum content area(s)" (p. 71). Their research demonstrated that comprehensive internationalization, with the ultimate goal of educating global citizens, must involve faculty.

Global collaborations and partnerships can take many forms between institutions of higher education and can be of great benefit to institutional members of both partners when done well. Bermingham and Ryan (2016) considered how global partnerships through student and faculty exchanges, scholarly research, and participation in international conferences are all important means of engaging the campus community on the global stage and how they can be transformative. In their single-case qualitative analysis of one community college, they shared campus stories of faculty development that occurred through scholarly exchange and contended that institutional priorities can impact faculty development. One outcome of faculty participation in the partnerships was an increased understanding of how ingrained mainstream national perspectives were in their curriculum. This new understanding pushed faculty to expand their classroom teaching to include global realities. Another outcome was the Center for Teaching and Learning developed a program to engage faculty to enhance cultural competencies in their curricula. In addition, these formal partnerships created opportunities for competing successfully for funding that may not have occurred without such robust global relationships.

Co-Curricular

International student enrollment is often seen as the path of least resistance to introducing global differences to campus. There are many benefits to exposing domestic students to students from around the world, especially as institutions strive to prepare graduates to enter a more global workforce; however, there are also challenges. Lee (2008) conducted research on college access for international students utilizing a case study-mixed methodology in which 501 international students responded to the initial 29-item survey, and 24 undergraduate and graduate students from the original 501 participated in a follow-up interview. Understanding international students' decision-making process is of value, especially when relying on this category of student population to help fulfill strategic comprehensive internationalization goals. Quantitative results included institution selection based on reputation, work study/graduate assistantships, and scholarships to name a few. The qualitative analysis, however, provided a deeper dive into motivations. For example, while reputation was high on the list of motivators, the qualitative data demonstrated that students selected the institution without first visiting campus or the region. Lee (2008) observed one particular student of color doubting her institutional choice as she had not anticipated experiencing discrimination. Other study participants noted feeling lonely, experiencing frustration with academic programs, and struggling to make connections.

Another important consideration would be the education experiences of international students. Glass (2012) posed two interesting research questions around such in a nation-wide quantitative study of over 29,000 students attending 55 U.S. colleges and universities that administered the Global Perspectives Inventory (GPI). First, he sought to discover the types of educational experiences linked with international student learning and development and the perception of the campus in a positive light. Second, he wanted to see if there were differences within international subgroups around the educational experiences. Glass (2012) considered whether there were "greater degrees of (a) thinking with complexity, taking into account multiple perspectives; (b) forming a unique sense of self that is value-based and authentic; and (c) relating to others with respect and openness" (p. 229). His findings indicated international students who "participate in leadership programs, community service, campus-organized diversity discussions, interact with people from diverse cultural backgrounds, and take courses with materials on race and ethnicity report greater levels of learning and development" (p. 246).

Glass's findings are consistent with what Soria and Troisi (2014) discovered in their research on IaH alternatives to study abroad. Their findings of greater interaction with international students in more socially focused settings like clubs and organizations, as well as the classroom setting, is much more likely to produce globally minded students versus globally faculty-led research or globally focused courses (i.e., international business). Soria and Troisi (2014) also found that global citizenship programs in which students earn a minor or certificate are less likely to produce globally competent individuals than one might think.

Well-framed alternative spring break excursions offer the opportunity for students to experience personal growth (Beatty, Meadows, SwamiNathan, & Mulvihill, 2016) that may include GII competencies should alternative spring break destinations within the homeland of the university serve migrant or first-generation immigrants, participants consisting of both domestic and international students, include social opportunities, group problem solving, and shared experiences. In 2006, Poole and Davis published a mixed-method study of graduate and undergraduate social work students from two universities. The researchers considered the idea of concept mapping as a way to measure learning outcomes of the students participating in a study abroad experience in Mexico that could be easily emulated by IaH alternative spring break co-curricular experiences. They found that concept mapping was a useful mechanism for both positing and measuring outcomes as it allowed for evaluation from beginning to end. The researchers unmasked the need to be intentional about global competency outcomes from the outset.

Mace and Pearl's (2019) research on comprehensive internationalization found that frequent co-curricular global education activities coordinated between the different offices and academic units were indicative of campuses with sustained internationalization and global education efforts. And Soria and Troisi's (2014) research notes the importance of social opportunities between domestic and international students.

Recommendations

While there is not a robust inventory of research around IaH curricular and co-curricular programs and activities, there is such that we can infer some "best practices" and make recommendations to institutional leaders based on the research that is available:

1 *Set and share the big picture of what global competencies graduates of your institution should possess.* Competencies would ideally come from the institution's president and/or chief academic officer and shared through a variety of possible mechanisms including the institution's mission, vision, or strategic plan.
2 *Appoint a task force/global education (or internationalization) committee.* A task force or committee that represents a wide swath of campus stakeholders who can consider the multiple facets of global education in the context of the institution's commitment.

    a *Conduct an assessment of internationalization efforts* using the IARCIHE to establish a baseline and understand the institution's global education landscape. Doing so will provide a clearer picture of where connections can be made to develop global education opportunities.
    b *SWOT analysis.* Based on the IARCIHE baseline assessment, identify the campus's strengths, weaknesses, opportunities, and threats.
    c *Develop a strategic internationalization/global education plan.* Consider every facet of the campus community from food service to programs of study and be strategic with short and long-term goals.

3 *Align resources appropriately to goals.* Resources come in different forms: (1) operating budget, (2) personnel, and (3) physical space. Think through what can be reimagined without adding costs if an additional budget allocation is not available immediately.
4 *Educate faculty.* Work with faculty senates, deans, department heads, and individual faculty members to align the education outcomes for courses, programs of study, and degrees with the university's big picture goals. To bring faculty along, offer workshops, conference attendances, faculty

fellows programs, and research/publishing opportunities. Take the time to understand faculty pressures and align global education goals to faculty promotion and tenure requirements.

5 *Educate staff.* As important as educating faculty, educating staff – all staff – on why global education is important and what it might look like in each area of the campus. It is critical to understand that everyone has a role to play in successful global education endeavors. Do department policies and procedures align with global education goals?

6 *Design co-curricular programs with intention and measure the outcomes.* Use backward design, just like faculty, to develop co-curricular activities and programs with outcomes that match the strategic global education plan.

7 *Assess, assess, assess!* Utilize freshman success seminar courses to launch GII competency goals. Most colleges and universities now employ a freshman seminar course to help launch students' successfully and increase the likelihood of retention. A course in which every freshman student is enrolled is also ideal for administering an assessment such as the GPI or IDI. In addition, exit survey in the final semester of a student's undergraduate career is a good option for collecting data to determine if growth in GII competencies occurred. The IARCIHE tool should be revisited annually to see if and how the campus has progressed on global education measures.

Discussion and Conclusion

The research positively links the development of global competencies to what occurs in the classroom, supplemented by meaningful co-curricular activities that help students engage across differences in a more social setting. The challenges to graduating a higher percentage of students with GII competencies rely heavily on the institution's top leader: the president. The institution's lead administrator conveys the importance, or lack of importance, based on the message s/he communicates to the campus community. The importance will likely reveal itself in mission or vision plans, strategic plans, budgets, and structure.

The appointment of an SIO and task force to develop a campus-wide global education or internationalization plan is an essential step in the process. Prior to developing the plan, the task force should conduct a baseline assessment of disparate academic and co-curricular activities occurring across campus to better understand the landscape before making recommendations for action. It goes without saying that the task force members should be representative of the many campus stakeholders with the mandate to affect change.

It is also clear that faculty development around GII competencies and how they are infused into the curriculum in a manner that does not disrupt curricula integrity are critical. SIOs who work in tandem with chief academic officers and centers for teaching and learning to offer workshops and develop robust global education faculty fellows programs are more likely to see widespread global education adoption in the curricular realm with early adopters transitioning into leaders among their faculty peers.

While the research cited in this chapter did not affirm the value of global education certificate programs, they should not be discounted. The underlying question may very well be why they were not successful in developing GII competencies. The answer may be in the intentionality of the design and the failure to prioritize the desired outcomes when developing the program. Consider that speakers' series, workshops, social activities, and curricular components are key components to successful competency development and make sure that they are an integral part of the program.

Additionally, the importance of assessment cannot be overstated. Assessment of student development through administration of the GPI of IDI surveys and assessment of the institution with the IARCIHE tool are essential in moving the campus toward graduating students with GII competencies. Institutions willing to follow the above recommendations and do the hard work of building a robust global learning ecosystem are more likely to produce graduates truly prepared to function as citizens in an ever-evolving global society.

References

Aktas, F., Pitts, K., Richards, J. C., & Silova, I. (2017). Institutionalizing global citizenship: A critical analysis of higher education programs and curricula. *Journal of Studies in International Education, 21*(1), 65–80. doi:10.1177/1028315316669815

American Council on Education. (2017). *Mapping internationalization in U.S. campuses*. Washington, DC: Author.

Anderson, P. H., & Lawton, L. (2011). Intercultural development: Study abroad vs. on-campus study. *Frontiers: The Interdisciplinary Journal of Study Abroad, 21*, 86–108. https://eric.ed.gov/contentdelivery/servlet/ERICServlet?accno=EJ991044

Beatty, S. H., Meadows, K. N., SwamiNathan, R., & Mulvihill, C. (2016). The effects of an alternative spring break program on student development. *Journal of Higher Education Outreach & Engagement, 20*(3), 90–118. https://eric.ed.gov/contentdelivery/servlet/ERICServlet?accno=EJ1117707

Beelen, J., & Jones, E. (2015). Redefining internationalization at home. In A. Curaj, L. Matei, R. Precopie, J. Salmi, & P. Scott (Eds.), *The European higher education area: Between critical reflections and future policies* (pp. 59–72). Cham, Switzerland: Springer.

Bermingham, J., & Ryan, M. (2013). Transforming international education through institutional capacity building. *New Directions for Community Colleges, 16*(1), 55–70. doi:10.1002/cc.20048

Childress, L. K. (2009). Internationalization plans for higher education institutions. *Journal of Studies in International Education, 13*(3), 289–309. doi:10.1177/1028315308329804

Childress, L. K. (2018). *The twenty-first century university: Developing faculty engagement in internationalization*. New York, NY: Peter Lang Publishing.

Choi, S., Khamalah, J. N., Kim, M. H., & Burg, J. E. (2014). Internationalization of a regional campus: Faculty perspectives. *International Education, 42*(2), 7–24.

Ewy, A., Geringer, S. D., & Taylor, J. (2015). Perceptions of university business students in relation to foreign-accented faculty. *International Journal of Education Research, 10*(2), 54–65.

Glass, C. R. (2012). Educational experiences associated with international students' learning, development, and positive perceptions of campus climate. *Journal of Studies in International Education, 16*(3), 228–251. doi:10.1177/1028315311426783

Global Perspectives Inventory. (2019). Three dimensions of GPI. https://www.gpi.hs.iastate.edu/dimensions.php

Green, W., & Mertova, P. (2016). Transformalists and transactionists: Towards a more comprehensive understanding of academics' engagement with 'internationalization of the curriculum.' *Research in Comparative & International Education, 11*(3), 229–246. doi:10.1177/1745499916662372

Hudzik, J. K. (2011). *Comprehensive internationalization: From concept to action.* Washington, DC: NAFSA: Association of International Educators. https://www.nafsa.org/professional-resources

Institute of International Education. (2019). Report on international educational exchange. U.S. Department of State. Washington, DC: Institute of International Education. http://iie.org/opendoors; https://p.widencdn.net/5i0s78/OD19_graphics_handout-2019

Intercultural Development Inventory. (2019). The roadmap to intercultural competence using the IDI. https://idiinventory.com/

Jones, E. (2013). The global reach of universities: Leading and engaging academic and support staff in the internationalization of higher education. In R. Sugden, M. Valania, & J. R. Wilson (Eds.), *Leadership and cooperation in academia: Reflecting on the roles and responsibilities of university faculty and management* (pp. 161–183). Cheltenham, UK: Edward Elgar.

Korhonen, V., & Weil, M. (2015). The internationalization of higher education: Perspectives on self-conceptions in teaching. *Journal of Research in International Education, 14*(3), 198–212. doi:10.1177/1475240915615447

Leask, B. (2009). Using formal and informal curricula to improve interactions between home and international students. *Journal of Studies in International Education, 13*(2), 205–221. doi:10.1177/1028315308329786

Lee, J. (2008). Beyond borders: International student pathways to the United States. *Journal of Studies in International Education, 12*(3), 308–327. doi:10.1177/1028315307299418

Mace, M. K., & Pearl, D. (2019). Rubric development and validation for assessing comprehensive internationalization in higher education. *Journal of Studies in International Education*. OnlineFirst. doi.org/10.1177/10283153198657790

Mertova, P., & Green, W. (2010). Internationalising teaching and learning: Perspectives and issues voiced by senior academics at one Australian university. In F. Fallon (Ed.), *Conference proceedings of the 21st ISANA international education conference, engaging the wider community*, Melbourne, paper 37. August 13, 2017. http://isana.proceedings.com.au/docs/2010/paper_mertova.pdf

Philipsen, M. I. (2008). *Challenges of the faculty career for women: Success and sacrifice.* San Francisco, CA: Jossey-Bass.

Philipsen, M. I. (2010). Female international scholars: "I feel many times I live between the cracks." *International Education, 39*(2). http://trace.tennessee.edu/internationaleducation/vol39/iss2/5

Poole, D. L., & Davis, T. S. (2006). Concept mapping to measure outcomes in study abroad programs. *Social Work Education, 25*(1), 61–77.

Soria, K. M., & Troisi, J. (2014). Internationalization at home alternatives to study abroad: Implications for students' development of global, international, and intercultural competencies. *Journal of Studies in International Education, 18*(3), 261–280. doi:10.1177/1028315313496572

11 Studying Abroad While Staying at Home in Australia

Diverse Intercultural Learning and Teaching through Partnerships

Dawn Joseph and Richard Johnson

Setting the Scene

Study abroad programs and internationalization in higher education institutes are not a new phenomenon. While internationalizing may be considered strategic by universities, there is no clear blueprint about what drives internationalizing (de Wit, 2019). Jones and de Wit (2012) argue that we can learn from western and non-western environments to fully understand how best internationalizing benefits students, universities and employers rather than a few. In the main, internationalizing is associated with experiences of international students studying overseas (Altbach & Knight, 2007; de Wit, 2020). Study abroad programs generally attract a small subset of elite and privileged students and faculty members rather than meeting "global and intercultural outcomes for all" (de Wit, 2019, p. 13). Study abroad programs and internationalizing are about providing global and cross-cultural viewpoints, "to better students' lives as a result of their participation in culturally diverse experiences" (Jenny, Chung, Rademaker, & Almond, 2017, p. 458).

Recruitment agents play a key role in attracting international students, mainland China being the highest source of overseas students (Bodycott, 2009). Much has been written about internationalization and international students (Barton, Hartwig, Joseph, & Podorova, 2017; Blackmore et al., 2014; Knight, 2004; Liyanage & Nima, 2016; Postiglione & Altbach, 2013) and study abroad programs (Dockrill, Rahatzad, & Phillion, 2015; He, Lundgren, & Pynes, 2017; Medina, Hathaway, & Pilonieta, 2015; Shiveley & Misco, 2015). Many international students undertake study programs for a variety of reasons, for example, to experience life and study in a new country, to gain new experiences and interactions, to improve job opportunities, to enhance their personal development, to advance their status and to gain permanent residency visas (Barton & Hartwig, 2017; Jenny & Jenny, 2016; Salisbury, Umbach, Pausen, & Pascarella, 2009; Thirolf, 2014). In addition, their study programs are met with challenges such as a lack of finance, family support, language and cultural barriers (Barton & Hartwig, 2017; Joseph & Rouse,

2019; Khawaja & Dempsey, 2008). The study abroad programs seldom cater for students with disabilities (Link, 2016) and are often not accessible and inclusive for all students (de Wit, 2019).

The authors Dawn (author one) at Deakin University and Richard (author two) at RMIT University are academics working within initial teacher education (ITE) programs at two different universities in Melbourne (Australia). In an effort to contribute to an equitable pathway to internationalization, we recognize the need and importance for our students to have equal opportunities of 'internationalizing the curriculum at home' (IaH). We take into consideration the diverse economic circumstances of our students addressing the exclusive nature of 'pay your own study abroad' with a more inclusive prospect for students and staff. We do so within the Bachelor of Education (Primary) (BEd) program and within our teaching units (subjects). Dawn teaches in music education and Richard in education studies. We offer our students an experiential learning environment that takes them out of their comfort zones (Jones, 2013). Within this environment, they encounter intercultural and international teaching and learning experiences (Leask, 2009; Thomson, 2014). Our students engage in what we refer to as a blended learning environment that includes face-to-face and technology-mediated experiences such as Skype, computer-assisted learning, virtual and web-based learning (Anderson & Elloumi, 2004; Bliuc, Goodyear, & Ellis, 2007; Helm & Guth, 2010).

Dawn draws on student comments on building collaborative partnerships with academics, teachers and performing artists from Australia, Spain, South Africa, Sri Lanka and New Zealand. Richard draws on student comments from the eTutor project where his ITE students tutored school students in Asia. IaH offers our students the chance to increase their cross-cultural knowledge, skills and understandings with the view of having respectful intercultural engagement and dialogue with people outside of their daily surroundings.

We argue that by providing an alternative option of IaH at our respective workplaces is no cost to the university or to the student. We see this option as a fair, equitable and accessible opportunity for our students. According to Leask, Jones and de Wit (2018), there are isolated examples of good practice of IaH that are not exclusive and elitist. Hence, our examples contribute to the broad knowledge base regarding IaH as an alternative to study abroad. Our alternative is not linked to a compulsory placement (practicum). Rather, we explore pedagogies and experiences as a way to IaH within our teaching units. Dawn, by teaching multicultural music with local and international musicians, academics and culture bearers, and Richard, by working with international academics and school students in Asia.

For this chapter, through our reflections, interviews and questionnaires, we discuss benefits and challenges that emerged as overarching themes by exploring partnerships as a form of IaH. In this way, all benefit, "not just individuals who gain study abroad experience" (Jackson, 2018, p. 133). We argue that the experiences foster effective, inclusive and equitable ways to IaH. It also promotes intercultural and international experiences that support short-term and sustained internationalized curriculum. As we prepare our ITE students for future classrooms, we anticipate that the international learning experience may change attitudes and stereotype thinking to advance social change in educational settings and the wider community (Baxter, 2018).

What Does the Literature Say?

Internationalization is broadly defined as "the process of integrating an international, intercultural or global dimension into the purpose, functions or delivery of post-secondary education" (Knight, 2003, p. 3). Many articles written on internationalization focus on the institutional aspects (enhancing the status of the institute through quality programs and league tables). Academics have argued that there is little research on internationalization in Australia in relation to curriculum or pedagogy despite Knight's widely based notion of internationalization (Lee, 2005; Sanderson, 2011). Knight focuses "on organisational approaches to internationalisation and does not attempt to instruct at the level of, for example, a university teacher" (Sanderson, 2011, p. 663). Eisenchlas and Trevaskes (2003, p. 89) point out that Knight's (1997) notion of internationalization

> does not provide concrete examples of how educators, focusing on interculturality, implement the internationalisation of the curriculum. It does not specify learning aims. It gives no suggestion to the kind of learning tools that might be involved in specific programs. It ignores the importance of communication as crucial to the process of internationalisation, particularly in relation to student interactions.

In light of the above, our IaH promoted interculturality, engaged students in dialogue that fostered mutual respect and understanding as they came into contact with cultural others (Rozbicki, 2015). Interculturality as pedagogy is complex, and it considers a range of diversities, societies and cultures (Dietz, 2009). We agree with Harman (2005, p. 131) that "there is almost a complete absence of material on the active involvement of academics in internationalization, their perceptions of other cultures and people, [and] the value they place on internationalization".

In preparing curriculum, academics need to consider the multicultural and intercultural capabilities of students in relation to engaging other cultures and their different value systems (Clifford, 2009; Joseph & Johnson, 2019). Harman (2005, p. 141) finds working with international staff offers Australian staff "a unique opportunity for collaborative work and collaborative curriculum development" which enables intercultural experiences to be located within a learning context. The engagement with other internationals offers teaching staff the opportunities "to work with colleagues overseas, to learn about the backgrounds of their students" (Harman, 2005, p. 141). They gain access to a range of resources working in a "cosmopolitan space" (Sanderson, 2011, p. 666).

As the world becomes more interconnected and borders blur, the scholarship across teaching, learning and research fields has progressively become international (Altbach, 2015). Developments in technology have significantly contributed to making communication possible. While setting up collaborations with local and international schools/communities, and practitioners takes time, the experience is worth the effort in relation to sharing and advancing knowledge (Shiveley & Misco, 2015). International educational projects need to be planned carefully based on mutual trust (Teutsch, 2012).

Internationalizing at Home: Experiences within the BEd (Primary) Program

Deakin University Student Experience

Dawn includes multicultural music with a focus on intercultural understandings within a core Arts Education unit and within music electives units. Over the years, she has collaborated with musicians, performers and music educators offering her students an intercultural intervention locally. These relations took time and effort to set up in relation to building trust (Young, O'Neill, & Mooney Simmie, 2015). She connected with people locally and internationally through Skype, telephone conferencing and face-to-face teaching from Australia, parts of Africa, Malaysia, Spain, Sri Lanka and New Zealand. They taught about their culture, heritage, history and music. Studying about music by an authentic person from that country created the opportunity for students to engage with multicultural music (Joseph, 2016; Joseph, Nethsinghe, & Cabedo-Mas, 2019).

All students were able to interact with musicians, performers and music educators at the same time. When an invited external person (culture bearer) comes into the class either through Skype, telephone conferencing or face-to-face, students have the opportunity to look, listen and learn about the country, genre of music and culture in real-time. The three-hour workshop time across ten weeks of the semester allowed students to have an equitable 'study abroad alternative'. All students had the same window of opportunity to ask questions in-class from an expert in the field when viewing PowerPoint or website presentations about the country and people. In this way, all students gained a different cultural and pedagogical approach to teaching songs, instruments and movements (dance) without having to travel abroad.

RMIT University Student Experience

Richard has been running the eTutor project over many years. The eTutor began as an eChatter with school partners in Nepal and India (Johnson & Jumani, 2009). Each week, his RMIT students (eTutors) interact with school students from Asia (Malaysia, Nepal, India and Pakistan) using a dedicated website. Richard's students spend half the year to assist school students in

Asia with their English language skills within a core education unit. The teaching occurred during class-time on-campus. Through the project, all participants had the opportunity to learn more about other cultures in an authentic learning and teaching online environment. The eTutors (RMIT students) were allocated international school students by Richard to teach and interact with online. The RMIT students had to focus on creating effective learning environments with international participants from culturally diverse settings. For the school students, this meant having the unique opportunity to be involved with first-language English speakers in an interactive English language program.

In setting up the eTutor project for intercultural exchanges, academic staff had to work closely with schools and the technical support services. While the project was offered concurrently with in-country school placement opportunities, comparisons between the two initiatives are not made in this chapter. While the online environment allowed informal discussion, Richard preferred asynchronous discourse consistent with the research findings in that it facilitated in-depth communication (Tallent-Runnels et al., 2006). Synchronous chats provide a direct and immediate environment for responses, whereas in an asynchronous environment, responses were delayed but more focused and purposeful (Davidson-Shivers, Tanner, & Muilenburg, 2001). Weekly, the students kept a diary of their experiences making note of "critical incidents, successful intercultural interactions, communication breakdowns" (Jackson, 2018, p. 148).

Method

We use a qualitative approach that allows us to describe, illuminate and interpret the data in our natural setting (Creswell, 1994; Flick, 2014; Williams, 2007). As reflective practitioners, the alternative to study abroad offers us a way to learn through and from our experience and that of our students (Findlay, 2008; Mathew, Mathew, & Peechattu, 2017). We independently gained ethical approval to conduct our research at our respective workplaces for our wider studies. It is beyond the scope of this chapter to report on all aspects of the data in our wider studies. Dawn draws on pertinent student data (questionnaires) to inform her findings that specifically explored the teaching and learning of multicultural music in her wider studies undertaken between 2010 and 2018 (*Attitudes and perceptions of Arts Education Students: preparing culturally responsive teachers [2010–2014]*, *Pre-service teacher attitudes and understandings of Music Education [2013–2017]* and *See, listen and share: Cultural practices in music teaching and learning* [2015–2018]). Richard reflects-on-action and in-action and student feedback through questionnaires to inform his findings from his wider study eTutor study that took place over a period of six years (Schön, 1983). Through our case studies (Stake, 1995; Yin, 2003), our partnerships have been a positive learning experience that promoted intercultural and international awareness.

Research Tool and Data Collection

Across our separate projects, we employed purposive sampling to gain an understanding of the phenomena being explored (Patton, 2002). Our students served as a convenient sample, were easy to access and were available to participate (Etikan, Musa, & Alkassim, 2016; Gay, Mills, & Airasian, 2012). For each of the wider projects, we provided a Plain Language Statement and Consent Form to the students outlining the projects and their involvement. We chose questionnaires as they provided meaningful data and were easy to administer and code (Bird, 2009; Rowley, 2014). All questionnaires were anonymous and participation voluntary. We draw on some open-ended questions as they provide "more in-depth insights and allow respondents to use their own language and express their own views" (Rowley, 2014. p. 314).

In the case of Dawn, questionnaires were handed out at the last music workshop for the wider studies (*Attitudes and perceptions of Arts Education Students: preparing culturally responsive teachers [2010–2014]* and *Pre-service teacher attitudes and understandings of Music Education [2013–2017]*. Students dropped off completed questionnaires into a box placed in the room. For the project *See, listen and share: Cultural practices in music teaching and learning (2015–2018)*, students completed an anonymous web-survey. Questions asked across all the wider projects included: what aspect of multicultural did you enjoy? What was difficult? Explain what you learnt about the new culture and music? In what ways did learning music from other cultures enhance your intercultural understanding?

In the case of Richard, questionnaires were completed by all students overseas and in Melbourne at the end of the semester. Interviews were voluntary and conducted with the eTutors. A deductive coding method was used to guide the analysis (Yi, 2018). The eTutor project codes broke the text into smaller categories of achieving a better understanding of the English language skills and intercultural understandings. Student engagement was a central theme, and the data was evidence for the continuation of the project. Identification of benefits coming from the student feedback was a key code relating to the success of the project. The critique of the programs was coded as challenges with nuanced pointers to cultural issues, sustainability and pedagogy.

Data Analysis

In preparing the data for this chapter, we initially had meetings (through email and telephone conversations) about how we would collate our data (Joseph et al., 2019). We independently extracted our relevant data and met face-to-face to discuss our initial findings in relation to student experiences of 'staying home and studying abroad'. As we each were immersed in our own data, we read and re-read our data searching for meanings and patterns. We used thematic analysis as an organizing framework and tool to analyse the data by writing "down [of] ideas and potential coding schemes" (Braun & Clarke, 2006, p. 86). Once the data had been initially coded and collated, we combined

Table 11.1 Themes

Initial Coding	*Emergent Themes*	*Overarching Themes*
Time and trust Teaching and learning about a new culture Building partnerships	Understanding the teaching	Benefits
English language Enculturation Collaboration and partnership	Understanding cultural diversity and language	
Organizational engagement with academics, school environments and professionals Mentors Support Structures	Independent communication in a new context	Challenges
Skype connections Language difficulty Playing, moving, singing Parents perceptions Cross-cultural	Technical, social and academic	

them to form overarching themes across our sites (Braun & Wilkinson, 2003; Maguire & Delahunt, 2017). We only report on two overarching themes that emerged (see Table 11.1) and use direct quotations from our data (Biggerstaff & Thompson, 2008).

Findings and Discussion

From our reflections, the importance of partnerships played a significant role in the success of our studies. In this section, we present key benefits and challenges that emerged from our overall data at our different sites.

Deakin University: Internationalization at Home

Benefits

Travelling to different parts of Africa when teaching about African music or around the globe when teaching multicultural or community music is not a practical option for on-campus study. Rather, by inviting academics, performing artists and teachers to speak to the students gave them the chance to experience different music and genres locally as a way to IaH. Students felt the experience of sharing by knowledgeable culture bearers "an authentic learning experience". They found that engaging first-hand with someone from a particular country and culture helped them learn the language and meaning of the song". Students "experience [d] different polyrhythms" and felt that they "understand more about the culture" when someone explained it to them through employing images, video footage and practical hands-on demonstrations. Students had the opportunity to "listen to someone [culture bearer] play on an authentic instrument" live in the classroom or through Skype. The cultural teaching and learning experiences were invaluable for students and Dawn. We were transported to different geographical regions (Campbell, 2016). Students experienced culture bearers from Africa who demonstrated their authentic instruments from different countries (kora, mbira, dud dun, Kpanlogo and djembe drums) and discussed with the students the role of music in their community.

Students had the opportunity to ask questions and engage with academics, teachers, performing artists in a safe and trusting environment. In the case of learning African music with indigenous African musicians, students saw the links between culture and music and the need to preserve and promote culture as an oral tradition (Joseph, 2016). Students found that they learned new and different ways to teach a song when engaging with different music educators and culture bearers (Joseph et al., 2019). They had the chance to learn about a new genre, music, country, culture and its people within a domestic learning environment (Joseph, Nethsinghe, & Cabedo-Mas, 2018).

Challenges

Organizing the partnership was challenging when scheduling the timetable. The sharing of music and culture by musicians, performers and music educators is not paid for by the university. When teaching from countries like South Africa, Spain and New Zealand, the difference in time is another consideration to take into account. Some presenters from Guinea, Ghana, Malawi, Mozambique and Sri Lanka live locally in Melbourne which was convenient to IaH. In this way, they integrated an intercultural and international dimension into the formal curriculum locally (Beelen & Jones, 2015). When using technology, technical glitches impacted the flow of the lesson from Spain, for example (Joseph et al., 2019).

While teaching and learning multicultural songs with someone from another country is advantageous, students found it hard to understand their accent. Therefore, trying to pronounce the words of the songs was not always easy. Some of the challenges students commented on was "trying to sing in Spanish" or "trying to learn the African song without the words". They also found that there was a lot to absorb in a three-hour workshop about a different culture and music. While playing on the instruments was fun and exciting, students were not as confident to sing and move their bodies at the same time. For some, the challenge offered them a chance to create their own rhythms (body percussion or movement), yet for others, they felt "creating the rhythm with our [their] bodies and the drum was scary". Learning a range of multicultural songs as a non-music specialist was pedagogically challenging.

RMIT University: Internationalization at Home

Benefits

Engaging interactions on eTutor was challenging for some of the RMIT students. One found it hard to believe that there were real overseas school students on the other side of her screen that wanted to interact and learn. She asked, "Are these students real? Are they real people or are we simulating an Asian learning environment?" The most successful eTutor partnership was with St Thomas School in Kuantan (Malaysia) with a classroom teacher (Madam Khor Got Hun). This partnership took time and trust (Young et al., 2015). She was committed to the eTutor project, made it part of her classroom pedagogy and had the support of her principal to recruit other teachers to the project.

The most satisfying aspect of the eTutor project was that students in Melbourne were given the opportunity to communicate with people from diverse cultures in an authentic learning and teaching environment (Shadiev, Hwang, & Huang, 2015). They responded enthusiastically to the opportunity of developing a greater cultural appreciation of Pakistan and Iran, respectively. One summed it by saying "they're just like us"! The faceless nature of the discourse minimized any prejudice that may have been there if the skin colour and English accents of the participants were more evident. Table 11.2 reflects the responses of school students showing that the program helped them improve their English. The intercultural encounter took place in a space where students negotiated their social position in the open-ended questions they remarked "I can write freely and share my experiences or culture", "I like to chat with my group members", "the pictures shared speak more than words" and "we can share videos with others". When asked if they liked online or face-to-face learning, one student summed it by saying "I like online learning as I can make more friends from other countries, I can write freely. I am not afraid of making mistakes and I can write and read anywhere I like". Another preferred "face-to-face learning because of the feedback from teachers". The teachable moments serve as stimuli to develop intercultural competence which facilitated what may have been "culture shock into culture learning" (Bennett, 2008, p. 17).

For school students, the experience was a breath of fresh air, different from the didactic and rote-dominated teaching style to which they were accustomed. The principals and teachers needed to trust the value of the eTutor project in order for it to contribute to their students' learning. Once they crossed the trust threshold, then the project was a significant professional experience for teachers and students. Trust was a crucial element in building and sustaining partnerships (Teutsch, 2012).

Challenges

The eTutor program seemed to be the perfect solution to improve students' levels of literacy in English in Asia. However, in practice, it was hard work

Table 11.2 Evaluation of eTutor by Students from St. Thomas School, Kuantan, Malaysia

	Statements Relating to eTutor	*Strongly Agree (%)*	*Agree (%)*	*Agree (%)*	*Strongly Disagree (%)*
1	The eTutor program allows me to use English without fear.	59	39	2	0
2	My eTutor helped me to improve my English.	66	32	2	0
3	I am more confident to give my opinion now after taking part in the eTutor program.	44	49	7	0
4	The eTutor program encourages me to think critically.	41	37	22	0
5	I make many friends in the eTutor program.	39	51	10	0
6	The allocated time for eTutor of two periods per week is sufficient.	44	39	17	0
7	I feel safe to give my opinions in the eTutor program.	44	44	12	0
8	I look forward to every eTutor class.	56	34	10	0
9	I learned about Australian culture through the eTutor project.	56	24	20	0
10	The tasks given in eTutor were appropriate.	44	39	12	5
11	eTutor was easy to access online.	41	39	15	5
12	eTutor gave me the opportunity to use English.	63	37	0	0
13	There are a variety of tasks.	51	37	12	0
14	I got feedback from my tutors.	57	39	2	2

maintaining the relationship between the tutor and tutee online. In all the cases where the eTutor project worked was because the classroom teacher was committed to the program and used the eTutor 'as a teacher from Australia', and school students were given classroom time to communicate with their eTutors. This required a particular pedagogy that could not be taken for granted as the majority of Asian teachers that Richard worked with found it difficult to be flexible enough to include eTutors into their classroom teaching. They had a very traditional, didactic classroom teaching style (Tan & Reyes, 2016). Madam Got Han and her small group of Malaysian teachers were able to do this over a period of years. They saw the opportunity of this interaction beneficial to their students.

For the ITE students, the eTutor project was a challenge to engage, communicate, teach and mentor school students whom they were unlikely to meet, was of a different culture, spoke different languages and spent their lives in vastly different conditions. The students anticipated the difficulties in starting such a cross-cultural discussion with participants who were not confident in using English text as the medium of discussion. They said, for example, "how will we greet the students", "will the school students be able to understand our Aussie language" and "how much do we need to know about Islam in order to communicate with our school students". These questions were raised and addressed in preparation for the online tutoring so that the Australian students (eTutors) would be mindful and aware of cultural sensitivities. Below are examples of communication from the eTutor Pakistan project to illustrate cultural sensitivities and differences that served as an intercultural learning experience:

> Hi dears,
> My name is Nisar I'm joining you first time today. first of all i introduce me to you. i am bachlor from sindh university in islamic culture, economics, muslim history and sindhi. i live in 'crystal city', jamshoro. my city is 8km off from hyderaba . . . Urdu is national language of pakistan . . . I describe u about languages in my country next time i am going to tell u different things about culture.

Tutors quickly picked up the culturally appropriate forms of addressing their international partners and also the significance of referring to the family.

> Asslamu alaikum . . ., Wow . . . I'm surprised you speak so many languages. I find it very interesting too that you change language depending on the environment . . . I would love to learn another language, but I think it would be very challenging . . . I think one other language would be enough though, not 5!!

The response:

> Let me tell you something about Pakistan. But before that may I ask you what do you know about Pakistan and what kind of information do you expect about Pakistan?
> . . . today it is 2nd day of the Holy month of Ramadan. Muslims celebrate it with an extreme level of their joys and they fast from dawn to dusk. They don't eat, don't drink and all other physical urges are prohibited.

From the above communication, it was evident that Nisar was upfront about his culture and Islamic faith and was open to share with his tutor about this. The tutor valued the depth of his diverse language experience and ability. He was sensitive in remarking about it in a positive way that built trust and respect for the partnership to grow.

The Australian tutors were quick to respond to the politeness and respect shown by their international partners by reflecting those values in their own responses. There was a great interest in exchanging cultural information. The challenges, mistakes and adjustments made proved worthy as a great intercultural learning experience while staying in one's home country.

Concluding Thoughts

We acknowledge that discussing two universities in Melbourne is a limitation in itself; therefore, generalizations about ITE programs or 'internationalizing at home' in Australia cannot be made. Our alternative to study abroad allowed for authentic learning experiences to take place through a blended environment (face-to-face and through technology) where our students were able to reflect on their intercultural understandings and learn from it across the semester (Medina et al., 2015). While our programs were met with some challenges, overall, they fostered "intercultural sensitivity, empathy, and global-mindedness" for all concerned (Jackson, 2018, p. 168). Setting up partnerships takes time and effort, and all parties concerned need to have a shared commitment and goal. We were able to keep our focus on intercultural learning without our students being distracted by the new cultural environment and the starkness of its difference. Rather than a tourist experience for what usually is a three-week international visit that may include a visit to an orphanage, or the Taj Mahal, we initiated a sustainable intercultural experience for all our students at no cost, bearing in mind the destructive green-house emissions of air travel.

While some study abroad programs "unintentionally promote otherization . . . ignoring commonality" (Jackson, 2018, p. 167), for our students and ourselves, our alternative option of internationalization at home proved to be a rich cultural and linguistic learning experience where the process of integrating an international and intercultural dimension was intentional (Knight, 2003). This chapter contributes to the growing body of research on study abroad initiatives. Based on our findings, we recommend more wide-ranging alternatives and opportunities of study abroad for students in other faculties where intercultural understanding is purposefully developed to enhance internationalization of the curriculum at home.

This chapter was prepared when the coronavirus was announced as a global pandemic by the World Health Organization (WHO, 2020), and travel bans in place to many international destinations have subsequently impacted higher education institutes. The alternative to study abroad programs lends itself to support diverse teaching and learning partnerships during uncertain times that lie ahead.

References

Altbach, P. (2015). Perspectives on internationalizing higher education. *International Higher Education*, *27*(2), 6–8.

Altbach, P. G., & Knight, J. (2007). The internationalization of higher education: Motivations and realities. *Journal of Studies in International Education*, *11*(3–4), 290–305.

Anderson, T., & Elloumi, F. (Eds.). (2004). *Theory and practice of online learning*. Athabasca, Canada: Athabasca University Press.

Barton, G., & Hartwig, K. (Eds.). (2017). *Professional learning in the workplace for international students: Exploring theory and practice*. Cham, Switzerland: Springer Publishers.

Barton, G., Hartwig, K., Joseph, D., & Podorova, A. (2017). Practicum for international students in teacher education programs: An investigation of three university sites through multisocialization, interculturalization and reflection. In G. Barton & K. Hartwig (Eds.), *Professional learning in the workplace for international students: Exploring theory and practice* (pp. 129–134). Cham, Switzerland: Springer Publishers.

Baxter, A. (2018). The benefits and challenges of international education: Maximizing learning for social change. In J. R. Dassin, R. R. Marsh & M. Mawer (Eds.), *International scholarships in higher education* (pp. 105–129). Cham, Switzerland: Palgrave Macmillan.

Beelen, J., & Jones, E. (2015). Redefining internationalization at home. In A. Curaj, L. Matei, R. Pricopie, J. Salmi, & P. Scott (Eds.), *The European higher education area: Between critical reflections and future policies* (pp. 59–72). New York: Springer.

Bennett, J. M. (2008). On becoming a global soul: A bath to an engagement during study abroad. In V. Savicki (Ed.), *Developing intercultural competence and transformation: Theory research and application in international education* (pp. 13–31). Sterling, Virginia: Stylus Publishing.

Biggerstaff, D., & Thompson, A. R. (2008). Interpretative phenomenological analysis (IPA): A qualitative methodology of choice in healthcare research. *Qualitative Research in Psychology, 5*(3), 214–224.

Bird, D. K. (2009). The use of questionnaires for acquiring information on public perception of natural hazards and risk mitigation-a review of current knowledge and practice. *Natural Hazards and Earth System Sciences, 9*(4), 1307.

Blackmore, J., Gribble, C., Farrell, L., Rahimi, M., Arber, R., & Devlin, M. (2014). *Australian international graduates and the transition to employment–final report.* https://www.deakin.edu.au/__data/assets/pdf_file/0010/365194/international-graduates-employment.pdf

Bliuc, A. M., Goodyear, P., & Ellis, R. A. (2007). Research focus and methodological choices in studies into students' experiences of blended learning in higher education. *The Internet and Higher Education, 10*(1), 231–244.

Bodycott, P. (2009). Choosing a higher education study abroad destination: What mainland Chinese parents and students' rate as important. *Journal of Research in International Education, 8*(3), 349–373.

Braun, V., & Clarke, V. (2006) Using thematic analysis in psychology. *Qualitative Research in Psychology, 3(*2), 77–101.

Braun, V., & Wilkinson, S. (2003). Liability or asset? Women talk about the vagina. *Psychology of Women Section Review, 5*(2), 28–42.

Campbell, P. S. (2016). World music pedagogy: Where music meets culture in classroom practice. In C. R. Abril & B. M. Gault (Eds.), *Teaching general music: Approaches, issues, and viewpoints* (pp. 89–111). New York, NY: Oxford University Press.

Clifford, V.A. (2009). Engaging the disciplines in internationalizing the curriculum. *International Journal of Academic Development, 14*(2), 113–143.

Creswell, J. W. (1994). *Research design: Qualitative and quantitative approaches.* Thousand Oaks, CA: SAGE Publications.

Davidson-Shivers, G., Tanner, E., & Muilenburg, L. (2001). How do students participate in synchronous and asynchronous discussion: What are the differences in the student participant? *Journal of Educational Computing Research, 25*, 351–366.

de Wit, H. (2019). Internationalization in higher education, a critical review. *SFU Educational Review, 12*(3), 9–17.

de Wit, H. (2020). Internationalization of higher education. *Journal of International Students, 10*(1), i–iv.

Dietz, G. (2009). *Multiculturalism, interculturality and diversity in education* (Vol. 8). Münster, Germany: Waxmann Verlag.

Dockrill, H., Rahatzad, J., & Phillion, J. (2016). The benefits and challenges of study abroad in teacher education in a neoliberal context. In J. A. Rhodes & T. M. Milby (Eds.), *Advancing teacher education and curriculum development through study abroad* (pp. 290–305). Hershey, PA: IGI Global.

Eisenchlas, S., & Trevaskes, S. (2003). Internationalization at home: Some principles and practices. In A. J. Liddicoat, S. A. Eisenchlas, & S. Trevaskes (Eds.), *Australian perspectives on internationalizing education* (pp. 87–102). Melbourne, Australia: Language Australia.

Etikan, I., Musa, S. A., & Alkassim, R. S. (2016). Comparison of convenience sampling and purposive sampling. *American Journal of Theoretical and Applied Statistics, 5*(1), 1–4.

Flick, U. (2014). *An introduction to qualitative research.* Thousand Oaks, CA: Sage.

Gay, L. R., Mills, G. E., & Airasian, P. (2012). *Educational research: Competentices for analsyis and applications.* Upper Saddle River, NJ: Pearson.

Harman, G. (2005). Internationalization of Australian higher education: A critical review of literature and research. In P. Ninnes & M. Hellsten (Eds.), *Internationalizing higher education: Critical explorations of pedagogy and policy* (pp. 119–140). Hong Kong, People's Republic of China: Comparative Education Research Centre.

He, Y., Lundgren, K., & Pynes, P. (2017). Impact of short-term study abroad program: Inservice teachers' development of intercultural competence and pedagogical beliefs. *Teaching and Teacher Education, 66*(1), 147–157.

Helm, F., & Guth, S. (2010). The multifarious goals of telecollaboration 2.0: Theoretical and practical implications. *Telecollaboration, 2*(1), 69–106.

Jackson, J. (2018). Intercultural interventions. In J. Jackson (Ed.), *Interculturality in international education* (pp. 129–156). New York, NY: Routledge.

Jenny, S., & Jenny, G. (2016). The impact of international service learning on teacher education students serving in a third world country. *Teacher Education Journal of South Carolina.* http://www.scateonline.org/pdfs/Journal.Final.2016.pdf

Jenny, S. E., Chung, J. J., Rademaker, S. M., & Almond, E. C. (2017). University students perceived and experienced challenges and benefits to studying abroad: Gender, class year, and length of experience comparisons. *Journal of Education Research, 11*(4), 457–476.

Johnson, R., & Jumani, N. B. (2009). Building cross cultural understandings through e-chatter. *Indian Journal of Open Learning, 18*(1), 17–27.

Jones, E. (2013). Internationalization and employability: The role of intercultural experiences in the development of transferable skills. *Public Money & Management, 33*(2), 95–104.

Jones, E., & de Wit, H. (2012). Globalization of internationalization: Thematic and regional reflections on a traditional concept. *AUDEM: The International Journal of Higher Education and Democracy, 3*, 35–54.

Joseph, D. (2016). Promoting cultural diversity: African music in teacher education. *Australian Journal of Music Education, 50*(2), 98–109.

Joseph, D., & Johnson, R. (2019). Colour, culture and difference in Australian teacher education: Voices from the edge. *Qualitative Research Journal, 19*(3), 324–343.

Joseph, D., Nethsinghe, R. & Cabedo-Mas, A. (2018) Creating multicultural music opportunities in teacher education: Sharing diversity through Songs. *Australian Journal of Teacher Education, 43*(5), 31–47.

Joseph, D., Nethsinghe, R., & Cabedo-Mas, A. (2019). "We learnt lots in a short time": Cultural exchange across three universities through songs from different lands. *International Journal of Music Education, 38*(2), 177–193.

Khawaja, N. G., & Dempsey, J. (2008). A comparison of international and domestic tertiary students in Australia. *Journal of Psychologists and Counsellors in Schools, 18*(1), 30–46.

Knight, J. (1997). Internationalization of higher education: A conceptual framework. In J. Knight, & H. de Wit (Eds.), *Internationalization of higher education in Asia Pacific countries* (pp. 5–19). Amsterdam, The Netherlands: European Association for International Education.

Knight, J. (2003). Updated internationalization definition. *International Higher Education, 33*, 2–3.

Knight, J. (2004). Internationalization remodeled: Definition, approaches, and rationales. *Journal of Studies in International Education, 8*(1), 5–28.

Leask, B. (2009). Using formal and informal curricula to improve interactions between home and international students. *Journal of Studies in International Education, 13*(2), 205–221.

Leask, B., Jones, E., & de Wit, H. (2018, December 7). Towards inclusive intercultural learning for all. *University World News*. https://www.universityworldnews.com/post.php?story=20181205093157690

Lee, A. (2005). Knowing our business: The role of education in the university. http://www.itl.usyd.edu.au/community/alisonlee.pdf

Link, T. C. (2016). Strategies and challenges for creating an inclusive study abroad program. *Journal of Postsecondary Education and Disability, 29*(3), 293–298.

Liyanage, I., & Nima, B. (Eds.). (2016). *Multidisciplinary research perspectives in education: Shared experiences from Australia and China*. Rotterdam, The Netherlands: Sense Publisher.

Maguire, M., & Delahunt, B. (2017). Doing a thematic analysis: A practical, step-by-step guide for learning and teaching scholars. *All Ireland Journal of Teaching and Learning in Higher Education, 9*(3), 3351–3354.

Mathew, P., Mathew, P., & Peechattu, P. J. (2017). Reflective practices: A means to teacher development. *Asia Pacific Journal of Contemporary Education and Communication Technology, 3*(1), 126–131.

Medina, A. L., Hathaway, J. I., & Pilonieta, P. (2015). How preservice teachers' study abroad experiences lead to changes in their perceptions of English language learners. *Frontiers: The Interdisciplinary Journal of Study Abroad, 25*, 73–91.

Patton, M. Q. (2002). *Qualitative research and evaluation methods* (3rd ed.). Thousand Oaks, CA: Sage.

Postiglione, G. A., & Altbach, P. G. (2013). Professors: The key to internationalization. *International Higher Education, 73*(3), 11–12.

Rouse, L., & Joseph, D. (2019). The theory–practice nexus: International early childhood education students making the connections. *New Zealand Journal of Teacher's Work, 16*(1&2), 31–47.

Rozbicki, M. (Ed.). (2015). *Perspectives on interculturality: The construction of meaning in relationships of difference.* New York, NY: Pulgrave Macmillan.

Salisbury, M. H., Umbach, P. D., Pausen, M. B., & Pascarella, E. T. (2009). Going global: Understanding the choice process of the intent to study abroad. *Research in Higher Education, 50*, 119–143.

Sanderson, G. (2011) Internationalisation and teaching in higher education. *Higher Education Research & Development, 30*(5), 661–676.

Schön, D. A. (1983). *The reflective practitioner.* New York, NY: Basic Books.

Shadiev, R., Hwang, W. Y., & Huang, Y. M. (2015). A pilot study: Facilitating cross-cultural understanding with project-based collaborative learning in an online environment. *Australasian Journal of Educational Technology, 31*(2), 123–139.

Shiveley, J., & Misco, T. (2015). Long-term impacts of short-term study abroad: Teacher perceptions of preservice study abroad experiences. *Frontiers: The Interdisciplinary Journal of Study Abroad, 26*(1), 107–120.

Stake, R. E. (1995). *The art of case study research.* Thousand Oaks, CA: Sage.

Tallent-Runnels, M. K., Thomas, J. A., Lan, W. Y., Cooper, S., Ahern, T. C., Shaw, S. M., & Liu, X. (2006). Teaching courses online: A review of the research. *American Educational Research Association.* ERIC: EJ751147.

Tan, C., & Reyes, V. (2016). Curriculum reform and education policy borrowing in China: Towards a hybrid model of teaching. In C. P. Chou & J. Spangler (Eds.), *Chinese education models in a global* age (pp. 37–49). Singapore: Springer.

Teutsch, R. (2012). Intercultural education and school partnerships. In J. Huber (Ed.), *Intercultural competence for all: Preparation for living in a heterogeneous world* (pp. 95–105). Strasbourgh, France: Council of Europe. https://rm.coe.int/intercultural-competence-for-all/16808ce20c

Thirolf, K. Q. (2014). Male college student perceptions of intercultural and study abroad programs. *Journal of Student Affairs Research and Practice, 51*(3), 246–258.

Thomson, P. (2014, August 14). Life as an international academic: It can mean feeling town in two. *Higher Education Network.* www.theguardian.com/higher-education-network/blog/2014/aug/14/international-academic-bring-competitive-advantage-british-universities

World Health Organisation. (WHO). (2020, March 11). Coronavirus confirmed as pandemic by World Health Organization. *BBC News.* https://www.bbc.com/news/world-51839944

Yi, E. (2018, July 24). *Themes don't just emerge—Coding the qualitative data.* https://medium.com/@projectux/themes-dont-just-emerge-coding-the-qualitative-data-95aff874fdce

Yin, R. K. (2003). *Case study research: Design and methods* (3rd ed.). Thousand Oaks, CA: Sage.

Young, A. M., O'Neill, A., & Mooney Simmie, G. (2015). Partnership in learning between university and school: Evidence from a researcher-in-residence. *Irish Educational Studies, 34*(1), 25–42.

12 Developing an Experiential Virtually Abroad Program to Ensure Mobility Access

A Quick Guide

Sharon Glazer and Rita G. Berger

Introduction

Global mobility has historically been an expensive endeavor, one that only a small number of people were fortunate enough to enjoy. Although the opportunity to travel abroad has extended to students receiving financial aid, it is still not always feasible for students to travel for a semester, summer, or even a month abroad. Students from lower SES, frequently of a sociological minority group, students with physical limitations, and non-traditionally aged students are often at a disadvantage for partaking in study abroad activities due to financial challenges and other responsibilities they may have both in their home (e.g., caring for a family member) and at work. As a result, although these groups of individuals, by virtue of their disposition, might have developed skills that enable them to cope with being "different" from the norm, they may be disadvantaged when it comes to developing international and cross-cultural competences. Cross-cultural competence refers to developing expertise on cross-cultural issues through changes in cognitive, affective, and behavioral responses as well as personal characteristics in order to more easily adapt to various intercultural interactions (McCloskey, Behymer, Papautsky, Ross, & Abbe, 2010; Rasmussen & Sieck, 2013).

In today's workforce, students with some international experiences are more competitive than those without (Anderson, Lawton, Rexeisen, & Hubbard, 2006; Marcotte, Desroches, & Poupart, 2007). The aim of this chapter is to present an innovative experiential solution with a unique pedagogical design to global mobility, a Virtually Abroad Program (VAP), that provides nearly every student an opportunity to gain international cross-cultural competences. The VAP draws on Kolb's (1984) Experiential Learning Theory (ELT), which stipulates that people learn by doing. Six important components of experiential learning include (1) constant feedback, (2) relearning key concepts through discussion, (3) learning through conflict (i.e., conflict that challenges old ideas and creates new ones), (4) a process of thinking, perceiving, feeling, and behaving, (5) interacting and adjusting one's schema according to one's environment, and (6) constructing knowledge

(Kolb, 1984; Kolb & Kolb, 2005). The VAP incorporates the aforementioned six components of ELT. And, to demonstrate that the approach has utility, we present data gathered before and after a VAP to demonstrate immediate changes in cross-cultural competence. It is important to note that this chapter is not presenting a research or experimental study with control groups. Instead, it is a guide or tool for how to design a VAP and also demonstrates the VAP's incremental utility.

What Is a 'Virtually Abroad Program'?

A VAP is a kind of experiential activity that allows students across multiple universities to work together on projects (short-term or long-term) in cross-cultural global virtual teams (GVTs). Drawing on organizational approaches to conducting global business, the VAP introduces students to GVTs, which are temporary groups made up of individuals in different parts of the world that make use of technology-supported communication to complete shared, complex tasks (Jarvenpaa & Leidner, 1999; Maznevski & Chudoba, 2000). Although some GVTs have some permanency (even if individuals come and go, like in other teams), many are temporary in the sense that team members may not have worked together in the past and they may not necessarily expect to work together again in the future (Jarvenpaa & Leidner, 1999).

The assignment of the VAP, as created for a cross-cultural organizational psychology course in one university and an introduction to industrial and organizational psychology course in another, requires that students prepare a training guide meant for expatriates working abroad. Along the way, students must gather information about a third country and a course-specific topic, both of their choosing, and collaborate with teammates in different countries using communication and information technology. The VAP can easily be modified to address any field of interest—for example, collaborating with students from another university to create a smartphone application, collaborative creative writing, or developing an international marketing strategy. This chapter presents the guide on the basis of the course for which it was created, a cross-cultural organizational psychology course, and, therefore, the remainder of this guidebook presents information from that context, though the VAP content can easily be crafted to suit the needs of other courses and disciplines.

Why Take Part in a VAP?

A large benefit of a VAP is that it offers a real experience with working in GVTs. Organizations are increasingly utilizing GVTs in order to better facilitate collaboration among geographically dispersed employees while cutting down on time and money spent on traveling for face-to-face meetings (Powell, Piccoli, & Ives, 2004). Almost half (46%) of all organizations, and two-thirds (66%) of multinational organizations, use virtual teams (Geller, Lee, Alonso, Schmit, & Esen, 2012). During the novel coronavirus disease

(COVID-19) pandemic, the need has been made all the more evident, as the pandemic conditions have made international face-to-face engagements nearly impossible. It is likely that students will, at some point in their future careers, find themselves taking part in GVTs, and the VAP offers students real, immersive experience with them. Participants are given a firsthand look at the benefits of working on such a team as well as the potential challenges that they may expect.

A VAP also offers students an alternative to taking part in a semester abroad program, which may not be offered by their institution or may be too expensive or time-consuming (Glazer, Moliner, & Carmona, 2014). Students in a VAP have an opportunity to gain international exposure by interacting with people from different cultural backgrounds, which might increase students' cultural intelligence or the ability to interact effectively in culturally diverse situations (Crowne, 2008; Earley & Ang, 2003; Glazer et al., 2014). Despite its strengths, it is not a replacement for study abroad, which is a cultural immersion experience. Still, for those who cannot travel, the VAP offers opportunities to develop cross-cultural collaborative skills.

Findings from a similar classroom GVT program called X-Culture support these assertions (Taras et al., 2012, 2013). In X-Culture, business students enrolled in universities around the globe worked for two months in GVTs to develop a business proposal (Taras et al., 2012, 2013) and researchers evaluated participants' understanding of the challenges of GVTs before and after they took part in the program (Taras et al., 2013). Students' cultural intelligence was evaluated in the same way (Taras et al., 2013). As a result of taking part in X-Culture, students had a more accurate understanding of the challenges of working in GVTs and experienced higher levels of cultural intelligence (Taras et al., 2013). Further, students who took part in X-Culture as part of a business course performed significantly better on course-related examinations compared to other students in the same business courses that did not take part in X-Culture (Taras et al., 2013). This suggested that the immersive experience that the X-Culture students had with the course material helped with their comprehension.

A VAP can also be a useful part of cross-cultural competence development that complements study abroad. Along the lines of the Theory of Met Expectations (Porter & Steers, 1973), participating in a VAP could help prepare study abroad students for some of the intercultural experiences they will have. Furthermore, if connections continue post in-person experience, it can sustain one's newly developed international network of peers and cross-cultural competences.

Student Competencies

The value of a VAP is not merely an exposure to people from other countries and to technology that support virtual interactions, but more generally strengthening global business acumen. Glazer et al. (2014) present an Integrated International Learning model that focuses on several educational approaches to enhancing cross-cultural competence. These approaches include traditional (face-to-face) classrooms or virtual classrooms and stationery or international scope. They present the idea of a VAP as one experiential teaching opportunity that combines an international scope with the virtual platform as particularly beneficial because the workforce is increasingly connected through computer-mediated communication. Students who participate in a VAP develop valuable competencies in several areas:

1 By interacting with peers in other countries, students become more aware of their own cultural biases. Having to reflect on their own reactions or responses to their partners' comments or activities, students are compelled to reflect on how their own cultural perspective shapes their understanding of their partners' behaviors as well as their own.
2 Throughout a VAP, students learn project management and time management skills. Since partner students are supervised by a different instructor, evaluated globally on different criteria, and have different content knowledge, students need to learn flexibility, adaptability, and project coordination. Moreover, part of project management is planning or anticipating barriers. Students develop a repertoire of alternative electronic communication in order to fulfill deliverables and milestones.
3 In terms of a simulated workplace, students learn how to clarify roles and responsibilities (i.e., role management), identify personal and team level goals, delineate guidelines for interactions, and develop predictable patterns of communication/interaction. To ensure communication flow, students also learn about the importance of timely and detailed feedback to their partners (this is a skill that is hard to develop and requires experience and a high degree of maturity).
4 Students in the VAP learn how to negotiate with their partners on the notion of professional presentations, for example, how much or how little content needs to be prepared on a PowerPoint slide. They learn that there are different norms for visual presentation of materials and have to negotiate with each other the extent to which they are willing to compromise. As a result, students begin to appreciate the dynamics of working with partners from different countries and learn to recognize and handle potential conflict.
5 Students develop skills in critical thinking as they navigate the intricacies of computer-mediated human interaction. In particular, they often question whether differences observed are a matter of personality or a matter of personality as influenced by culture.
6 Students begin to build competencies in identifying responsible, dependable, independent, and self-sufficient partners, a skill that is necessary when one is in a management position and needs to organize teams.
7 Students develop competencies necessary for cross-cultural interactions, including developing tolerance, navigating through language barriers, and managing time-zone differences.

Application Example of the VAP to Teach Cross-Cultural Organizational Psychology

With a focus on cross-cultural organizational psychology, the course instructors from University of Baltimore, U.S.A. (13 students: two of whom were international or first generation and three of whom were Black) and University of Barcelona, Spain (17 students, whose demographics were not captured), organized, implemented, and evaluated a VAP. The VAP component of the U.S.-based courses was a required graded component of the course. More than half the students had already taken and completed an IO Psychology course; the other half were in the current course for five weeks before the VAP project began. At the University of Barcelona in Spain, 17 English-speaking undergraduate students who were enrolled in different sections of an introductory course on Work, Organizational, and Personnel Psychology were given the option of taking part in the VAP. Unlike the U.S. students, the Spanish students were not expressly required to complete the VAP as part of their course; however, those who opted to take part were graded and given extra points from their instructor for their efforts.

Students at both universities worked together in GVTs to create a training guide aimed at U.S. and Spanish expatriates working abroad in a third country of each group's choosing. At the end of the project (which aligned with the end of the semester in the U.S.A.), each team presented their training synchronously through the use of videoconferencing technology in each classroom. In addition, the instructors sought to utilize the videoconferencing technology to team-teach two joint lectures in front of classes at both universities. After finishing the project, participating students received a certificate of completion signed by the instructors and deans of both universities.

Creating a VAP

Finding a VAP Partner

When designing a VAP, the first step is to identify at least one other instructor at another university and country who is also interested in taking part in the project and is, ideally, teaching a course on the same, similar, or complementary topic. This guide is written under the assumption that a VAP will consist of instructors and students at only two universities. It is possible to involve more than two universities in the project; in fact, this may allow for a more enriching experience for students due to larger, more diverse workgroups. However, administering a VAP across more than two universities may present additional challenges with video conferencing software. VAP partners should meet with their respective university's Information Technology (IT or technology support) departments early in the process to ensure that technological needs will be met and identify alternative arrangements should the technology not support all components needed for the experience. Meeting with IT before additional planning is essential. Therefore, we recommend the first interaction with IT be held around the same timeframe as identifying and coordinating with a partner(s).

Approximately 8–12 months in advance, VAP partners should agree upon:

- The program's overall topic of focus and its format;
- Participating students' education level (Bachelor's, Master's, Ph.D.);
- VAP teams' composition and size;
- Specific assignments and deadlines;
- Dates and times for joint lectures and final presentations (remember to carefully calculate scheduled times based on time-zone differences).

VAP partners would also find it useful to identify holidays, reading days, or other periods in which either university will be closed during the course of the VAP. This information will be helpful in scheduling the start and ending times of the VAP as well as assignment due dates. It would also prove useful for students during the teamwork phase of the project, as they will need to be reminded and considerate of the project timeline.

If the VAP partners wish to collect data from students taking part in the project, they should also use this time to agree upon the number of surveys that students will receive, the time intervals at which they will receive them, and the specific measures that will comprise each survey. These authors administer the survey three times: at the project's onset, midpoint, and end (preferably about one week after it ends, but prior to the students dispersing for holiday breaks). Prior to distribution, all surveys should then be submitted to each university's Human Research Ethics Board or Institutional Review Board (IRB) for approval, and therefore, adequate time for IRB approval needs to be accounted for in the VAP planning. VAP partners' agreed-upon terms will be used to create a general, flexible outline of the project.

Advertising VAP to Students

Instructors who choose to offer a VAP would benefit from advertising the program. At the University of Baltimore (UB), flyers were posted around buildings (the authors would be happy to share their flyers with interested parties), and the Psychology program's student advisor was informed of the VAP in order to encourage qualified students to participate. Qualifications included an average grade or mark in a research methods and statistics course and having successfully completed an additional psychology or business course such as Industrial and Organizational (IO) psychology or organizational behavior. At the University of Barcelona, about 450 students were registered for the undergraduate psychology course in Organizational Behavior. Flyers were posted around buildings informing students of the program. Students in Spain who wished to participate were required to be comfortable communicating (writing and speaking) in the English language and participated in an extra instructor-led tutoring session to prepare them for the subject matter of the VAP.

Identifying and Fulfilling Technological Needs

Communication technology is a crucial component of the VAP; without its proper implementation, the program cannot function. Because different universities have different sets of tools at their disposal, it is necessary that both VAP partners meet with IT staff at their universities to identify the best technology to facilitate the program. Each class needs an audio-visual system to communicate with one another during joint lectures, and student teams need a communication platform to work with one another on a day-to-day basis. Despite best efforts to identify the kinds of technology available on a campus to support a VAP, it is imperative that the faculty permit flexibility in their technology needs and assignments (or methodology for carrying out assignments) in order to align them with available technology. In other words, course instructors and students must be prepared to accommodate (sometimes unexpected) variations in course requirements, needs, methodology, and technology capabilities.

Audiovisual equipment. Audiovisual equipment is necessary to facilitate synchronous lectures and presentations between classrooms. For the example VAP, both classrooms at the two universities contained (a) a Polycom VoIP videoconferencing system to communicate with the other class and (b) a separate computer, projector, and projection screen to view presentations. If your (or your partner's) university does not have access to a VoIP videoconferencing system, video chat software such as Zoom, Skype, Google Hangouts, or ooVoo may be used instead.

At the time the courses in all locations are scheduled, the rooms, fitted with all technological equipment, in which the course will be delivered, must be reserved too. At least one month preceding the start of the program, IT teams at both universities should contact one another and attempt to connect via their audiovisual system of choice. Testing audiovisual connections is important, as scheduling all people's time across time zones can be quite difficult. It is possible, particularly when starting a new VAP, that there will be a need to change classrooms, equipment, or computer-mediated technology, and the instructors would need time to update and modify their course syllabi to reflect those changes.

Team communication platforms. A reliable communication platform is necessary for day-to-day communication amongst teammates. The platform should allow for instantaneous messaging, video or voice chat, file sharing, and collaborative file editing and must be available for use at both universities. It should also allow course instructors to view the ongoing development of each team's project as the semester progresses.

For the example VAP, we ultimately decided on the Google suite of communication tools (Google Drive, Talk, and Hangouts), as it fulfilled the program's needs and had the additional benefit of being free of charge. Further, most students were already familiar with the use of each of these applications. Students who were not familiar with these applications were provided instruction on the use of each component of the toolkit. Each team also had access to Campus Obert, a learning management system offered by the University of Barcelona. Students from both countries received mass notification through Campus Obert, and other useful information was posted on the site. Other potential options for future VAPs include Zoom, Skype, Moodle, WhatsApp, and a host of other communication applications and learning management systems.

During the VAP: Content

Joint Lectures

Using videoconferencing technology, joint lectures are delivered synchronously to all students across all participating VAP classes. The benefits of joint lectures include an experience much like that of an invited guest speaker to a classroom, observing possible cultural differences in student–instructor interactions, as well as content of interactions, and an opportunity for students to have another shared experience. When different instructors present information, students benefit from different or converging points of view on a given topic. Because all VAP instructors may be experts in different subject areas let alone of different cultural backgrounds, they may use their expertise to complement one another. Joint lectures also allow for each class of students to meet and hear from one another. Further, they showcase and familiarize students with the audiovisual equipment that they will later use during their team presentations.

Two joint lectures were originally scheduled for the example VAP: one on the first day of the project and one at its mid-point. Due to unforeseen circumstances (related to civil unrest), however, the second joint lecture could not be held. During the first joint lecture, instructors at both universities used the VoIP videoconferencing system to introduce themselves to each of the two classes, have students introduce themselves, and discuss the goals, deliverables, timelines, and cautionary notes regarding the VAP project.

Project Assignments and Milestones

Selecting project topics and creating teams. Because the University of Baltimore's spring semester started prior to the University of Barcelona's, it was decided that U.S. students would first select project topics to ensure that students would be working on topics of interest. Topics needed to relate to the course topic: cross-cultural organizational psychology. Students submitted at least three topics in priority order to the course instructor, and final topic assignments were relayed to the students via email. Once the U.S. students were assigned to their project topics, a list of those topics was sent to the Spanish students, who then submitted their priority list based on available project topics. Instructors then created teams of students in the U.S.A. and Spain based on shared topic preferences. There were a couple of students who needed placement or reorganization of placement (e.g., because too many people prioritized the same one topic). Ultimately, there were nine teams of two students and four teams of three students, as there were more Spanish students involved in the VAP than U.S. students. Moreover, for the teams of three, typically, one of the students from Spain was a non-U.S. international student studying in Spain. These teams consisted of one U.S., one Spanish, and one international student, with the international student providing a richer experience by reflecting on his/her own culture, too, throughout the project.

"Getting to Know You" activity. The "Getting to Know You" activity was the first assignment that students were required to complete in their teams and consisted of three parts. First, teammates interviewed one another via video chat about their personal background, beliefs, values, behaviors, and personal schedules. Second, teammates discussed two scenarios that were meant to foster further discussion about values, and how these values might differ from person to person and culture to culture.

The main goal of these discussions was for teammates to familiarize themselves with one another. Across organizations that utilize GVTs, 51% report that building team relationships was one of the large obstacles to GVT success (Geller et al., 2012). Some students taking part in the example VAP echoed these sentiments, stating that prior to speaking to their teammates, they were worried about interpersonal problems. However, these same students reported that the "Getting to Know You" activity helped alleviate these fears and establish trust between them and their teammates. Therefore, although the activity did not create a typical experience of "feeling" a stranger in a foreign country, per the above comment regarding reducing fears, as the team members had to create a new and ambiguous team culture, it appears that the activity had added value even in a non-immersive intercultural experience.

Finally, teammates were instructed to agree upon three possible countries on which they would ultimately do their presentations. Their only requirement for this was that the countries could not be the ones with which any person on a team had significant experience. For example, if a team was composed of one individual from Spain and one individual from the U.S.A. who had also spent several years living in Germany, then this team's country of focus could not be Spain, U.S.A., or Germany. This ensured that all students in the program were required to research a national culture with which they were not initially familiar. Using each team's list of three choices, the student assistant assigned each team the country they would focus on to ensure that there were no duplicate countries studied. The student assistant then sent an email to notify students of their assigned country.

At the conclusion of the "Getting to Know You" phase, as proof of completing the assignment, students submitted a summary of key points from their conversations. The student assistant reviewed the content of the summary and raised any concerns with the course instructor. Example concerns include a one-sided summary of the interaction or a report that lacked examples and relevant details.

Interim notes. At the project's midpoint, each team submitted a progress report of their activity through that point in time. The requirements for this assignment were relatively loose; students could submit a presentation outline, detailed notes about the team's focal topic, a list of relevant references accrued from the literature, and so on. The purpose of this assignment was to ensure that teams were making progress on their projects. Given the number of challenges faced by VAP teams throughout the project, it is imperative that teammates complete work in a timely fashion; requiring interim notes increases the likelihood that progress is being made. Instructors (or student assistant) should review the progress of each team and connect with any teams appearing to underperform to gather more information about their performance progress. Example indicators of underperformance included only a handful of articles related to the team's topic and country and no other supporting materials; having a crude outline of the content of the presentation, following mostly the outline in the syllabus, but no other supporting information (e.g., articles, references, URLs).

Student presentations. The final team assignment of the VAP was the presentation of a PowerPoint (deck) training guide meant for expatriates from Spain and U.S.A. working as managers in the team's host country. Three presentation times were scheduled to take place at the end of the semester in Baltimore (near to mid-semester in Spain), utilizing the same VoIP technology used by the instructors during the joint lecture.

Each presentation consisted of the following:

- Information about the dominant cultural values, beliefs, and managerial practices within the host country;
- Differences in cultural values between the host culture and the team members' cultures;
- Discussion of the team's topic of choice in the context of the country;
- Analysis of how expatriates from U.S.A. and Spain would best adapt to the core managerial practices of the host country;
- A summary of the training guide and recommendations for expatriates' adaptation to the host culture with regard to the team's topic;
- Sources that validated the information presented by the team.

In addition to the training guide, teams also discussed (debriefed) the team processes they underwent throughout the semester, highlighting any challenges they may have faced and explaining how they were able to overcome them.

VAP impression paper. At the end of the project, students wrote a paper detailing their experiences with the program as well as a fuller literature review of their chosen topic and country. Part of the literature review was also meant to guide students' training guide. Thus, each student's paper included a summary of his or her team's project, including the personal background of each team member, a description of the team's focal topic, a review of the literature used to create the final presentation as well as the overall impression the student had about the VAP experience. Students also presented their perceptions of advantages and disadvantages of participating in the VAP, challenges they faced, and how they overcame them. Further, they were asked about how they imagined their teammates felt about the project. The impression paper was also an opportunity for students to offer ideas about how the VAP might be improved in the future.

Writing impression papers gave students an opportunity to reflect upon what they learned firsthand about working in a GVT environment. They also provided students with another avenue to give feedback about the VAP, which could be used to make improvements to the program in the future. Below is a summary of students' feedback.

Evaluation

Advantages and Opportunities

On the basis of data collected to assess cross-cultural competence development (McCloskey et al., 2010; Rasmussen & Sieck, 2013) through the experiential study design, specifically, the VAP (Glazer et al., 2014; Kolb, 1984), we conclude that the VAP was a success. Although students expressed some frustrations with the process, such emotions are normal when put into an uncertain environment. U.S. students tended to have explicit assignment requirements and specific guidance; however, this VAP purposefully had many ambiguous decision points for the students to work through. For the U.S. students, this might have been unsettling. Nonetheless, the success of the VAP is observed in both student comments and student feedback to the surveys. While sample sizes for the example VAP were too small to make assertions of statistical significance, mean differences do point to several potentially promising trends.

As shown in Table 12.1 and Figure 12.1, U.S. students' overall global and local identities, openness to cultural diversity, and cultural intelligence improved from Time 1 (gathered at the start of the VAP, immediately after team formation) to Time 3 (survey completion was solicited one day after oral presentations had been delivered and closed three weeks later). Moreover, the U.S. students rated participation in the VAP as more valuable during Time 3 than they did during Time 1. It is possible that the U.S. students' coursework content, along with the VAP activity influenced their responses, thus biasing final conclusions. For Spanish students, mean differences from Time 1 to

Table 12.1 Changes in U.S. and Spanish Students' Cross-Cultural Competences

		Global Identity		*Local Identity*		*Openness to Cultural Differences*		*Cultural Intelligence*		*Improve General Performance*	
Country		M	SD	M	SD	M	SD	M	SD	M	SD
U.S.A	Time 1	4.87	1.16	4.15	1.54	5.42	1.27	5.39	1.36	4.63	1.92
	Time 3	5.57	0.86	5.00	1.35	5.48	0.95	5.57	0.62	5.13	1.64
Spain	Time 1	5.66	0.75	5.20	0.83	5.67	0.62	5.65	0.56	5.88	1.36
	Time 3	5.68	0.84	5.31	1.05	5.70	0.93	5.75	0.52	4.75	1.69

Note: Time 1 data were collected at the project's start, and Time 3 data were collected at its end.

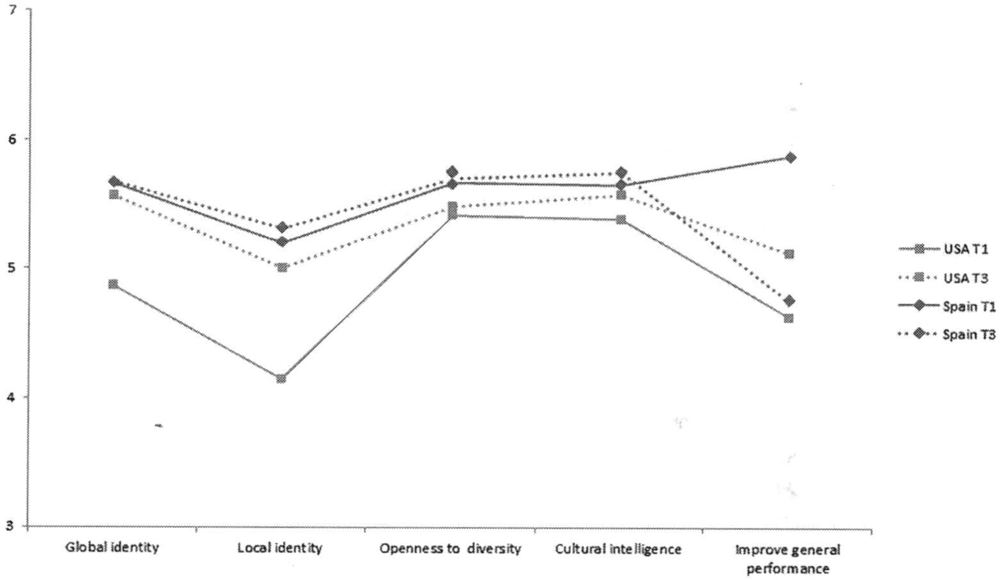

Figure 12.1 Changes in U.S. (USA) and Spanish (Spain) students' global and local identities, openness to cultural diversity, cultural intelligence, beliefs about the VAP's role in improving performance on general life activities, and approach to working with people from different countries. *Note.* Time 1 (T1) data were collected at the start of the project, and Time 3 (T3) data were collected at its end.

Time 3 were smaller, but there were slight improvements in respondents' global and local identities, openness to cultural diversity, and cultural intelligence. It is worth noting that at Time 1, Spanish students' ratings for these constructs—particularly global and local identity—were much higher than the U.S. students'. This may be because the VAP was voluntary for the Spanish students but not for the U.S. students. Spanish students who took part in the project chose to do so on their own accord. Thus, it may have been that those students who already had well-established global and local identities were more likely to take an interest in a cross-cultural project like the VAP. This explanation may also apply to why mean differences for the constructs were smaller for Spanish students between Time 1 and Time 3: there may have been less room for improvement within these constructs for Spanish students because they initially responded relatively highly across all of them. In the future, instructors may wish to test this hypothesis by surveying both Spanish students who volunteer for the VAP and students who enroll in the introductory IO psychology class but do not volunteer for the VAP to see whether those who volunteer for a VAP indeed rate more highly than their peers on global/local identity, cultural intelligence, and other constructs.

Several U.S. students commented that the experience made them realize that their assumptions about people of other cultural backgrounds had originally been stereotypical rather than fact-base. Together with the assigned reading materials, the U.S. students were able to process how they contributed to successful and unsuccessful practices. For example, they noted that clarifying roles and reevaluating them over time were essential and that more team interaction was better than less. U.S. students' overall recommendation was to continue offering the VAP, taking into consideration some of the challenges presented in the section.

The students from Spain also gave very positive overall feedback on the course. They enjoyed working with foreign students (i.e., students from the U.S.A.) and having the opportunity to interact with people from a different culture. To their instructor, the students mentioned that having the opportunity to witness different points of view, improving group-work skills, and gaining experience with virtual platforms were all great experiences. Their recommendation was to repeat the VAP and to include it into the regular study plan.

Challenges

In order to work together effectively, teammates must be cognizant of the many different challenges that are inherent to GVTs, such as problems with technology and scheduling, as well as issues arising from cultural differences, including language skills and work processes.

Technological issues. Of the 24 students who completed the feedback survey at the end of the project, 75% reported a problem with technology that affected their teamwork. Problems included general internet connectivity, struggles with specific applications like Google Hangouts, and hardware difficulties, such as microphones and web cameras. Some students dealt with technological barriers by using communication platforms outside of those recommended to them. For example, one group reported successfully using WhatsApp, a mobile messaging application, as their primary means of communication rather than the web-based recommendations.

Scheduling. Another major issue for students was scheduling time to speak and work with their teammates. Roughly 42% of students who completed the feedback questionnaire reported difficulties with scheduling. These were largely due to the six-hour time difference between U.S.A. and Spain and the full work and personal schedules of students. For example, each university's spring break occurred on a different week, and several students reported difficulties getting in touch with their teammates on the week of their break. In order to manage scheduling conflicts, some students found it easier to split up tasks for team members to complete individually so that team meetings only needed to occur once a week.

Cultural differences. On the feedback questionnaire, two respondents mentioned differences in views and ideas with their teammates as barriers. During in-class discussions, some U.S.-based students mentioned differences in work styles due to cultural differences impeded work at times. Another student mentioned that mutual misunderstandings were frequent and were likely due to a combination of the language barrier and cultural differences. Some teams found that using explicit and direct communication about project tasks helped alleviate some of these problems.

Educational differences. Another difference between the classes was level of exposure to the discipline of IO psychology. More than half of the U.S. students had an introduction to IO psychology course. U.S.-based students, who had not yet taken courses in IO psychology, however, were several weeks ahead in their studies of Cross-Cultural IO Psychology, as the spring semester began approximately five weeks before the spring term began in Spain. One recommendation, therefore, is to limit the course to students who are of similar educational levels, including course studies, making exceptions for certain students' participation only under certain conditions necessary.

Grading schemes. It is imperative that the grading schemes be comparable across universities. This guidance stems from challenges experienced in the example VAP, as grading differences might have affected the engagement levels. Specifically, completion of the VAP was central to the course in which the University of Baltimore students were enrolled; students could not pass the course without successfully completing the VAP. For students at the University of Barcelona, however, the VAP was optional, and in at least two cases, participation in the VAP might not have factored at all into students' course grades (the Barcelona students were selected from amongst 450 in the course, but there were several different instructors for those 450 students). The instructors learned only at the end of the VAP that this knowledge affected how the students related with each other; Baltimore students felt like they were the main persons responsible for fulfilling the VAP requirements. In fact, this feeling might be partly reflected in Spanish students' T3 self-evaluation on improved performance (see Figure 12.1). Further, U.S. students within certain teams felt as though they were doing more work than their teammates.

What Makes for a High-Performing VAP Team?

Because many students taking part in the VAP might not have had prior experience with a similar program or with GVTs, instructors may wish to advise students about how to best participate in a VAP team. Just as in the world of work, one does not always get to choose his or her teammates, so was the coordination of the VAP teams not purposefully created to ensure fit. The aim, as stated earlier, was to create an activity that somewhat replicated the way GVTs are created in a real global workplace—fit is not always assessed and coordinated. Instead, the team composition often depends on the task and other working conditions. Still, it may be worthwhile to see how efficient teams with similar cultural orientations (e.g., collectivistic) are compared to teams that are of opposing cultural orientations (e.g. individualistic) or varied cultural-orientations (Mason & Watts, 2012).

Another lesson to be learned from the experience is trust. According to both the academic literature and anecdotal responses collected during the example VAP, one major key to a high-performing VAP team is the establishment of trust among team members (Crisp & Jarvenpaa, 2006; Jarvenpaa & Leidner, 1999). Jarvenpaa and Leidner (1999) examined 350 Masters' students placed in self-managed, cross-cultural GVTs, and asked to complete three assignments over the course of six weeks. Of the 29 teams that sent the researchers usable data, 10 developed trust quickly and maintained it for the length of the project. Each of these teams had several qualities in common that facilitated the formation and maintenance of trust. Members of these teams all exchanged social, non-work-related messages with one another early on, introducing themselves and discussing hobbies, family life, and personal history (Jarvenpaa & Leidner, 1999). Team members also explicitly conveyed enthusiasm about the project. It is because of these two points that a task like the "Getting to Know You" activity is crucial, as it gives VAP team members an opportunity to introduce themselves on a social level and to express their enthusiasm about starting the project. Throughout the example VAP, teammates with high levels of trust engaged in predictable communication and warned one another about upcoming absences. Further, teammates delivered meaningful and timely responses throughout the project; other teammates' ideas received substantive feedback.

Conversely, two individuals taking part in the example VAP who reported a relatively low level of team trust by the end of the project explicitly commented on experiencing poor communication and team processes throughout the semester. According to a couple of studies (e.g., Krawczyk-Brylka & Piotrowski, 2008; Potter & Balthazard, 2004), virtual teams, compared to face-to-face teams, are less cohesive and solution-oriented. It is possible that the medium for communication, as well as the extent to which poorly performing GVTs chose to use asynchronous versus synchronous tools, might have affected the members' experiences. Indeed, high frequency contact increases connectedness with one's work group, which further reduces discomfort with any cultural differences. Indeed, according to the Social Presence Theory, it is important to align communication media and level of social presence and involvement in order to achieve an effective communication (Short, Williams, & Christie, 1976).

Though it is not possible with the evaluation we conducted to know how frequency of using various communication media affects team cohesiveness, it is worth considering if one chooses to prepare an experiment. Nonetheless, available data suggest that for the example VAP, high levels of team trust were correlated with effective communication strategies, such as exchanging non-project-related personal information with one another, openly discussing project issues, and careful consideration of others' viewpoints. See Table 12.2 for a correlational analysis of team trust and other items and constructs using data from the example VAP Time 3 survey.

Beyond effective communication strategies, members of highly trusting teams engaged in several helpful individual actions (Jarvenpaa & Leidner, 1999). Each member took a proactive approach to work and showed initiative. They were quick to create plans for dealing with technical issues or task uncertainty, such as creating and sharing work schedules. Members took on leadership roles based on skill or interest level and had different team leaders for different tasks. Based on anecdotal evidence, teams in the example VAP that established explicit procedures and roles early on experienced higher team cohesiveness and less personal frustration than did teams who did not. After establishing work procedures, the high-trust teams described by Jarvenpaa and Leidner (1999) did not allow disruptions to procedures (such as a missing team member) get in the way of completing tasks. In the example VAP, one team of three had an absent team member in the days leading up to the completion of the "Getting to Know You" assignment. In response, the two still-present team members completed the assignment with one another and waited for the return of the third team member to complete and discuss her portion. Finally, members of highly trusting teams remained unaffected by crises when they arose, such as missing a deadline, and simply continued to work (Jarvenpaa & Leidner, 1999). For example, one VAP team that reported high levels of trust was initially late in completing the interim notes assignment, but did not let this hinder completion of the final assignment.

Final Thoughts and Housekeeping

The VAP enables global mobility without having to leave one's home. It mimics the real-world of business operations today in a structured, guided environment that enables students to learn and grow without hurting their professional development. It is an accessible program for people of different physical and personal abilities, as so much of the program is supported by

Table 12.2 Descriptive Statistics for Items/Constructs on the Example VAP's Time 3 Survey, and Spearman's *r* for Correlations between Survey Items/Constructs and Final Level of Overall Team Trust

	Item/Construct	*M*	*SD*	*Correlation Coefficient between Item/ Construct and Team Trust*
1	How satisfied are you with overall team performance?	5.58	1.39	.64[a]
2	To what extent were the team outcomes of high quality?	5.62	1.10	.71[a]
3	To what extent were the team outcomes due to team performance?	5.58	1.45	.52[b]
4	To what extent were the team outcomes influenced by external constraints?	4.31	1.41	<.01
5	If the opportunity was presented, how willing would you be to work together again with your team?	5.27	1.54	.84[a]
6	My level of commitment was [high].	5.85	1.05	.31
7	Other team members' level of commitment was. . .	5.38	1.63	.70[a]
8	I expect to earn a grade that is [high].	5.65	1.02	.45[b]
9	Team members were willing to devote whatever effort necessary to achieve team success.	5.73	1.80	.48[b]
10	Achieving our team goal(s) was a higher priority than any individual objective.	6.19	1.74	.04
11	The members of my group were cooperative with each other.	6.85	0.73	−.08
12	Everyone on the team seemed to work well together.	6.62	1.24	.09
13	There were differences between group members in the extent to which they shared information with each other.	4.42	2.32	−.17
14	There were differences between group members in the extent to which they cooperated with each other.	3.65	2.35	−.13
15	There were group members who worked individually and did not coordinate their work with the group.	3.42	2.83	−.37
16	Members felt comfortable expressing their ideas and opinions.	6.04	1.11	.50[b]
17	We listened to each other and considered each other's opinions.	6.31	0.88	.59[a]
18	We listened carefully to minority viewpoints.	5.96	1.34	.53[a]
19	We tried to get everyone's input.	6.23	1.07	.59[a]
20	Some members had a difficult time being listened to.	2.12	1.63	−.25
21	Team members felt free to make negative comments.	4.62	1.72	.29
22	My team often reviewed its objectives.	4.12	1.95	.17
23	We regularly discussed whether the team was working effectively.	3.42	1.68	.07
24	In our team, we regularly discussed the flow of information between us.	4.42	1.77	.10
25	Team members were completely honest with each other.	5.69	1.26	.39
26	Team members could be trusted.	5.54	1.70	.83[a]
27	Team members took actions that were consistent with their words.	5.85	1.29	.69[a]
28	Team members were reliable.	5.65	1.62	.70[a]
29	I could rely on my team members to deliver their parts as promised.	5.62	1.86	.64[a]

	Item/Construct	*M*	*SD*	*Correlation Coefficient between Item/Construct and Team Trust*
30	Everyone had a chance to participate.	6.58	0.70	.58[a]
31	Team members were straightforward with each other.	5.73	1.25	.22
32	How much did you trust your fellow group members?	5.58	1.58	.81[a]
33	Were your group members truthful and honest?	6.08	1.02	.63[a]
34	How much did you respect your fellow group members?	6.23	0.91	.86[a]
35	How much did you respect the ideas of the people in your work group?	6.27	1.00	.74[a]
36	How much did you like your group members?	6.19	1.13	.62[a]
37	To what degree would you consider these people your friends?	4.27	1.54	.55[a]
38	How often did you discuss with your teammates matters that are not related to the project, such as weather, hobbies, friends, movies, or other topics?	4.27	1.64	.55[a]
39	How much open discussion of issues was there in your work group?	5.31	1.67	.45[b]
40	To what degree was communication in your group open?	5.96	1.04	.61[a]
41	To what degree was conflict dealt with openly in your work group?	4.58	1.79	−.04
42	How much competition was there in your work group?	2.00	1.33	.09
43	To what extent was your group cohesive?	5.23	1.31	.76[a]
44	How much do you feel like your team had group spirit?	5.04	1.75	.77[a]
45	To what degree would you talk up this group to your friends as a great group to work in?	5.00	2.00	.86[a]
46	This project contributed to my knowledge about cross-cultural/international work.	7.28	0.74	.44[b]
47	Interpersonal conflict	2.25	1.83	−.44
48	Task conflict	2.95	1.94	−.45
49	Cultural intelligence	5.64	0.53	.07
50	Burnout	5.40	1.38	.83
51	Overall team trust	5.56	1.05	*.87*[c]

Note: $N = 25$ for means and standard deviations of Item 46, interpersonal conflict, task conflict, and team trust; 23 for means and standard deviations of cultural intelligence; and 26 for means and standard deviations of all other items/constructs. $N = 23$ for all correlation coefficients. Items 1–5 and 32–45 were measured on a seven-point Likert-type scale ranging from 1 (Not at all) to 7 (Very much). Items 6–8 were measured on a seven-point Likert-type scale ranging from 1 (Very low) to 7 (Very high). Items 9–15 and 46 were measured on a seven-point Likert-type scale ranging from 1 (Strongly disagree) to 7 (Strongly agree). Items 16–31 were measured on a seven-point Likert-type scale ranging from 1 (Almost never) to 7 (Almost always). Lowest and highest possible values for each construct (47–51) were 1 and 7, respectively.

[a] Correlation is significant at the 0.01 level (two-tailed).
[b] Correlation is significant at the 0.05 level (two-tailed).
[c] Cronbach's α reliability estimate.

computer-mediated technology. The VAP provides university students with a culturally enriching experience and an opportunity to take part in a GVT. Students save on travel-related costs (e.g., direct costs, such as airfare, and indirect costs, such as loss of wages due to absence from work), while still developing intercultural experiences. Through learning in an immersive, team-based environment, students gain valuable knowledge about cultural and technological challenges that may arise in similar situations and are given an opportunity to overcome these issues. Implementing a VAP opens doors to students who would otherwise not have a chance to travel abroad. It ensures diversity and inclusion.

We encourage faculty wishing to implement a VAP to collect student feedback, as their feedback is crucial for the future improvement of the program. If the opportunity avails, we recommend an experimental study that manipulates various features of the VAP, and the GVTs specifically, in order to determine which VAP features are critical to retain and which should be modified. During the example VAP, students provided feedback in their impression papers, through an anonymous survey given to them at the project's close, and in person throughout the course. The VAP raised several logistical and technology-focused opportunities, too. For example, through this program, IT personnel at both universities were able to identify technological shortcomings that could be improved in the university. Specifically, the Dean at the University of Barcelona was so impressed with the results of the students' experiences and the cooperation between the two programs that he initiated technology improvements.

Finally, readers are invited to contact the first author for a one-page quick reference to the project timeline; an example of notes taken during initial discussions between partners, outlining a tentative project timeline, "to-do" list, and identifying the next steps that each partner needed to take toward creating the program; an example outline of tasks, deliverables/milestones, and deadlines required of students in the cross-cultural organizational psychology VAP, "getting to know you" activity scenarios, and an example training guide presentation.

Acknowledgements

The authors appreciate the support of Ivica Pavisic for compiling and organizing the authors' data and preparing some analytic results. The authors also thank the University of Baltimore Foundation's Fund for Excellence, the University of Baltimore's Helen P. Denit Honors Program funds, and the University of Barcelona Collaboration funds for supporting the work of the Virtually Abroad Program.

References

Anderson, P. H., Lawton, L., Rexeisen, R. J., & Hubbard, A. C. (2006). Short-term study abroad and intercultural sensitivity: A pilot study. *International Journal of Intercultural Relations, 30*, 457–469.

Crisp, C. B., & Jarvenpaa, S. L. (2013). Swift trust in global virtual teams: Trusting beliefs and normative actions. *Journal of Personnel Psychology, 12*, 45–56.

Crowne, K. A. (2008). What leads to cultural intelligence? *Business Horizons, 51*, 391–399.

Earley, P. C., & Ang, S. (2003). *Cultural intelligence: Individual interactions across cultures.* Stanford, CA: Stanford University Press.

Geller, D., Lee, C., Alonso, A., Schmit, M., & Esen, E. (2012). *SHRM survey findings: Virtual teams* [PowerPoint slides]. http://www.shrm.org/research/survey findings/articles/pages/virtualteams.aspx

Glazer, S., Moliner, C., & Carmona, C. (2014). Differences in educational training models and implications from international collaborations. In. R. L. Griffith, L. F. Thompson, & B. K. Armon (Eds.), *Internationalizing the curriculum in organizational psychology* (pp. 79–104). New York, NY: Springer.

Jarvenpaa, S. L., & Leidner, D. E. (1999). Communication and trust in global virtual teams. *Organization Science, 10,* 791–815.

Kolb, A. Y., & Kolb, D. A. (2005). Learning styles and learning spaces: Enhancing experiential learning in higher education. *Academy of Management Learning & Education, 4*, 193–212.

Kolb, D. A. (1984). *Experiential learning: Experience as the source of learning and development.* Englewood Cliffs, NJ: Prentice-Hall.

Krawczyk-Brylka, B., & Piotrowski, M. (2008). Using a computational model to compare objective negotiations in real and virtual environments. *International Journal of Production Research, 46,* 1315–1333.

Marcotte, C., Desroches, J., & Poupart, I. (2007). Preparing internationally minded business graduates: The role of international mobility programs. *International Journal of Intercultural Relations, 31*, 655–668.

Mason, W., & Watts, D. J. (2012). Collaborative learning in networks. *Proceedings of the National Academy of Sciences of the United States of America, 109*(3), 764–769. doi:10.1073/pnas.1110069108

Maznevski, M. L., & Chudoba, K. M. (2000). Global virtual team dynamics. *Organization Science, 11,* 473–492.

McCloskey, M. J., Behymer, K. J., Papautsky, E. L., Ross, K. G., & Abbe, A. (2010). *A developmental model of cross-cultural competence at the tactical level.* (Technical Report No. 1278). Alexandria, VA: U.S. Army Research Institute for the Behavioral and Social Sciences.

Porter, L. W., & Steers, R. M. (1973). Organizational, work, and personal factors in employee turnover and absenteeism. *Psychological Bulletin, 80,* 151–176. doi:10.1037/h0034829

Potter, R. E., & Balthazard, P. A. (2004). Understanding human interaction and performance in the virtual team. *Journal of Information Technology Theory and Application, 4,* 1–23.

Powell, A., Piccoli, G., & Ives, B. (2004). Virtual teams: A review of current literature and directions for future research. *The DATA BASE for Advances in Information Systems, 35,* 6–36.

Rasmussen, L. J., & Sieck, W. R. (2013). Metacognitive underpinnings of 3C development. In D. Schmorrow & D. Nicholson (Eds.), *Advances in design for cross-cultural activities 1* (pp. 332–341). Boca Raton, FL: Taylor & Francis.

Short, J. A., Williams, E., & Christie, B. (1976). *The social psychology or telecommunications.* London, UK: Wiley.

Taras, V., Bryla, P., Gupta, S. F., Jiménez, A., Minor, M. S., Muth, T., . . . Zdravkovic, S. (2012). Changing the face of international business education: The X-Culture project. *Academy of International Business Insights, 12*(4), 11–17.

Taras, V., Caprar, D. V., Rottig, D., Sarala, R. M., Zakaria, N., Zhao, F., . . . Huang, V. Z. (2013). A global classroom? Evaluating the effectiveness of global virtual collaboration as a teaching tool in management education. *Academy of Management Learning & Education, 12*, 414–435.

Index

Made in the USA
Las Vegas, NV
05 November 2024

688ed571-ec42-4ad9-950d-bb84d5038a8dR02